CW01496947

WOMAN'S HOUR

ALSO FROM WOMAN'S HOUR

*Woman's Hour: Words from Wise, Witty and
Wonderful Women (2017)*

WOMAN'S HOUR

DAILY MEDITATIONS

UNA McCORMACK

BOOKS

BBC Books

UK | USA | Canada | Ireland | Australia
India | New Zealand | South Africa

BBC Books is part of the Penguin Random House group of companies
whose addresses can be found at global.penguinrandomhouse.com

Penguin Random House UK
One Embassy Gardens, 8 Viaduct Gardens, London SW11 7BW

penguin.co.uk
global.penguinrandomhouse.com

First published by BBC Books in 2025
1

Typeset in 12.65/16pt Perpetua MT Pro by Jouve (UK), Milton Keynes
Printed and bound in Great Britain by Clays Ltd, Elcograf S.p.A.

The authorised representative in the EEA is Penguin Random House Ireland,
Morrison Chambers, 32 Nassau Street, Dublin D02YH68

A CIP catalogue record for this book is available from the British Library

ISBN 9781785945069

CONTENTS

JANUARY

1 JANUARY

MAKE SOMETHING OF YOURSELF

'Stay open to the world. Try to be kind to somebody else, because it becomes contagious. And hang out with positive people. Don't hang out with people who bring you down, who are negative and nasty and gossipy and mean. Cut those people out of your life. Find people who, like you, want to make something of yourself.'

Hillary Clinton, United States Senator, Secretary of State and First Lady, 2017

• • • • • •

The first woman to earn the presidential nomination by a major US political party, Hillary Rodham Clinton (b. 1947) is one of the most powerful women who has ever lived. In the 2016 US presidential election, she lost the electoral college (and the presidency) to Donald Trump, but took the popular vote, winning the third most votes of any candidate in US history.

Clinton's life and career have dramatised – on a vast public scale – the costs, compromises and challenges of being an ambitious woman, one living through a period where women, arguably, have enjoyed the most power and freedom than ever before. Her life and career have shown too, often painfully and publicly, the limits to women's power and freedom, from the revelation of her husband Bill Clinton's affair with his aide, Monica Lewinsky, to her electoral defeat in 2016.

Clinton's advice is simple, but not trite, advocating curiosity, open-mindedness and surrounding oneself with people who want to build rather than destroy; who recognise we only have one chance at life, and who want to make something of themselves.

2 JANUARY

GRUDGE MATCH

'I have a terrible tendency towards grudges.
I've given myself a three-year cut-off point on that.
So I'm trying to ditch any grudge I've had for longer
than three years – with mixed results! But that's
certainly the plan going forward. If they're older
than three years I have to let them go!'

Polly Vernon, journalist and columnist, 2017

• • • • • •

The New Year often brings a period of reflection about who we are, who we've been and who we would like to become. Sometimes this self-reflection leads us to make resolutions – perhaps there are habits that we would like to break, or changes in behaviour that we believe might make us happier. But, as we all know, our resolutions can be notoriously difficult to keep.

In recognising her tendency towards keeping grudges, journalist and feature writer Polly Vernon goes through exactly this kind of self-reflection – and also acknowledges how difficult it is for us to alter ingrained behaviours. A three-year cut-off puts her resolutions on a much more practical and realistic timescale.

Change is not something likely to happen overnight. Change is a small-scale process of nudging ourselves, noticing when we slip back into bad habits, and moving forwards step by step.

3 JANUARY

GETTING BACK INTO THE SADDLE

'I hadn't ridden in 32 years and I went down to pick up my motorbike – which is a big Triumph, 1200CC – I was nervous but I was like, "No, I'm not going to let fear stop me from doing things anymore", which I realised that I had been doing.'

Bridget Christie, comedian, actor and writer, 2023

• • • • • •

In the throes of menopause and a midlife crisis, Bridget Christie (b. 1971) got herself a motorbike. This image – of a middle-aged woman putting on leathers and powering off towards the horizon – forms the central image of her sitcom, *The Change* (about, perhaps not coincidentally, a woman who is in the throes of a midlife crisis).

Buying a machine with a huge engine is a wickedly subversive spin on stereotypical male midlife crisis behaviour of buying a new, fast car. But Christie is also tapping into something else very powerful: the idea of a middle-aged woman travelling alone, going hell for leather wherever she wants, without looking back at the responsibilities she has left behind.

Perhaps we don't have the desire to put on leathers and climb onto the back of a motorbike. But what kinds of risks did we take when we were younger that we have stopped taking? Are there fears or limitations that we have let set in, that stop us from doing things that we once loved to do? Or maybe there's something we always wanted to try, but never quite summoned up the nerve to do. Today is as good a day as any.

4 JANUARY

TELLING THE TRUTH

'Imagine the lack of problems we would have if people said what they thought. [H]ardly anyone does. That's why no one believes me.'

Fran Lebowitz, writer and essayist, 2021

• • • • • •

Fran Lebowitz's (b. 1950) sardonic wit was described by the *New York Times* in 1981 as a 'sour cream sensibility', and in an article that compared her to Dorothy Parker, another great source of acerbic asides. Lebowitz's influence on US culture has spanned decades.

Like Parker, Lebowitz is a New Yorker to the bone, and has been associated with many figures in the city's art scene, particularly Martin Scorsese, who has made her the subject of two of his documentaries. Her essays have been collected into a single volume, *The Fran Lebowitz Reader* (1994).

There's a risk to telling the truth, which is that it doesn't always make you popular. Cloaking it in humour is one way to smuggle the truth into the conversation – although perhaps it doesn't take away the sting.

How often do you find yourself speaking evasively? What might happen if we resolved to be more honest this year? To tell fewer lies, or half-truths? To equivocate less, and live more authentically?

Fran Lebowitz is ahead of you – or so she says.

5 JANUARY

BUILDING CONFIDENCE

'When I'm in the recording studio that's when I'm at my happiest, because that's when you can cut yourself off from people and really get into your songs . . . I love walking on stage. I love entertaining people, otherwise I wouldn't be here. Took a bit of work, building up the confidence.'

Susan Boyle, singer, 2012

· · · · · ·

Susan Boyle's (b. 1961) fame came not so much overnight as within a matter of seconds, when she began her outstanding performance of 'I Dreamed a Dream' on *Britain's Got Talent*. Tours and albums followed, bringing with it a sudden and very public profile, and the inevitable press attention. Her debut album was the best-selling album of 2009, and she has gone on to sell over 20 million records.

Boyle's comments remind us that behind the paraphernalia of performance and publicity, there lies something very simple – the pleasure of singing for the sake of it, and the pleasure of singing for others.

At the start of the year, take a moment to think about the kinds of creativity that most give you pleasure. We may sing, or draw, or paint, or write, or cook – but when and how do we most easily forget ourselves, in the act of making something beautiful?

6 JANUARY

THRESHOLDS

'It was such a big deal, because it's forever.
It's a trusted position, it's beyond the establishment.
The establishment we have now isn't going to be
the establishment we have in two hundred years'
time and the doors are still going to be there. So
there was an incredible amount of responsibility
and onus put onto me. I didn't take it lightly.'

Tracey Emin, artist, 2023

• • • • • •

Between 2020 and 2023, the National Portrait Gallery, London, was closed for a major renovation. One of the changes was a development of the north façade of the building to create an entirely new entrance and forecourt. As part of the new entranceway, three new doors were installed, and a permanent installation was commissioned by Dame Tracey Emin (b. 1963).

Emin's artwork comprises 45 etchings of women's faces on the bronze doors. In her original conception, Emin intended to depict famous women, to counterbalance and challenge the stone busts already carved into the façade, depicting figures such as Hans Holbein the Younger, Sir Joshua Reynolds and Sir Anthony van Dyck.

However, as the project developed, Emin began to draw faces from her imagination, representing women of all ages, ethnicities, backgrounds and historical periods. Her aim was for anyone to be able to look at the faces on the doors, and see someone familiar.

How often has a woman artist received a commission that has changed the face of a major city? Emin's women will be there for centuries.

7 JANUARY

THAT CLINKING CLANKING SOUND

'Money goes through our hands every day: we earn, we spend. But many of us don't quite understand what factors drive our behaviour with money and how we feel about it. Sometimes we know what we should be doing with money, but we don't make what we feel are the right choices. And sometimes that's because there are complex emotional factors driving them ... Once you start pulling that thread and start analysing your relationship with money, you start to find out a great deal about yourself.'

Vicky Reynal, financial psychotherapist, 2024

• • • • • •

This is a time of year when we might be reflecting upon how much we have spent over the festive period, looking ahead to a long and lean January.

We tend to think of money matters as driven by rational decision-making and logical choices. But money has symbolic and emotional significance too, in ways we rarely consider. There might be complicated family dynamics around an inheritance. Or we are overcome with anxiety when we think about financial planning or saving. Perhaps we quickly overspend, or we quarrel about managing the family budget with our partner.

Vicky Reynal is a psychotherapist who specialises in the psychology issues that we bring to our finances. Her work as a therapist focuses on helping clients to consider the deep-seated needs and fears that they bring to their relationship with money and their handling of their finances.

Considering how we relate to money emotionally might be stressful or painful, but it might also bring us more control over this aspect of our lives.

8 JANUARY

EVERYBODY'S TALKING

'There have been a couple of big meta-analyses
on this ... [T]he effect size is tiny [but] the situation
where a man will talk more than a woman most
is when one man is talking to one woman.'

Sophie Scott, professor and neuroscientist, 2017

• • • • • •

Chatterboxes, tongues a-wagging . . . The stereotype is clear enough. Men are goal-orientated, but women are more inclined to be relationship-orientated — which makes them talk more. But is it the truth?

Neuroscientist Sophie Scott (b. 1966) has examined the various meta-analyses done on this subject (that is, looking at the various analyses done in the field, to see what statistically reliable results can be drawn from across the body of research). It turns out that there's only one real difference between men and women when it comes to who talks more. It's a small difference, and dependent on context, but it's reliable. When one man is talking to one woman, he'll talk more.

Why, then, do the stereotypes of chatty women persist? One reason might be that when there are fewer women in the room (and it often happens), then it's more noticeable when they speak. Another reason might be that as the number of women in a given space increases as a result of efforts towards equality, then we hear more from each one of them. And if we're not used to hearing women's voices, then when they are given space, it can — to some ears — be more noticeable.

Or it may be that some prejudices die hard.

'ONE IS NOT BORN, BUT RATHER BECOMES, A WOMAN.'

'At the moment we're living at a time of such return to biological determinism, to essentialism: this idea that little boys and little girls come out of the womb differently. To read again [Simone de Beauvoir's] extraordinary statement [that one is not born, but rather becomes, a woman] of how we just don't know what men and women would be like if they were growing up in conditions of equality, I find that incredibly energising, empowering and inspiring.'

Natasha Walter, feminist, writer and human rights activist, 2008

· · · · · ·

Simone de Beauvoir — existentialist philosopher, writer and feminist theorist and activist — was born on this day in 1908. Among her vast literary and critical output, Beauvoir's *The Second Sex* (1949) was foundational to the emergence of second-wave feminism — and triggered angry reactions from across the establishment, from Camus to Kinsey to the Vatican.

Beauvoir's statement that 'one is not born, but rather becomes, a woman' is an early expression of a distinction between 'sex' and 'gender'; that 'womanhood' is not only a process of socialisation, but arises within particular social, economic and historical conditions.

In her 2009 book *Living Dolls*, Natasha Walter (b. 1967) documented the resurgence of sexism and essentialism in the twenty-first century. Walter, reflecting on Beauvoir's famous statement, brings us back to her radical vision of equality, which asks the question: how might relations between men and women be if we began — and continued — to be equal?

10 JANUARY

A BIT OF A TUMMY

'We've grown up to feel ashamed of this part of our body [the stomach]. Actually most women have a bit of a tummy! ... I tried to change my body for so long, did really dramatic things ... Even when I was dangerously thin, I still had a little bit of a tummy ... I thought, "If I've put myself through all of that, and I still don't look this way – that's not how my body's supposed to be." ... We don't sit and prod our elbows, or our wrists – it's just another part of our body.'

Lottie Drynan, blogger and campaigner, 2024

· · · · · ·

Our perceptions of what constitutes beauty change significantly over time, and while we have come some distance from the stick-thin models of the 1960s and the 'heroin chic' of the 1990s, thinness is still the standard. We don't regularly see Rubenesque women with full figures and rounded bellies. But isn't that how many of us look?

Lottie Drynan set up a blog, *The Tummy Diaries*, to document her experience of irritable bowel syndrome (IBS), and particularly the bloating that comes with the condition. She has used social media to connect with other women who are self-conscious about their stomachs, and to encourage positivity and self-acceptance.

Whether through pregnancy, reaching middle age, the menopause – or simply because of how we are shaped – our bodies tell the stories of our lives.

11 JANUARY

ON GOSSIP

'Everybody gossips. Humans gossip. There's quite a compelling argument that one of the main reasons we evolved language was so we could gossip.'

Sophie Scott, professor and neuroscientist, 2017

· · · · · ·

The word 'gossip' wasn't historically pejorative. It came from the Old English *god sibb*, a 'godparent', a close friend of the parents – usually of the mother. During the sixteenth century, perhaps associated with the rise of puritanism, the word began to take on the negative connotations that we know today: someone who likes to talk too much about others, who passes on tales – a living, breathing sidebar of shame.

Perhaps it should be no surprise that the word shifted in the context of women's friendships. Patriarchy has always been afraid that women might talk to each other, pass on unauthorised information and knowledge, form unsanctioned alliances.

There's a danger when women get together and speak without constraint. Miriam Toews takes this as the subject of her novel *Women Talking* (2018), which centres upon the covert meetings taken by the women within an isolated Mennonite community, who realise that they have been the subject of night-time attacks and rapes by some of the men. A group of women gather to talk urgently about what must be done.

We are social creatures; talking – communicating – is what we do. Language is the way we get to know each other better. Language is the way that we form friendships with each other, take care of each other, watch out for each other, warn each other – and plan an escape.

Sometimes that's the most revolutionary thing we can do.

12 JANUARY

ON SECRETS

'People who professionally hear secrets – like priests,
like therapists – go through to a lot of training to
try and work out how they can carry those secrets.
I've heard therapists talk about how they learn
to build a kind of chest inside them into which
they can put very sacred secrets.'

*Mark Vernon, psychotherapist, writer and
former Anglican priest, 2010*

• • • • • •

Mark Vernon has degrees in theology and physics, and a PhD in ancient Greek philosophy. He has written numerous books on topics ranging from spirituality and belief to friendship and love.

When we seek advice, or simply to offload, we might turn to friends, who know us well, and whom, we hope, will understand the nuances of our situation. Alternatively, we might turn to a stranger, someone trained to listen to us, take an objective view and bring a fresh perspective.

Sometimes, people approach us because they want to find a way through their difficulties; sometimes they simply want to be heard. We might have practical suggestions to make, if the other person wants to hear them. Or we might simply listen reflectively and empathetically, offering back our understanding of the other person's feelings, until they know they have been heard.

How do we react when we are asked to act as someone's confidant? Are we able to distinguish between when someone is looking for affirmation and when they are looking for advice? How can we best help?

13 JANUARY

BOOKS AND BABIES

'[M]ost of the women who have been canonized by the male critics have been childless women. And I think there's a bit of a wrong understanding going on there. You can have books and babies. They are not mutually hostile occupations. It leads to a busy life, I will say.'

Ursula K. Le Guin, writer, poet and critic, 1990

• • • • • •

Ursula Kroeber Le Guin (1929–2018) was born into an academic and literary family (her father was an anthropologist; her mother an author). Ursula Kroeber pursued graduate studies in French literature, and earned a Fulbright scholarship to study in France. On the boat, she met historian Charles Le Guin, and they married in Paris in 1953.

Marriage meant the end of Le Guin's plans for doctoral studies. Returning to the United States, she taught and worked as a secretary while Charles completed his PhD. As their family grew (they would have three children), Le Guin continued the work that was to make her internationally famous – writing science fiction. Her writing broke out of the genre ghetto and, in 2014, she won the National Book Foundation's Medal for Distinguished Contribution to American Letters.

Le Guin's remarks remind us that she began her writing career at a time when marriage more generally signalled the end of women's ambitions for their work and art. She reminds us that both work and home – books and babies – are achievable. That art is made from life.

14 JANUARY

THE POLITICS OF BIRTH

'A woman should be able to choose who she has with her and should bear in mind that she's not going to want a crowd, and in fact that they can be very intrusive and this is not a good idea. [She should be able to select] somebody who she feels in tune with and who is in tune with her, and who knows exactly what she wants, and what she wants if she doesn't get what she wants: that's very important.'

Sheila Kitzinger, writer and childbirth activist, 2010

• • • • • •

Sheila Kitzinger (1929–2015) was a founder member of the National Childbirth Trust. She was a campaigner for women having the right information to make decisions about childbirth, particularly their right to a home birth if medically possible, and also an advocate for breastfeeding.

Kitzinger saw birth as intrinsically political, bound up in questions of who was in control, who was making the decisions and how well women were informed in order to make choices that were right for them. Her work arose because of the unnecessary medical interventions she saw imposed upon women, and aimed to give those choices back to women, supported by midwives.

Choices about pregnancy, birth and breastfeeding, and the language we use to describe these experiences, remain deeply contentious. Breastfeeding in particular is an issue where many mothers may feel judged about the choices that they make.

How do we ensure people are able to make healthcare choices that are right for them? How do we avoid being judgemental when people make choices about their health and their bodies that are different from the ones that we would make for ourselves?

15 JANUARY

I HARDLY KNOW YOU (AND YOU'RE EATING A SAUSAGE)

'I just find it interesting how people feel that women's bodies are there to be talked about, and it's kind of public domain conversations. I could be standing at a barbecue and an older lady asks me, "Are you having children?" And it's just that thing of – I would never dream of asking you, "How is your menopause going?" I don't really need to talk about my private biological things with you. I hardly know you and you're eating a sausage.'

Sian Harries, comedian and writer, 2017

• • • • • •

Being child-free has become a meaningful choice for women only since the arrival of reliable contraception, and the removal (in law, if not in practice) of barriers to equality in employment. Perhaps at no point before in human history have women been able to exercise so much choice about whether or not they want to become mothers.

But the assumption remains that women will have children – that they will become mothers – and speaking about one's ambivalence towards motherhood still carries with it an air of transgression. Women find themselves in the double bind of understanding the financial and career penalties that come with motherhood, but being convicted in the court of public opinion for not wanting to face these penalties.

And some women simply do not want to be mothers.

BAFTA-nominated Sian Harries has explored and written

about the kind of remarks she has received when it has emerged in conversation that, despite being in her late thirties, she is not a mother.

What makes women's choices about whether or not to become a parent public domain, when men do not face such scrutiny? Why do many find it difficult to accept that when some women say they do not want to be mothers, they are speaking the truth?

16 JANUARY

SUPERWOMAN

'We were still full-throttle breastfeeding when the race started and I couldn't just go cold turkey ... It was a disadvantage at the start of the first couple of checkpoints because competitors tend to go through them quite quickly ... but further on it really didn't make much of a difference anymore because people slow down and get less efficient.'

Jasmin Paris, ultramarathon runner, 2019

· · · · · ·

For those people who find marathon running insufficiently demanding, there is the Spine Race, an ultramarathon clocking in at 268 miles, run along the Pennine Way. In winter. Runners have a week to complete the course, typically racing through wind, snow, ice and, for most of the time, in dusk and darkness.

In 2019, fell runner Jasmin Paris (b. 1983) completed the course while still breastfeeding her young daughter. Paris – who works as a vet – expressed at checkpoints throughout the course of the event in order to avoid mastitis. While the delays cost her time at the start of the race, when her co-competitors were fresh, the differences proved negligible as the race went on.

Paris ultimately completed the course in 83:12:23. This was the overall record across both men's and women's events until 2024.

Very few of us are likely to be called upon to carry out acts of such extreme physical endurance. But Paris's outstanding achievement reminds us that the myth of the delicate woman is exactly that – a myth.

17 JANUARY

THE CHILD WE STILL ARE

'I still have to work so hard to extract that [confident] persona. I have been so fortunate in my life and I've had so many good experiences, but I never feel that far away from the eleven-year-old girl who always stepped right out of her shoes.'

Sigourney Weaver, actor and film producer, 2016

• • • • • •

Sigourney Weaver's (b. 1949) career in film began with a minor part in *Annie Hall* (1977). She has gone on to appear in some of the highest-grossing film franchises of all time, including the *Ghostbusters* and *Avatar* series. But Weaver's most famous role is surely as the iconic Ellen Ripley, the resolute heroine of the *Alien* series. Beginning with *Alien* (1979), Weaver has played Ripley in four films, earning an Oscar nomination for *Aliens* (1986).

Ripley subverts multiple tropes: instead of a victim, stalked and murdered, she turns from prey to predator. She is arguably the first female action hero.

It is touching, then, to read of Weaver's personal journey towards self-confidence. Conveying strength, charisma and sympathy on screen, Weaver reminds us that the child we once were is still sometimes very present – awkward, shy, and not yet a heroine.

18 JANUARY

GRAND NATIONAL

'Quite honestly, my horses meant more to
me than close family members.'

Jenny Pitman, champion horse trainer, 1981

• • • • • •

Jenny Pitman (b. 1946) left school at the age of 15 to start working in stables. By 1977, she had been married, divorced and was the mother of two young sons. Opening her own stables, Pitman began her solo career as a racehorse trainer. Known for her toughness and plain speaking, she worked doggedly to establish herself in a world not always welcoming to women.

In 1983, Pitman became the first woman to train a Grand National winner, Corbiere (ridden by Ben de Haan). She trained a second Grand National winner, Royal Athlete, in 1995, and was also the first woman to train a Cheltenham Gold Cup winner, in 1994.

Diagnosed with thyroid cancer in the 1990s, Pitman won the inaugural Sports Personality of the Year Helen Rollason Award in 1999, given for 'outstanding achievement in the face of adversity'. She retired the same year, and took up writing novels set in the world of race training.

We often hear women talk about putting family first. It's refreshing to hear Jenny Pitman give priority to her career – and her horses.

19 JANUARY

THERE IS A SEASON

'I'm a big fan of friendship pruning, so if I have friends in my life and I come to realise that I don't get out of them what I want, and maybe vice versa, I tend to freeze them out. I don't do it brutally, I don't have a massive argument about it unless there was something in their behaviour that caused me to do that. But I would stop replying to texts, be very evasive about when to meet up again and be nice, but basically push them out gently. There's no point in having friendships in your life that don't make you feel good about yourself.'

Jo Carnegie, novelist, 2015

• • • • • •

Have you ever meant to reply to someone's message or text, and then found the moment passed (maybe months), and that you never quite got around to getting back in touch?

It is easy to feel guilt when friendships drift in this way, to think that with a little more effort on your part (or more time in the day), you might have been able to meet and rekindle the relationship.

But it might also be that your friendship had come to a natural end. Perhaps neither of you are now the people that you were at its height. Sometimes people are with us for only a while, at just the right moment for both parties.

Sometimes, when friendships end, it's nobody's fault. It's part of life.

20 JANUARY

A BIT RANDOM

'When everything begins to look a bit random,
hit the gym running. That's my advice.'

Felicity Kendal, actor, 2016

• • • • • •

Felicity Kendal (b. 1946) began acting as a child in her father's touring repertory company; her career on stage and (particularly) television now stretches over 70 years.

Kendal is best known for playing Barbara Good in the BBC sitcom *The Good Life* (1975–8). *The Good Life* follows the exploits of Tom and Barbara Good, a married couple who are trying to become self-sufficient after Tom (Richard Briers) quits his stressful and unfulfilling job. Their conventional neighbours, Margo and Jerry Leadbetter (Penelope Keith and Paul Eddington), provide a foil for stories involving escaping pigs, hungry goats, animal-derived methane and home-made clothes. Margo (a social climber) is horrified by her neighbours' messy lifestyle; Jerry is sure they will fail, but wistfully admires their nerve and their newfound freedom.

The cast of four are in perfect harmony and Kendal's portrayal of Barbara, cheerfully going along with her husband's midlife crisis, laughing at his more self-important moments and the ridiculousness of their situation, but ready to give anything a go, made her a 1970s sex symbol. How heartening to learn that Barbara Good, too, later in life, finds that things can go a bit random, and nips down to the gym.

THAT'S NOT WHERE THE COLANDER GOES

'There is always time to make sure [the loo roll] goes over ... But I don't think I could sleep with somebody who had a system for loading the dishwasher. I don't know if I could be with somebody who said, quite seriously, "You know, that's not where the colander goes, love."'

Claudia Winkleman, television and radio presenter, writer and journalist, 2022

• • • • • •

Claudia Winkleman (b. 1972) is one of the most recognisable faces on British television. A graduate of New Hall, Cambridge, Winkleman has co-hosted the BBC's Saturday night flagship show *Strictly Come Dancing* since 2014 (having since 2010 co-presented the Sunday results show). Since 2022, she has been the host of the reality television programme *The Traitors*.

Here Winkleman turns her attention to those burning questions that can divide even the most harmonious household. Should the eggs be put in the fridge? Is there a right way to fill the dishwasher? Should milk go in before or after the tea? Do you have a system for forks? Is it right to tidy up in other people's houses? And – of course – which way round should we hang the loo roll?

Sometimes a line must be drawn. What are your household red lines?

22 JANUARY

HIT THE ROAD

'I remember going into work and saying to everybody,
"That's it. I'm going to get rid of my home, my
possessions, I'm going to buy a motor home and
I'm going to hit the road and find my happy place"
… I felt in society we were working long hours to
earn lots of money to clutter our lives, fill our lives.
My flat was full of beautiful things. And on the
surface it looked great. But I was so unhappy.'

Siobhan Daniels, motor-home dweller, 2024

• • • • • •

At the age of 60, Siobhan Daniels former reporter and current motor-home dweller gave up her house and possessions, bought a motor home and set off on the road. She's still journeying, five years later.

We are not all in a position to make such drastic changes to our lives, but Daniels's example provides the opportunity for a thought experiment.

What would we bring with us, if we were to pack up and hit the road, and what would we leave behind? What is truly essential to our lives, and to our wellbeing?

23 JANUARY

CLEARING OUT

'I used to have a lot of stuff myself ... When I was on the
path to having less, minimalism made me feel terrible.
Anything I kept felt wrong ... This need for perfection,
this push to purge.'

Jenn Jordan, professional organiser, 2024

• • • • • •

Minimalism, decluttering, sparking joy – it seems that you could stuff
a house full with books advising you how to remove stuff from your
house. But how practical are these guides? Do we simply fall into a trap
of having grand ambitions – and then feeling like a failure when we can't
keep up?

Jenn Jordan is a professional organiser and declutterer who loves
to come into people's homes and help them empty the boxes that have
remained unpacked for years, or clear out a wardrobe, or transform
a spare room from a storage unit into a useable space. Even so, she
advises caution in trying to do too much all at once, or setting off in
pursuit of yet more unattainable goals.

We will never have the perfect house – nor, perhaps, would we like
to live in such a space, as uninhabitable as any too-full, overly cluttered
home. But a modest goal or two – putting away the washing, clearing
a pile of paperwork that's lingered for too long – might give us a sense
of relief.

24 JANUARY

WHAT PLANET ARE YOU ON?

'Men and women have brains that are much more similar than they are dissimilar. [T]he really important thing about how your brains are affected is your experience ... Whether you're a man or a woman is almost one of the least interesting parts of that.'

Sophie Scott, professor and neuroscientist, 2017

• • • • • •

We've all heard of how men's brains and women's brains are different. How men are better at maths and women are better at multitasking. We might even observe this is in our day-to-day life, in our families, among our friends and at work.

Sometimes, however, our observations are not the most reliable source of data. It's easy for 'observer bias' to be at work, our tendency to see what we want or expect to see. We like to have our opinions confirmed. But there's a risk to assuming that there are fundamental differences between men's and women's brains: it's a short step to 'neurosexism', that is, saying that there are tasks for which women are innately unsuited.

Instead, we should ask ourselves: what does the data say?

Sophie Scott's research has looked into the neuroscience of speech. For her, the scientific evidence is clear. Our brains are more similar than not, and what matters most is the experiences that we have — our opportunities, or the languages we speak, or whether or not we have learned to read.

Mars and Venus have nothing to do with it. We're all from planet Earth.

THE BETTER PART OF VALOUR

'I think within successful relationships that you do
have secrets. You say, "I tell my partner everything!"
I don't think it's true. I think that privacy within a
relationship is actually very important for the health
of that relationship. Maybe to take the sting out of
it you should call it privacy rather than a secret, but
I think if you reveal to your partner all the dark
things that go through your mind about them
it could destroy a relationship.'

Linda Kelsey, writer, 2010

• • • • • •

Advice on better communication with your partner is a staple of life-style magazines and website listicles. And it's true – working out how you feel so that you can explain it to your partner, and listening as they communicate back their own feelings and position, is without doubt critical to making a relationship work.

But do we have to tell all? Do we have to be completely open? Linda Kelsey (b. 1952) suggests that sometimes discretion is the better part of valour and that we don't need to reveal some of our darker thoughts. Perhaps, too, the occasional white lie or lie of omission can save someone's feelings or dignity.

Sometimes people use the excuse of being 'an honest person' to allow them to bypass considering the opinions or feelings of others. When does honesty become too honest?

26 JANUARY

HAVING IT ALL

'I get up pretty early so I do my training essentially when my daughter and my husband are asleep in bed. That way I don't really feel like I'm missing out on time with them. I just generally think that if there's something you really want to do, you make it fit in.'

Jasmin Paris, ultramarathon runner, 2019

• • • • • •

Jasmin Paris's chosen sport of fell racing and ultramarathons involves multiday events across gruelling terrain, and her outstanding success has earned her an MBE. Paris combines her athletic career with her job as a vet and being the mother of a young daughter. She speaks with simplicity about how she organises her time, and how she prioritises what is important to her. It's humbling, in very many ways.

Sometimes we might look around and see other women performing at levels that leave us exhausted just to contemplate. But in fact most of us spend our days juggling a series of almost impossible and competing tasks, splitting our time and attention between caring responsibilities, work requirements and the many other sudden demands that are made upon us.

Perhaps we are closer to being superhuman than we imagine. Perhaps rather than judging ourselves about what is not yet done, we can stop and give ourselves credit for everything we *have* achieved.

27 JANUARY

A STORY THAT NEEDS TO BE TOLD

'They were a big inspiration to me. These were a group
of women that showed the extraordinary qualities
that us women have ... What the women did was such
an extraordinary feat of bravery and determination, I
thought, "This is a story that needs to be told." I don't
know many people remember or knew that four women
spent four nights, five days, down a mine with not
very much preparation, and just, off the cuff,
thought, "We're going to give this a go."'

Maxine Peake, actor and activist, 2012

• • • • • •

Maxine Peake (b. 1974), one of Britain's best-known actors, is perhaps
most recognised for her role as Twinkle in Victoria Wood's sitcom *din-
nerladies*. Peake has also starred in television series such as *Shameless* and
Silk, and taken on demanding parts such as serial killer Myra Hindley.

Born in Bolton to a working-class family, Peake is a committed socialist. Typically, she chooses projects with a strong political core, such as Mike
Leigh's *Peterloo* (2018), a dramatisation of the events of the Peterloo Massacre (1819), in which a crowd of thousands who had gathered in St Peter's
Field, Manchester, to demand voting reform was brutally put down.

Peake's play *Queens of the Coal Age* draws upon the Parkside Colliery
demonstration in 1993, in which a group of four women occupied the
colliery for four days to protest its imminent closure.

The Miners' Strike of 1984–5, and the years of closures and
decline that followed, fundamentally reshaped the landscape and social
fabric of Britain. In retelling this piece of working-class history, Peake
reminds us of the central part played by many women in this defining
post-war era. We are left reflecting upon what other similar hidden
histories remain untold.

28 JANUARY

HANDS-ON PARENTING

'I could literally pull my fingernails out and carve them into toys and no one would call me a "hands-on mother"!'

Nell Frizzell, writer and journalist, 2023

• • • • • •

Nell Frizzell has written extensively on parenting, notably in her *Vogue* column, 'Bringing Up Baby', and her memoir of the first years of motherhood, *Holding the Baby*.

Frizzell's writing tracks the isolation and frustrations of caring for a newborn, which go alongside the small and incandescent joys of watching a small personality unfold. She rails against the structural inequalities that penalise mothers more than fathers, and the gendered assumptions made about task allocation.

Mothers are frequently asked to live up to impossible standards. Frizzell points out the unfairness in the language we use to refer to mothers and fathers. That a father who plays with his child, changes nappies or shares caring responsibilities is referred to as 'hands on' is one example of these different and gendered expectations. For a mother, performing these tasks is simply par for the course.

Do we have double standards when it comes to parenting? Do we make assumptions about what a mother should do and what a father might do? Are we better thinking of mothering not in terms of perfection, but in terms of being 'good enough'?

29 JANUARY

SLEEPLESS NIGHTS

*'You are so aware of the fragility of your child
that you can't sleep even if they are asleep. Sleep
when your baby sleeps is the biggest load
of baloney I've ever heard in my life.'*

Nell Frizzell, writer and journalist, 2023

• • • • • •

Conversations about sleep, thinking about sleep and daydreaming about sleep can consume the thoughts of the parents of a newborn child.

Apps will track, in minute detail, the baby's sleeping hours, and parents will pore over them looking for patterns, in the hope of spotting a window of opportunity to get some much-needed kip themselves. Books will offer failsafe regimes for getting a newborn to sleep on demand. And everyone seems to have (often conflicting) advice.

Nell Frizzell is robustly frank about the advice she was given as the mother of a newborn to sleep when the baby sleeps. She describes precisely the overwhelming consciousness that parents of newborns have of the fragile human being that has been put in their care.

Parenting a small child is so specific to the particular child and the particular parent that offering advice seems almost to be doomed from the start.

How else can we support a new parent? What else can we do? Can we offer to take the baby out in the pram for an hour or two, perhaps?

30 JANUARY

WORKING HOURS

'There's one type of conversation that literally makes me feel rage and it's when I hear dads talk about how they have to sleep in the spare room because they have to be rested for their day of work. We don't value looking after a newborn baby as work.'

Paul Morgan-Bentley, journalist, 2023

· · · · · ·

When Paul Morgan-Bentley became the father of a newborn baby, he experienced what all new parents go through: sleeplessness, exhaustion, the struggle to keep up with work demands alongside the new and utterly overwhelming responsibilities for a vulnerable and completely dependent human being.

Morgan-Bentley has explored his experiences of attempting to share parenting responsibilities with his husband in his book *The Equal Parent: How Sharing the Load Helps the Whole Family Thrive*. As a family comprising two dads and a baby, Morgan-Bentley has a fresh eye on the double standards that apply to mothers and fathers.

The presence of a newborn child completely overturns our idea of what constitutes work. The physical labour of caring for a newborn – combined with the erratic hours – most certainly counts as work, albeit entirely unpaid and largely unappreciated.

When we acknowledge this, the boundaries between home life and work life become less stable; we have to admit their interdependence, as well as the ramifications of this for all of us with caring responsibilities.

31 JANUARY

TIRED ALL THE TIME

'When we're exhausted, we tend to reduce down our activities ... That is intuitive, that we want to avoid expending energy, but it's also dangerous, because we cut out what has the potential to re-energise us, to nourish us ... we need to do things for ourselves that are purely joy giving, that just serve the function of making us feel alive, of giving us some respite, of allowing us a moment of peace and joy in our lives ... Rather than just cutting everything out of our lives, when we feel very depleted, we need to remember what makes us feel alive.'

Anna Katharina Schaffner, academic and executive coach, 2024

• • • • • •

Fatigue, burnout, exhaustion – a survey by YouGov, conducted in 2022, suggested that one in eight Britons felt permanently tired, and a quarter felt tired most of the time. The feeling is so ubiquitous that it has an acronym: TATT, or 'tired all the time'.

Parents of young children unsurprisingly reported being more tired – and women were, in general, more tired than men. And the pandemic has undoubtedly had an impact on us all, whether or not we are struggling with symptoms of long COVID.

Burnout has a negative impact upon our whole life. Anna Katharina Schaffner was a professor of cultural history when she realised she was suffering from fatigue, and that stress at work was taking the pleasure and enjoyment from her whole life, making her irritable and bitter. She prepared an exit from her job, and, after leaving, wrote a book on her experiences, with advice for those in the same situation: *Exhausted: An A–Z for the Weary* (2024).

One recommendation Schaffner offers is to make space again for hobbies. While this might in itself feel like an insurmountable task, the benefits are enormous, reminding us that at least some of our time must be devoted to rest and relaxation, to doing something that isn't serving our work life. Even doing a jigsaw puzzle – gentle, meditative and with no purpose other than itself – can have a beneficial effect.

As the new year is settling in, are you remembering to take time to rest, to nourish yourself?

FEBRUARY

1 FEBRUARY

PARENTAL LEAVE

'[C]ompulsory parental leave, particularly for MPs
and business owners. I want them to . . . change nappies,
change bedding, wipe sick up off the floor,
get peanut butter out of a plug socket.'

Nell Frizzell, writer and journalist, 2023

• • • • • •

There are strong financial reasons for supporting working parents through the early weeks and months of having a newborn. If companies have invested in people, then losing them makes no sense.

But how to make policymakers and employers understand the reality of the situation in which many working parents find themselves, not simply the exhaustion of those early months, but the expense of childcare?

Nell Frizzell's suggestion that MPs and business owners in particular should be compelled to take parental leave is aimed at the people who make and benefit from policy. But her point goes beyond asking policymakers to enter imaginatively into the lives of working parents. Frizzell is clear that this is a matter of restructuring the gender imbalance in domestic labour.

Equality at home leads to equality in the workplace, with all the social, cultural and political changes that implies.

2 FEBRUARY

LONG-DISTANCE FRIENDSHIPS

'My best friend lives in Australia and when I see her we just "are". It's lovely. It's the one relationship where if we don't see each other for three years there's no explaining to do. We just fit into this way of being which is very neutral, very easy and very lovely. I think for a woman it's very important to have that solidarity with somebody.'

Dawn O'Porter, writer, director and television presenter, 2014

. . . . . .

Historically, friendships have often taken place at long distance. Marriage might mean a woman moving some distance away from her former circle of friends, as well as from her family. In an age before mass communication, letter writing was an important means of contact, a way of keeping in touch with one's former life, and one of our most important sources of information on how women used to live.

We move away for different reasons now — to study, to work, to travel — and it's easier to remain connected than ever before, something we all learned during lockdown, when video calls and email became crucial means of connecting with our loved ones. And there are those friendships where time away or lack of day-to-day contact seems not to interrupt the natural flow of being together again.

Have you spoken to an old friend recently? Is it time to reconnect?

3 FEBRUARY

RAGS TO RICHES

'So you see what purposeful daydreaming can accomplish. My advice is, try it. Dream of what you want most and dream of it really hard, when you're tackling the washing, when you are cleaning out the ashes, when your hands are full of cinders and your teeth are on edge, or when your back is breaking in the garden.'

Catherine Cookson, author, 1950

• • • • • •

Dame Catherine Cookson (1906–98) was one of Britain's best-selling and most prolific writers, with sales estimated to be in excess of 120 million copies. She was also – for a time – the most borrowed author from British libraries (overtaken in 2001 by Jacqueline Wilson). Hers is a quintessential rags-to-riches story – but with a fairy godmother replaced by hard work.

Cookson's books were inspired by the deprivation of her childhood in South Shields, then in County Durham. The illegitimate child of an alcoholic and a bigamist, she was brought up by her grandmother, believing her mother was her sister. Leaving school at 14, she worked first in 'service' and, later, having moved south, ran the laundry of Hastings workhouse.

She married in her mid-thirties and, after a series of devastating miscarriages, took up writing as a means to help with her depression. Her first novel, *Kate Hannigan*, was published in 1950. Televised adaptations of her novels were a staple of ITV's schedule, with 18 of her books serialised between 1989 and 2001.

In later life, Cookson returned to the north-east, where she died, aged 91, in 1998. Her husband of 50 years, Tom, died shortly afterwards. Since the 1980s, her charitable foundation has made donations to numerous causes, particularly to young and disadvantaged children in the north-east.

4 FEBRUARY

ON EMPATHY

'The route that EmpathyLab uses is books, which
is really based on the science that when we identify
with book characters and their feelings, we're expanding
our real-life empathy. And that's exciting because
of course books are in homes and schools and libraries.
And so it means that families can springboard
off books to teach empathy skills.'

Miranda McKearney, social justice entrepreneur, 2020

· · · · · ·

Miranda McKearney founded the Reading Agency in 2002; the charity runs a Summer Reading Challenge through local libraries, in which more than 800,000 children participate each year. McKearney's interest in childhood literacy led her to a body of psychological research which shows that reading can improve our ability to empathise with others.

Research suggests that empathy, our capacity to imagine and share the feelings and points of view of others, is not an innate skill, but one that can be learned. McKearney founded the social enterprise scheme EmpathyLab to improve empathy in children and young people through better access to books and reading schemes.

It makes intuitive sense that reading improves our ability to empathise with others. When we read, we're being asked to enter the minds of others, experience the world in the way that they experience it, and – perhaps – learn to hold back on judging too quickly.

Do we push ourselves beyond our comfort zone in what we read? Do we tend to stay with the same sources, or the same authors, who represent what is safe and familiar? How could we go beyond what is familiar? What new insights might that open up to us?

Seeing the world from someone else's point of view is not the same as condoning it. It's possible to agree to disagree.

5 FEBRUARY

MUSCLE TRAINING

'I tend to find myself going from a novel to short stories ... There is a difference in focus in them, and you come out of one with your muscles all trained for the other, as if your whole body's been used rather than just using one part of your body or one part of your brain.'

Ali Smith, writer, academic and journalist, 2008

• • • • • •

Over her 30-year career, Ali Smith (b. 1962) has published 12 novels and five collections of short stories. Her novels have won the Orwell Prize for Political Fiction and the Women's Prize for Fiction, and have been shortlisted for the Booker Prize and the Goldsmiths Prize. She is one of Britain's most technically assured and accomplished prose writers.

Smith's description of alternating between writing short stories and writing novels shows how she has to switch between processes depending on the form. What works for one doesn't work for the other, but part of the pleasure comes from having to make other parts of her brain work out after being at rest.

How repetitive are we in the ways we think and work? Can we experiment with different forms of cognitive workout? Is it time to try something new? Could we pick up a new language, or an instrument, or a paintbrush? The brain is a muscle too; you need to use it – and train it – if you want to keep it in shape.

6 FEBRUARY

A NATURALIST'S EYE

'I was trained as a scientist and I suppose I still think as a scientist. I still see the world through a naturalist's eyes. I want to describe the relationships between things that I see ... I have to know what it smells like, what it sounds like after rain, what's blooming at the time of year that this character is walking this earth.'

Barbara Kingsolver, novelist, essayist and poet, 2010

• • • • • •

American author Barbara Kingsolver (b. 1955) has written nine novels, as well as volumes of poetry, essays and short stories. Her novel *Demon Copperhead* won the Pulitzer Prize for Fiction in 2023; it also won the Women's Prize for Fiction that year, making her the first writer to win twice (she had won previously with *The Lacuna*, in 2010).

Kingsolver started out as a science writer, and her novels are exquisitely pitched between accessibility and literary ambition. Many of her books draw extensively on her affinity for the natural world. *Flight Behavior* (2012) follows a group of characters studying monarch butterflies in rural Appalachia, and the effects of climate change upon the population. *Prodigal Summer* (2000) evokes the landscape of rural Virginia. The human narratives are inextricably linked to the wider web of nature.

Take the time to step outside today. Pay attention to the small details of what's around you. The cracks in the pavement and the moss that grows there. Feel the sun, or the rain; take a deep breath. All life is linked.

7 FEBRUARY

BEING ORDINARY

'I find it quite easy to shut [the fame] out. I'm an ordinary person, you know. I wasn't a showbiz person, I was a photographer and just a person, I haven't been brought up in the showbiz world, I didn't start young in the public eye. So I like truth, you know, I like just being ordinary.'

Linda McCartney, photographer and musician

• • • • • •

Linda Eastman (1941–98) was recently divorced with a young daughter and establishing herself as a photographer when she met Paul McCartney in 1967. They were married in 1969 (to some negativity from fans – McCartney was, after all, the last 'unattached' Beatle). Her relaxed attitude to life – and her distance from 'Beatlemania' – was a significant part of the success of their marriage.

After the break-up of the Beatles in 1970, McCartney formed Wings (with Linda and Denny Laine), but the 1970s was also a period when the couple focused on their domestic life. Linda brought her daughter from her first marriage, and the couple had three further children together. McCartney's farm on Kintyre became a place of retreat.

A retrospective of Linda's photographs from this period was held at Kelvingrove Art Gallery in Glasgow in 2019, showing pictures of rural and family life alongside portraits of celebrity visitors such as Jimi Hendrix and Aretha Franklin.

Linda McCartney died of breast cancer in 1998 at the age of 56. A commemorative garden, with a bronze sculpture by Jane Robbins, is in Campbelltown, Kintyre; a memorial that speaks more to her connection to the local community than to her fame.

8 FEBRUARY

WEBS OF CONNECTION

'I lived 20 years right on the Mexican border. So border
culture was quite salient; I received
my political education from living in Tucson, learning
about border issues and refugees,
and what one country does to another.'

Barbara Kingsolver, novelist, essayist and poet, 2010

• • • • • •

As well as environmental and ecological themes, American writer Barbara
Kingsolver (b. 1955) frequently turns to themes of progressive change and
social justice. These novels are large and capacious, covering long periods
of time, and reminiscent of nineteenth-century social novels – in fact, her
2022 novel *Demon Copperhead* transfers the action of *David Copperfield* to
contemporary Appalachia.

The Lacuna (2009) revolves around the lives of painters Frida Kahlo
and Diego Rivera, their association with Leon Trotsky, and McCarthyism
during the 1950s. *Unsheltered* (2018) is concerned with the increasing
precariousness of the American middle class, and the fragility of
American institutions, particularly in the face of natural disaster.

Kingsolver uses the novel to trace our interconnections, our mutual
dependencies, all of which rely upon the environment of which we are
a part. She draws our attention to the gaps in our safety nets – and the
people who fall through those gaps.

It's easy to say to whom we feel most connected. But what are the
interdependencies – the connections – that we rely on that are more
obscure, less obvious?

9 FEBRUARY

FORWARDS AND IN FLATS

'I was crying and everyone had gone to lunch, and some legs appeared in front of my face ... and a voice said, "What is it, little girl? What's the matter?" And I said, "Well, I can't learn all this. It's impossible!" ... He said I could watch him rehearse ... He threw his cane, he broke his cane, he cursed at the drummer ... It was equally as hard for Mr Astaire.'

Debbie Reynolds, film star and singer, 1989

• • • • • •

Debbie Reynolds (1932–2016) shot to fame at the age of 19 when she starred opposite Gene Kelly in *Singin' in the Rain* (1952), arguably the greatest film musical of all time. Her career spanned seven decades; her last screen performance was in *Behind the Candelabra* (2013), Steven Soderbergh's biopic of Liberace, in which she played Liberace's mother, Frances.

Reynolds was a product of the Hollywood 'star system', in which studios created and promoted actors as glamorous personalities, and one of the very last to come through MGM Studios. Her private life, particularly her divorce from her first husband, singer and actor Eddie Fisher, was the subject of huge public interest, not least the revelation of Fisher's affair with Elizabeth Taylor.

Her daughter from that marriage, Carrie Fisher (1956–2016), herself became a superstar at a young age, filming the role of Princess Leia, in *Star Wars: Episode IV – A New Hope* at 19 years old. Carrie Fisher later became one of the most in-demand script doctors in Hollywood, as well as the author of several brilliant memoirs of growing up in and surviving Hollywood. Carrie Fisher died on 27 December 2016; Debbie Reynolds passed away the day afterwards.

Reynolds's memory of filming *Singin' in the Rain* gives a glimpse at another great studio star; a man who made his talent seem effortless. If even Fred Astaire found his day job hard, then we can all – like Debbie – take comfort.

10 FEBRUARY

THE SCIENCE OF DATING

'Different age groups have different expectations. Younger people are much more focused on looks ... There's that moment they walk [in] and we can see from their faces they don't fancy each other. Whereas someone in their thirties or forties ... they want to settle down ... They're much more open to seeing why we've matched them and exploring all those other things. And then the older generation – they still want the spark and connection but they're looking for companionship and shared interests ... There is a science to it, but there's an instinct ... in just imagining those two people together.'

Lana Salah, TV executive and producer, 2017

· · · · · ·

What do we really want from romantic relationships?

Lana Salah has been involved in the production of Channel 4's long-running reality show *First Dates,* in which two people are brought together for the first time at a restaurant, and their date is filmed. At the end of the evening, they're asked whether they would like to meet again.

Salah describes the different expectations we have of our relationships across the course of our life. From sexual and physical attraction in our twenties, to looking for a partner in our thirties, to looking for someone with whom to be companionable as we grow older, there is a knack, Salah believes, to putting couples together.

How do our expectations change over the course of our relationships? Are we able to reconfigure these, or do we inevitably drift apart?

One thing remains true – most of us are looking to be loved, to have someone beside us with whom we feel comfortable and compatible.

11 FEBRUARY

HERE COMES THE BRIDE

'So many weddings now are in a registry office or have a humanist element ... My second wedding was in a church and I just walked down the aisle myself ... That was fine. The world kept turning.'

Anna Burnside, humanist celebrant, 2018

• • • • • •

Government statistics show that around a quarter of a million of us got married in 2022, a return to pre-COVID levels. Weddings, it seems, are as popular as they have ever been.

The reality is that marriage in the twenty-first century is very different from how it was only a couple of decades ago. Civil partnerships between same-sex couples became legal in 2004, and the Marriage (Same Sex Couples) Act of 2013 legalised same-sex marriage in England and Wales. A record number of same-sex marriages took place in 2022 (about 3 per cent of the overall total).

We also spend more time living together before committing to marriage: nine out of ten couples who married in 2021 and 2022 had been cohabiting before the wedding – the highest rate since records began in 1994.

How we choose to celebrate has changed dramatically, too, as Anna Burnside points out. Every part of the ceremony is evidently open to alteration.

Whether it's a best woman's speech, walking yourself down the aisle or eschewing any religious component, it seems that we are more than able to maintain something of the traditional nature of the wedding while bringing our own interpretation to the ceremony. And why not?

It is, after all, our own very special day.

12 FEBRUARY

REGRETS

'I wish I had been a teenager. But when I was that age the concept didn't exist, or if it did it didn't come my way. So I never wore my hair in a pony-tail, or danced to rock 'n' roll until I was ready to drop, or wore drainpipe trousers (not then, anyway), or shrieked when I saw pictures of film stars, or wore bright pink luminous socks. I dare say I was well enough off without the shrieking and the socks, but the rest I regret.'

Iris Murdoch, novelist and philosopher, 1957

. . . . . .

Fiercely intellectual and wickedly subversive, Dame Iris Murdoch's (1919–99) novels contemplated the nature of good and evil, and the power of sex and the subconscious.

Murdoch's novel *The Sea, The Sea* (1978), which won the Booker Prize, charts the attempt by Charles Arrowby, a playwright and director, to retire to the coast to write his memoirs, an endeavour thwarted by the reappearance in his life of his first love, and his own self-absorption.

During her life, Murdoch's novels eclipsed her reputation as a philosopher (she was a fellow of St Anne's College, Oxford from 1948 until 1963). More recently, her work has been reappraised; she forms one of the four female colleagues discussed in *Metaphysical Animals: How Four Women Brought Philosophy Back to Life* (2022) by Clare Mac Cumhaill and Rachael Wiseman, a study of women philosophers at Oxford after the war.

In later life, Murdoch was diagnosed with Alzheimer's disease. This period of her life was documented by her husband, John Bayley, to whom she was married for over 40 years, in his memoir *Iris* (1998).

13 FEBRUARY

PUSH EACH OTHER AROUND

'He is my toyboy . . . I don't know why we got married but we both decided it was the right moment. I suppose it's something to do with commitment, the idea that yes, we are prepared to push each other around in our Zimmer frames and bath chairs and we want to spend the rest of our lives together.'

Prue Leith, restaurateur, broadcaster, presenter and writer, 2016

· · · · · ·

Dame Prudence Leith's (b. 1940) energy is enviable. Starting out in her early twenties as a supplier of high-quality business lunches, she moved into events catering before opening her first restaurant in 1969. Based in Notting Hill, Leith's eventually won a Michelin star. Her first catering training school, Leith's School of Food and Wine, opened in 1975, and was turning over millions before she sold it in the late 1990s.

Alongside her catering and cookery school businesses, Leith moved into journalism and food criticism, writing for various national newspapers. Cookery books naturally came next, and, latterly, a career in television, first as a judge on no article in the title *Great British Menu* and then on *The Great British Bake Off*.

Widowed in 2002, Leith subsequently met John Playfair, a retired clothes designer, and they married in 2016. After a period of living in their own houses, they moved in together in 2020.

14 FEBRUARY

LOVE AND MARRIAGE

'I'm a very romantic person. I definitely was one of those
people who was just going to keep on getting married
until I finally got it right. If this one hadn't worked out,
I'd be married to the next one, and trying with the
next one. It only took three tries to get it right.'

Nora Ephron, screenwriter and director, 1998

• • • • • •

Nora Ephron (1941–2012) was the genius behind some of the most
beloved films of the 1980s and 1990s.

Starting with screenplays such as the hard-hitting *Silkwood* (1983,
which won Meryl Streep an Academy Award nomination for her
portrayal of the murdered union organiser Karen Silkwood) and the
near-flawless script for *When Harry Met Sally . . .* (1989, which earned
the writer her own Oscar nomination), Ephron went on to directorial
triumphs with romantic comedies such as *Sleepless in Seattle* (1993)
and *You've Got Mail* (1998).

Ephron's humour is tender but sharp; her characters witty but
self-deprecating. In her own life, Ephron's second marriage to Water-
gate journalist Carl Bernstein ended over the revelation of his affair
with Margaret Jay (the daughter of British Prime Minister James Cal-
laghan), who was at the time married to the British ambassador to the
United States.

Ephron's account of her own relationship is funny and yet vulnerable, recasting her own life into the shape of one of her films. Yet even
as she undercuts the whole notion of romantic love, we hear the ache
for partnership, and understand how we too might wish for the happy
ending.

15 FEBRUARY

AN EFFORT OF WILL

'[Love] is not easy. And it shouldn't be. It's
not a muscle response, it's an effort of the will
and an act of intelligence. And so it really
should be a difficult thing to do.'

Toni Morrison, writer, editor and Nobel laureate, 1992

• • • • • •

Toni Morrison (1931–2019) was one of the greatest writers of the twentieth century. A graduate of Howard and Cornell, where she completed a Master's on Virginia Woolf and William Faulkner, Morrison moved from academia into publishing. In 1967, she joined Random House, becoming the first Black woman at the publisher to become senior fiction editor.

At Random House, Morrison began a process of bringing African-American literature into the mainstream, publishing writers such as Toni Cade Bambara and Angela Davis, as well as non-fiction volumes depicting African-American lives. Morrison's first novel, *The Bluest Eye*, written when she was the mother of two small children, was published in 1970.

Morrison has described her works as being about 'love under duress'. In situations of terrible grief and horror, her characters find the capacity to love each other fully. Love in her books is not romance or an arrow's strike; it is a conscious and continuing choice.

16 FEBRUARY

FRIENDS INDEED

'I love collaborating, and I love collaborating on movies, and I love working with [her sister, producer and screenwriter Delia Ephron] . . . It was Meg Ryan's idea that after that scene where she and Billy Crystal talked about orgasms she would have one in the delicatessen. That's her idea and therefore she's probably entirely responsible for my whole career.'

Nora Ephron, screenwriter and director, 1998

• • • • • •

Nora Ephron's best-known films are romantic comedies, stories about men and women trying to make sense of each other. At the heart of *When Harry Met Sally . . .* lies the question, 'Can men and women ever be friends?'

Conventionally, narratives about love and romance place women in competition with each other, rivals for the hand of the most eligible man in the vicinity. The women in Ephron's films gently subvert this. They are friends with other women. They are competing chiefly with their own inadequacies and insecurities.

Speaking about her professional life, Ephron highlights the collaborative nature of her working relationship with her sister, Delia, and with the star of several of her films, Meg Ryan. Ephron attributes what must be the most famous moment in *When Harry Met Sally . . .* to Ryan.

While the world around us might tell us that we are competitors, women know better. We succeed more through collaboration.

17 FEBRUARY

LONG-TERM THINKING

'When you enter into a long-term relationship [you think]
that it's going to be the same relationship. But . . .
sometimes a marriage has to die in order to be reborn.'

Emma Thompson, actor and screenwriter, 2018

• • • • • •

Dame Emma Thompson (b. 1959) has been married twice. Her first
marriage, to Kenneth Branagh, ended in the mid-1990s after he began
an affair. Thompson subsequently met actor Greg Wise on the set of
Sense and Sensibility in 1995, a film which she wrote and starred in.
Thompson and Wise have been married since 2003 and have two
children together.

If we ourselves change as individuals, why would we expect our
relationships to stay the same? Our priorities alter; our circumstances
vary. This holds true of all our relationships in life, not just our marriage or partnership. As parents grow older, we might find ourselves
taking over caring for them. As children move on, we may have to adapt
to their absence, to the fact that their world no longer centres around
the family life that has been built up.

Every long-lasting relationship has its highs and lows. Can we adapt,
and meet our partner on these new terms? If we feel our relationship
is ending, can we see a way to make a new one from everything that has
gone before?

18 FEBRUARY

WE ARE NOW FREE

'I wanted to explore what people can do whose bodies have literally been owned, and was not yours ... Part of freedom is the freedom to fall in love, to choose whom you love, to inhabit your body, to express things through your body. And it may appear – as it did during the Jazz Age – to be a little naughty and perhaps even in some cases illegal, but it was the way in which many people ... were able to say, "We are now free."'

Toni Morrison, writer, editor and Nobel laureate, 1992

• • • • • •

In 1993, the Nobel Prize in Literature was given to Toni Morrison, 'who in novels characterized by visionary force and poetic import, gives life to an essential aspect of American reality'. She was the first Black woman of any nationality to win the award.

Morrison was, at the time, partway through a major trilogy of connected novels depicting African-American history, beginning with *Beloved* (1987), which narrates the haunting of a mother pursued by slave hunters who is driven to murder her baby, and followed by *Jazz* (1992), set during the 1920s Harlem Renaissance and reaching back into the bloody history of the American South. (The third book in the trilogy, *Paradise*, was published in 1997.)

Morrison's novels invite us to consider questions such as: what does it mean, to be unfree? What scars does this leave? What do people do with their freedom? And if they choose to do something that we would not do – who are we to judge?

19 FEBRUARY

THE SUBVERSIVE STITCH

'My mother sewed. She made our clothes. We used to have a Christmas pantomime at the church, and my mother was always making clothes for that. So there was a sewing machine in our little cottage . . . and I was sewing dolls' clothes as a child, making models. Always sewing. Learning to knit. So then I made my clothes as a teenager. As a young person, I spent my money on shoes and made all my own clothes.'

Vivienne Westwood, fashion designer and businesswoman, 2014

• • • • • •

Dame Vivienne Westwood (1941–2022) was one of Britain's most influential fashion designers. The description of how she learned to sew is oddly domestic for one of the architects of punk. But sewing – for all its association with the private sphere and female decorousness – has always had a rebellious side.

Art historian Rozsika Parker's classic feminist text *The Subversive Stitch: Embroidery and the Making of the Feminine* (1984) examines how women's arts – particularly textile arts – were separated from the domain of 'fine art' and marginalised as craft. At the same time, embroidery and textile arts were a source of deep pleasure and creativity for the women who practised them – not to mention a source of income.

Westwood's work was steeped in her knowledge of the history of fabric and design. Her *Pirate* collection of 1981 (as worn by Adam and the Ants) drew extensively on her research into eighteenth-century costume and traditional tailoring techniques and fabrics. The stitch was now openly subversive.

20 FEBRUARY

ANYTHING GOES

'The most important thing that's happened is complete freedom from fashion rules. This is the great thing. We can wear all the hemlines. There's no obsession with "this is what is in, this is what's out". The same girl can wear the most frivolous and flamboyant female clothes and then very boyish clothes. We can all have such fun. No rules anymore.'

Mary Quant, fashion designer and businesswoman, 1971

• • • • • •

Hotpants, skinny rib sweaters and (possibly) the miniskirt, Dame Mary Quant's (1930–2023) designs epitomise an era. A self-taught designer (she had originally studied illustration), Quant created a 'scene' around her boutique, Bazaar, on the King's Road, Chelsea. People came for the drinks, late nights and music as well as for Quant's fresh, contemporary and wearable styles.

Equally commercially minded, Quant struck lucrative deals that pushed her clothes and cosmetics onto the high street; the Victoria and Albert Museum reports that by the end of the 1960s, up to 7 million women had a Quant product in their wardrobe. Although most likely not the inventor of the miniskirt (Quant herself said that she took the look from what the girls on the King's Road were already wearing), it became in many ways her signature design, as worn by model Twiggy.

Youth, sexiness, fun – above all, the miniskirt symbolised freedom – the freedom to move, to run about, to be alive in the world.

What do you wear that makes you feel free?

21 FEBRUARY

TAKEN IN ONE'S STRIDE

'One just looked at a map of Europe and had no
passports to think about and no currency questions
and went wherever one liked ... We were carried
across the Dolomites, my sister and I, when I was about
two-and-a-half, by the guides, so that we began very
early. I think travel was taken in one's stride in those days.'

Freya Stark, writer and traveller, 1965

• • • • • •

When Dame Freya Stark (1893–1993) died at the age of 100, she
had lived through the height and decline of the Empire, two world
wars, the creation of the Commonwealth, and the emergence and
rise of the post-war political intra-national consensus known as the
European Union. She had travelled widely throughout the Middle
East – including Syria, Arabia, Iraq and Turkey – capturing her journeys in over a dozen volumes of travel writing, autobiography and
collected letters.

Where her predecessor in the region, archaeologist Gertrude
Bell (1868–1926), had an eye for the more obviously scholarly,
Stark's knack was in capturing the everyday life of the people upon
whom she descended, an ethnographic approach requiring imaginative sympathy and a recognition of the poverty and disease rife
throughout the region.

The freedom to move that Stark describes undoubtedly arose
from the fact of Empire, and her own status as a white Englishwoman,
and a biography by Molly Izzard published shortly after Stark's death
inevitably paints a more complicated portrait than appears in Stark's
own accounts of herself. But there is no doubt that she paved the way
for a later generation of women writers who have struck out on their
own, including Dervla Murphy, Robyn Davidson and Sara Wheeler.

22 FEBRUARY

WORLD SCOUT DAY

'If getting girls to do fun, adventurous things every day, getting them to learn leadership skills, helping them to develop character and boys doing that with them as well is a feminist thing – then let's have more boys and girls who are feminists, I say.'

Ann Limb, educationalist, 2015

· · · · · ·

Dame Ann Limb (b. 1953) is an educationalist whose career in further education institutions spanned from the mid-1970s until the start of the millennium. In 2015, she became Chair of the Scout Association, the first woman to hold the position since the organisation was founded by Robert Baden-Powell in 1907.

In 1910, Baden-Powell created an entirely separate organisation for girls, the Guides. Girls were not permitted in the Scout Association until 1976, when they were allowed to join the Venture Scouts. Across the next 30 years, girls were admitted piecemeal to various parts of the Scout Association. In 2007, full admission across all parts of the organisation became compulsory. Within a decade, more than one in four scouts identified as female.

From exclusion to leadership in less than 40 years is a triumphant story of second-wave feminism. A single generation can be enough to transform an organisation – but the willingness to change must be there.

23 FEBRUARY

OTHER POINTS OF VIEW

'The kind of issues they look at collectively [at scouts],
seeing each other's points of view in an informal
learning environment out of the classroom [means that
scouts] is probably a safer place for boys and girls to
learn about how best to work together.'

Ann Limb, educationalist, 2015

• • • • • •

Can girls and boys benefit from having separate spheres? Certainly
there is a case to be made for dedicated spaces which can enable children and young adults to flourish by meeting people who share similar
experiences. But do these benefits outweigh learning to work together?

Ann Limb, who in 2015 became the first woman to chair the Scout
Association, oversees an organisation that has moved from admitting
only boys in 1976 to the full admission of girls in 2007. She makes the
case for shared spaces beyond the classroom, where all children can
work together collectively.

Our assumptions about sex and gender begin very young. One
benefit of full integration is that boys, from an early age, get to see
girls act as leaders, and that gendered assumptions of who is fit to lead,
whose voices are given the most weight, are not given the chance to
take root and develop.

Boys who have learned young to respect girls will – we would
hope – grow to be men who respect women.

24 FEBRUARY

ACTING OUT

'People aren't really able to understand their feelings. I think we see more and more that feelings are driving us. We're supposed to be in the age of the enlightenment and the age of rationality but you've got the whole world seemingly acting on their feelings.'

Deborah Orr, journalist and writer, 2017

• • • • • •

Deborah Orr's (1962–2019) memoir, *Motherwell: A Girlhood*, about growing up as a working-class girl in Motherwell, near Glasgow, was published in 2020 shortly after her death from breast cancer at the age of 57.

In 2016, Orr began treatment for complex post-traumatic stress disorder (complex PTSD). Complex PTSD arises from experiencing repeated or long-term traumatic events; symptoms may include those of PTSD, such as flashbacks and nightmares, but also difficulties in relationships, a sense of disconnection and feelings of guilt, shame and low self-esteem.

Inspired by Carrie Fisher's openness about her experiences of bipolar disorder, Orr too wrote about her diagnosis and subsequent therapy.

Are we able to understand why we react the way that we do? Do we know what can trigger anger, or guilt, or sadness? Can we put a name to our emotions when we experience them?

25 FEBRUARY

HOW TO DEAL WITH DIVORCE

'Some people get drunk, some people become
promiscuous and I decided to get on a stage in
front of strangers and tell them all about it.
And luckily they thought it was hilarious.'

Sarah Millican, comedian, writer and presenter, 2017

• • • • • •

When Sarah Millican's (b. 1975) husband left her, she turned the
experience into stand-up comedy, took her show to the Edinburgh
Fringe, and won the award for Best Newcomer. She is now one of the
most popular and recognisable comedians in Britain. Her memoir, *How
to Be Champion*, was published in 2017.

We might not all want to turn to something as dramatic as becoming a stand-up comedian in order to work through a devastating change
in our lives. We might, in fact, prefer to retire hurt, hide in a corner
or climb under the bedclothes to nurse our wounds and try to heal.
Grieving is essential after any loss – but what happens next?

How do we deal with unexpected blows? What happens when life
throws us curveballs? How do we find a way to treat ourselves kindly
while picking ourselves up and dusting ourselves down? Who are the
people that we know we could rely on to help, to give us a way through?

And what hidden resources might reveal themselves to us? What
are we capable of that we never previously imagined?

26 FEBRUARY

HELICOPTER PARENTING

'We're driving ourselves completely and utterly mad.
My waiting lists are full of people who ... think
that unless they fulfil every last one of their
children's needs they'll be letting them down.'

Andrew G. Marshall, author and family and marital therapist, 2013

• • • • • •

'Helicopter parenting' refers to a parenting style in which parents and caregivers are closely involved in every aspect of their child's life. Whether it's overseeing homework, monitoring offline and online friendships, managing schedules or directing choices, it's characterised by intervention or, less positively, interference.

It's true that social media has brought about many unanticipated dangers for children. And it's true, too, that it's not as easy to play outside independently as it used to be when the streets were less full of traffic, and families tended to live more within tightly knit local communities.

Ultimately, however, children need to learn self-sufficiency and independence. They need to learn how to function in the world – and be keen to get out there.

Are there ways in which you might be able to let go a little more?

27 FEBRUARY

DO UNTO OTHERS

'My parents dragged us kicking and screaming to Hebrew school and I must say we didn't take to it very well. We didn't get much out of it, but we did get "do unto others". That was really important. That's all we got but I do believe that's all you need. That's what they're all peddling and it's a good thing so I took it to heart.'

Bette Midler, singer and actor, 2014

• • • • • •

Sometimes referred to as the 'Golden Rule', the idea that you should behave towards others in the way that you hope they will behave towards you appears throughout human history in multiple philosophies and religions.

A mosaic entitled *Golden Rule* (1985), created by Norman Rockwell (and based on his 1961 painting of the same name), was presented to the United Nations as a gift by First Lady Nancy Reagan, and is held by the UN in their New York headquarters. The painting and mosaic depict more than 30 people, representatives of multiple faiths and belief systems from around the world, all of which have the Golden Rule as one of their principles.

You may have been brought up in a faith – or not – and still hold those beliefs – or not. But have you found that the Golden Rule still stands?

28 FEBRUARY

HE'S JUST KEN

'I'd love to see more women win things and be
nominated for different awards for directing, because
I think the work is so worthy . . . [What] I try to focus
on is that the work is getting done, the work is
beautiful, it's going to keep getting made
. . . Progress is being made.'

Greta Gerwig, actor, screenwriter and film director, 2019

• • • • • •

The Academy Awards – known universally as the 'Oscars' – are given out at a star-studded ceremony that takes place in either late February or early March. Awards are given based on the votes of the membership of the Academy of Motion Picture Arts and Sciences.

At the 2015 Oscars ceremony, the lack of diversity (no actors of colour had been nominated across their categories) led to the #OscarsSoWhite campaign, a hashtag created by activist and writer April Reign. When there was no change in 2016, a number of high-profile stars, including Spike Lee, boycotted the ceremony. The Academy subsequently embarked on a membership drive, raising the numbers from around 6,000 to closer to 10,000 by 2024.

As yet, no Black director has won in their category. And the statistics for women directors are similarly dispiriting. Only two women have won in the category to date: Kathryn Bigelow for *The Hurt Locker* (2008) and Chloé Zhao for *Nomadland* (2020), who was also the first Asian woman to win. Jane Campion has earned two nominations for best director, the first woman to do so.

As for *Barbie* (2023), both Margot Robbie in the title role and Greta Gerwig, the director, missed out. The film's single Oscar was for Best Original Song (written by Billie Eilish and Finneas O'Connell). At least it didn't go to Ken.

29 FEBRUARY

MOMENT TO MOMENT

'[My daughter] changed my perspective drastically. I'm much calmer now ... She has made me realise the truth of something I'd heard all my life but never really understood, which is what's important is the moment. Moment-to-moment living. And that life is right now. It's not tomorrow. It's not six months from now. Because she's such a spontaneous moment-to-moment little being herself.'

Glenn Close, actor, 1989

• • • • • •

The leap year. What are you going to do with this gift of more time? Are you glad to have an extension on a deadline? Or frustrated that this month's pay cheque is delayed?

Glenn Close's (b. 1947) acting career has spanned five decades and she is the recipient of multiple awards and awards nominations. Throughout the 1980s in particular she was a dominant presence on screen, earning back-to-back Oscar nominations for Best Actress in a Supporting Role for *The World According to Garp* (1982), *The Big Chill* (1983) and *The Natural* (1984). She unforgettably played 'bunny boiler' Alex Forrest in the psychological thriller *Fatal Attraction* (1987), securing her 'leading lady' status.

Speaking here after one year as a mother, she reminds us that time passes very quickly, and that life is happening right now.

Remember to relish this extra day.

MARCH

1 MARCH

HISTORY IS HER-STORY

'For me it's always about the narrative, the social history, the emotional undercurrents . . . I have a memory of working in the field of domestic abuse, for Women's Aid, and going one night to a concert, to hear a singer called Gordeanna McCulloch sing a 400-year-old song about domestic abuse, and I was shocked and moved by this kind of lineage of experience across time.'

Karine Polwart, singer-songwriter, 2019

• • • • • •

March is Women's History Month, but when we think about the study of history, we can perhaps too easily fall into thinking primarily about the actions of Great Men (and Women) or the reigns of kings (and queens).

Karine Polwart (b. 1970) is a Scottish folk singer, songwriter and spoken word performer whose lyrics tap into the long folk tradition of giving voice to history's quieter and more easily unheard lives. She recalls how a centuries-old song directly connected to her day-to-day work in the field of domestic abuse.

The power of folk songs to bring ordinary people back to such vivid life enables us to draw connections across time. This, in turn, lets us give voice to our own experiences, knowing that others before us have struggled and have, perhaps, found a way through.

Women's solidarity at its best makes coalitions across class, gender and ethnicity. We can find allyship, too, across time, bringing alive voices from the past that can illuminate our present.

2 MARCH

MIND-BLOWING

'[The Oscars are] kind of mind-blowing. They have you come in early in the morning and rehearse and then you see the seats have been designated for, who's gonna sit in them, and it's just like one gigantic movie star name after another.'

Aimee Mann, singer-songwriter, 2013

• • • • • •

Aimee Mann's (b. 1960) career as a singer-songwriter has spanned five decades, from the 1980s cult new wave band 'Til Tuesday to her solo career from the 1990s onwards. As a solo artist, she has released ten studio albums, and is known for her sophisticated and dry lyrics, which – touching on themes such as addiction and loneliness, and centring on outsider characters – often read like short stories. She has also won two Grammy Awards.

Mann's glimpse inside the Oscars ceremony came in 2000, when 'Save Me' was nominated in the Best Original Song category. The song was written for the film *Magnolia* (1999), directed by Paul Thomas Anderson and with a hugely talented ensemble cast including Julianne Moore, Philip Seymour Hoffman, Tom Cruise – and a storm of frogs. The script was inspired by Mann's music.

In the event, 'Save Me' – a beautifully crafted and worded piece about lonely people reaching out to find salvation through love – lost out to Phil Collins's 'You'll Be in My Heart', from the soundtrack to *Tarzan* (1999).

3 MARCH

PERSONAL SPACE

'You feel that sense of threat even if it's something as simple as someone sitting next to you on a bus.'

Grace Thomas, Anglican priest, 2024

• • • • • •

In 2024, Reverend Grace Thomas stimulated an online debate when she complained on social media about a man taking the seat beside her on a largely empty bus. What is the right response in such situations? Should she simply ask the man to move? Or is it too risky to initiate a conversation? And why should the woman be expected to regulate her behaviour? Why not the man?

Research conducted in 2017 by a team of psychologists suggests that while the concept of personal space is universal, there are some broadly cultural or national differences when it comes to respecting personal space. And the British, on the whole, prefer to keep a distance.

Leaving aside cultural misunderstandings (or simple thoughtlessness), women cannot help but go on alert in such situations. According to Rape Crisis, one in four women have been sexually assaulted or raped as an adult (the figure is one in eighteen for men). It can profoundly alter the way in which we move and operate in the world.

4 MARCH

WASHED UP BY FOURTEEN

'I've already been a has-been – by 14, which isn't easy to accomplish ... I think every person in their profession has that fear that one day it's all going to go away. But when it actually does, you're left to realise you will survive.'

Drew Barrymore, actor, producer, talk-show host and author, 2007

• • • • • •

Even Drew Barrymore's (b. 1975) name points to her family's long connection to the acting profession: her great-grandfather Maurice Barrymore was a British stage actor; his wife Georgiana Drew an American actor and comedian. Her godfather is Steven Spielberg, who cast her as Gertie, the baby sister of protagonist Elliott, in *E.T. the Extra-Terrestrial* (1982). Barrymore's performance is a delight – natural, charming and funny – and *E.T.* became the highest-grossing film of the 1980s.

The dream rapidly turned sour, with Barrymore struggling with substance abuse from her teens and entering rehab, as described in her memoir *Little Girl Lost* (1990), written when she was only 13, and published when she was 14, and entering rehab for the second time.

Throughout, Barrymore has continued to act and produce, and, in 2020, she began hosting her own talk show, *The Drew Barrymore Show*. In 2023, *Time* magazine named her one of the 100 most influential people in the world.

Few of us will lead so quintessentially Hollywood a life, but Barrymore's ability to pick herself up, again and again, and talk frankly about her life and her troubles speaks to our capacity for survival.

5 MARCH

I MIGHT NOT BE HERE TODAY

'If I had been one of those 12-year-old boys, if I had
been an anonymous working-class Egyptian woman
who did not have a Twitter account, who did not have
thousands of people following on Twitter, I might not be
sitting on this couch talking to you today.'

Mona Eltahawy, journalist and activist, 2018

• • • • • •

Mona Eltahawy (b. 1967) has written extensively on feminism and
women's rights within the Middle East, particularly in Egypt, where
she was born.

Eltahawy's book *Headscarves and Hymens: Why the Middle East
Needs a Sexual Revolution* (2015) is a feminist manifesto for the Middle
East and North Africa; her second book, *Seven Necessary Sins for Women
and Girls* (2019), encourages women to embrace deadly sins such as
anger, ambition and lust. Eltahawy's newsletter, *Feminist Giant*, reports
on feminist activism from a global perspective.

In November 2011, Eltahawy was arrested while covering the pro-
tests in Cairo's Tahrir Square. She was held for over 12 hours, during
which time she was physically and sexually assaulted. Her followers on
Twitter, where Eltahawy had a significant presence, mobilised to draw
media attention to her arrest.

Eltahawy's experience – and her global perspective – reminds us
of the struggles for self-determination faced by women around the
world. Feminism is, and remains, a global battle.

6 MARCH

WOMEN, ART, COMMERCE, MONEY, AMBITION

'When I [reread *Little Women*] as an adult I was
just completely gobsmacked by how modern
it was, and how pressing it was, and it felt like the
entire undercurrent of the book, the themes that
were running under it, were about authorship, ownership,
women, art, commerce, money and ambition. And
those are the things I am thinking about!'

Greta Gerwig, actor, screenwriter and film director, 2019

• • • • • •

Greta Gerwig's 2019 adaptation of Louisa May Alcott's *Little Women* (1868) smartly reorders the events of the familiar story, foregrounding Jo's trajectory from scribbler of family entertainments to hard-nosed professional fighting to retain copyright in the face of her publisher's pressure to give it away.

The scenes of Jo working on her book is a unique visual insight into 'being a writer', capturing the restlessness of what is commonly imagined to be a static process. The character of Amy, often portrayed as selfish and immature, is here another woman making her way in the world, forced to accept that her talent for painting is insufficient, and making choices guided by the need to support her family.

Little Women earned Gerwig a second Oscar nomination for Best Picture, following her nomination for her coming-of-age drama *Lady Bird* (2017). A third nomination for *Barbie* (2023) made her the first director in history to be nominated in that category for their first three solo films. *Barbie*'s success made her the first woman director to gross over $1 billion. Art, commerce, ambition – the Oscar is surely to come.

7 MARCH

PARENTING AND PARTNERING

'It's strange that whereas people are perfectly happy to knock on their teenager's door before they go in, they allow their children to wander into their bedroom at any time. And what I'm trying to say is it's very important to give role models to your children which say that adult relationships are important and they should be able to have a private space.'

Andrew G. Marshall, author and family and marital therapist, 2013

· · · · · ·

The requirements of parenting can often push other relationships to the periphery; not only friendships, but also one's relationship with one's partner. Sometimes it may seem that conversations have become primarily about administration: who's handling pick-up from school; who will fill in the forms for an upcoming school trip; whose turn it is to cook dinner; who's responsible for sports kits going into the wash.

But it can take nearly 20 years to launch a child into the world. That's a very long time to go without having a real conversation with your partner – and lives lived in parallel are not truly shared.

Andrew G. Marshall has over 30 years of experience as a marital therapist. His book *I Love You But I'm Not in Love with You: Seven Steps to Saving Your Relationship* (2010) offers advice to couples who, for whatever reason, have begun to decouple.

Have you had the chance to really talk to your partner recently? Can you find some time to yourselves to reconnect?

8 MARCH

INTERNATIONAL WOMEN'S DAY

'I'm a [young person] doing what I believe in, which is campaigning for girls' education around the world, and now focusing more on refugee girls. Sometimes it is quite overwhelming, when you see so many people out there supporting you ... Even if I change my look, wear jeans or a cap, people still recognise me.'

Malala Yousafzai, female education activist and Nobel laureate, 2019

• • • • • •

8 March is International Women's Day. Emerging from socialist and labour women's movements of the early twentieth century, the date has become a focus for women's rights, and campaigns for reproductive rights, gender equality and the eradication of violence and abuse against women and girls.

Malala Yousafzai (b. 1997), the youngest Nobel laureate in history, has campaigned for the rights of girls and young women to have access to education. From the age of 11, she kept an online diary about life under the Taliban in north-west Pakistan. She was shot by the Taliban in 2012, aged 14; her subsequent treatment in Pakistan and, latterly, the UK brought her to international attention.

The Malala Fund was founded in 2013 to promote the rights of girls to receive an education, particularly in Pakistan; more recently, Malala's focus has turned to the plight of refugee girls and women.

Women of the world, unite. Solidarity to us all.

9 MARCH

SUPERIOR BRAIN POWER

'There is no psychological test yet that indicates that either one of the sexes has a superiority of brain power. What we need is a combination and utilisation of the best talents and brain power of the two sexes. But we get ourselves lost and completely hung up on whether a person wears pants or a skirt. It's ridiculous.'

Shirley Chisholm, United States Member of Congress, politician, 1971

• • • • • •

In 1968, Shirley Chisholm (1924–2005) was the first Black woman to be elected to the United States Congress. In 1972, she ran for the Democratic Party nomination for president; she was the first woman to do so and the first Black candidate for a major party.

Dynamic, passionate and indefatigable, Chisholm was a staunch defender of minorities, speaking up not only for women and Black people, but for the gay community. She saw discrimination as wasteful, as much as it was unjust; a failure on the part of the United States to nurture and make use of the talents of the whole country. She argued that government should be representative – including Black, white, young, old, male and female voices, and not simply those of old white men.

Chisholm earned the support of enough delegates to be able to speak from the podium at the 1972 Democratic National Convention, but not enough to secure her the nomination. Senator George McGovern became the Democratic Party candidate, losing to Richard Nixon in a landslide victory for the Republican Party.

A trailblazer, Chisholm forced open the door for the candidates who came after her: Barack Obama, Hillary Clinton, Kamala Harris.

10 MARCH

THE MARCH OF THE WOMEN

'At all times Mrs Pankhurst was adamant in
her ruling that our militancy be against property
only. At no time endangering human life.'

Mary Richardson, suffragette, 1957

• • • • • •

Canadian-born Mary Richardson (1882/3–1961) became active in the
British suffrage movement as a member of the militant Women's Social
and Political Union (WSPU).

The WSPU was founded in 1903 by Emmeline Pankhurst and her
daughters Sylvia and Christabel, and was born out of frustration that
the Independent Labour Party (in which they had been involved) was
not advancing the cause of women's suffrage.

Eschewing the democratic methods of existing suffragist movements, members of the WSPU (dubbed 'suffragettes') used direct
action and civil disobedience, including criminal damage and arson.

Richardson's activities epitomised this approach. Most famously,
on 10 March 1914, Richardson entered the National Gallery in London
armed with a chopper, which she used to slash the *Rokeby Venus* by
Diego Velázquez. Richardson was sentenced to six months in jail. The
painting was successfully restored – and was more recently the subject
of an attack in 2023 by two environmental activists from Just Stop Oil.
More than a century apart, these acts of direct political action derive
from the same sense of urgency and outrage at the status quo.

11 MARCH

DEEDS NOT WORDS

'As the race started, I saw Emily look at her race card.
Her hand was steady, yet she knew that death was
galloping toward her. Darting onto the course from under
the rail, she obtained her objective, as if by a miracle.
She got the king's horse bridle rein, it came to its knees,
the jockey was thrown but merely shaken. Emily rolled
over twice. People rushed onto the course to molest
her. One of the first to arrive tore open her jacket.
There was a purple, white and green emblem
of our militant movement.'

Mary Richardson, suffragette, 1957

• • • • • •

Mary Richardson provided an account of one of the most dramatic and tragic episodes in the history of the women's suffrage movement, the death of Emily Wilding Davison (1872–1913) when she walked onto the racecourse during the 1913 Epsom Derby.

Davison, like Richardson, had adopted fully the principles of the WSPU's motto: 'deeds not words', engaging in assault, stone-throwing, planting bombs and arson. She hid several times overnight in the Palace of Westminster, notably on the night of the 1911 Census, to be able to give her address on the census as 'House of Commons'. She was imprisoned multiple times and force-fed repeatedly.

On 4 June 1913, Davison stepped out in front of the king's horse, Anmer, during the Epsom Derby. Taken unconscious from the track, Davison died two days later from her injuries.

12 MARCH

BELIEVE IN OURSELVES

'Above all, don't think of yourself as "only a woman".
Say instead: "I am a woman and proud of it" . . .
Once we get that idea into our heads and learn
to believe in ourselves, we shall stop using men
as yardsticks and stand on our own feet.'

Vera Brittain, writer, pacifist and socialist, 1953

• • • • • •

Vera Brittain (1893–1970) was part of the generation of 'surplus women', the young unmarried women who greatly outnumbered the equivalent cohort of men in the aftermath of the First World War. The phrase 'new woman', used from the late nineteenth century onwards, was particularly applicable for this generation, looking to earn a living in their own right.

Brittain herself had to fight her father's objections to earn the right to study at Somerville College, Oxford (at the time a women-only college); with the outbreak of war, she left Oxford in 1915 to join the Voluntary Aid Detachment (VAD), serving as a nurse for the remainder of the war. Her fiancé, two of her close male friends and her brother were all killed in the conflict; these tragedies formed the basis of her memoir of this period, *Testament of Youth* (1933), which brought her to national prominence.

Throughout the 1930s, her increasing pacifism put her at odds with the prevailing mood; during the 1950s and 1960s she turned her attention to campaigning for nuclear disarmament and against apartheid.

We are often drawn to the second wave as representative of the women's movement, but in the 1920s and 1930s, after women acquired the vote, there are women whose lives might echo strongly with our own.

13 MARCH

SECOND SELF

'[My mother, Vera Brittain,] was there throughout Winifred's pretty awful death. They were very different characters but they were hugely supportive to one another and through the whole period from when they first met until Winifred died [aged 37] there was a colossally intimate relationship. It was a very deep friendship of the type that has always been accepted for men but never for women.'

Shirley Williams, politician and academic (daughter of Vera Brittain and adopted 'niece' of Winifred Holtby), 2014

• • • • • •

Winifred Holtby (1898–1935) was a novelist and journalist, a pacifist and socialist, and a campaigner on behalf of Black union organisers in South Africa.

At Oxford, Holtby formed an intense friendship with a fellow undergraduate, the writer and peace campaigner Vera Brittain. Part of the generation of 'surplus women' (after the death of so many young men in the First World War), the two women were thrown upon each other for support and solidarity in a wholly new way.

Brittain's marriage to philosopher George Catlin in 1925 temporarily disrupted these collegiate arrangements; Holtby eventually moved into the Catlin-Brittain household, and was instrumental in bringing Brittain's memoir, *Testament of Youth*, through its final, difficult stage of composition. As Shirley Williams (1930–2021), Brittain's daughter (and Holtby's adopted 'niece'), points out: these were friendships that had received very little attention before, and certainly not in fiction.

After Holtby's early death in 1935, Brittain oversaw publication of her masterpiece, *South Riding* (published posthumously in

1936). The book has been televised and filmed several times, and has remained steadily in print since original publication, most recently as a Virago Modern Classic. The book's longevity is a testament both to the author's deep friendship with Brittain, and her own vivid genius.

14 MARCH

A GOOD FRIEND

'Ellen [Wilkinson] was older than me, and we were next-
door neighbours. And she was so kind to me. She
could have been jealous of a younger woman who
was taking part of the limelight. But Ellen was
a very good friend and I loved her.'

Jennie Lee, politician, 1980

• • • • • •

Jennie Lee (1904–88), Baroness Lee of Asheridge, entered the House of Commons for the first time in 1929, winning a by-election to become the MP for North Lanarkshire. She was one of only a handful of women at the time, from across all parties. Lee lost her seat in 1931, but returned to Parliament in 1945.

Recalling those early days in the House of Commons, Lee particularly remembered her colleague, the Labour MP Ellen Wilkinson (1891–1947).

Wilkinson had entered Parliament in 1924, winning the seat of Middlesbrough East, and was, at the time, the only woman Labour MP. She lost her seat in 1931, and returned to Parliament in 1935, as MP for Jarrow. This was a period of extreme unemployment and deprivation, which led to the Jarrow March of 1936, a protest march to London to plead for the right to work. The march took place with Wilkinson's assistance. After the war, Wilkinson became Minister of Education in the Attlee administration, until her death in 1947.

Lee lovingly remembered Wilkinson's kindness to her in those early and disorientating days in the House of Commons.

Who are the people that have shown us friendship, and mentorship? Who has eased our way? Are there people in our own lives to whom we can show the same kindness, who might benefit from what we have learned?

15 MARCH

A LITTLE HELP FROM YOUR FRIENDS

'It's one of the essential things, like food and drink and work and children ... Life is hard. You need help to get through it, and friendship is one of the things that helps.'

Marilyn French, feminist and writer, 2006

• • • • • •

Marilyn French's (1929–2009) most famous novel, *The Women's Room* (1977), documents the lives of a group of female friends in the United States from the 1940s to the 1960s. Central to the narrative is the feminist awakening of the lead character, Mira, as she leaves an unhappy marriage and acquires a circle of friends who are involved in the women's movement.

There is still something transgressive about centring women's lives and loves, rivalries and loyalties, relationships and friendships. But what is it that makes depicting these friendships so powerful? Perhaps it is that alliances and coalitions among women strike at the heart of patriarchy. Perhaps it is that in representing many and varied women we stop being a monolith; we become diverse.

We become, undeniably, people.

16 MARCH

IT HURTS MORE

'Female friendship is one of the most important things
about being a woman . . . When you fall out with your
female friends, it can hurt more than a relationship.'

Rose Ayling-Ellis, actor and model, 2022

· · · · · ·

The friends we make as we are growing, whether we've known them
since school or met at college or university, are the ones we often feel
inseparable from, given how closely interwoven our emerging identities and sense of self are with theirs.

And then, somehow, the friendship falls apart. Perhaps they move
away. Perhaps they find a partner and start to spend more time with
them. Perhaps they become parents and their life completely revolves
around their family. Perhaps they've found a new job or vocation that
means their focus has turned intensely elsewhere.

When we drift apart from friends – particularly if we are the one
that feels left behind – a gap opens where closeness has been. It can be
saddening or baffling – why don't they want to be with us any longer?
It can feel like a blow. Like abandonment – even betrayal.

Sometimes we grow and change at different paces. Sometimes we
are no longer in sync. Sometimes what the friendship needs is that
space for us to become different people. We might come back, in years
to come, to see where life has taken the other person. With the passage
of time, and as we grow older, those friendships may come to mean
something to us again.

17 MARCH

MAKING THE TRADITION

'I didn't know that it would cause such furore. I knew that as a woman and a young woman in her twenties in Ireland that I was treading danger water by writing a book at all, even if it was a book about – I don't know, gardening. 'Cause there were no women writers ... There was no tradition of women writers. There was no room for women writers, and above all there was no respect for women writers.'

Edna O'Brien, novelist, short story writer, playwright, poet and critic, 2019

• • • • • •

Edna O'Brien (1930–2024) was Ireland's pre-eminent female writer from the 1960s onwards. Her first novel, *The Country Girls* (1960), concerned two young women from rural Ireland – Kate Brady and Baba Brennan – and shocked what was at the time a deeply conservative and repressive country with its frank depictions of sex and female sexual desire. The first part of a trilogy, the following books follow Kate and Baba to Dublin, then London, and their complicated affairs and marriages.

O'Brien's last novel, *Girl* (2019), was inspired by the Chibok kidnappings in Nigeria by the Islamic terrorist group Boko Haram. She was the winner of many awards, including the Irish PEN Award, the Frank O'Connor International Short Story Award and the David Cohen Prize, the last given for recognition of an entire body of work.

In 2015, O'Brien was elected to Aosdána, the Irish academy of arts, whose membership is limited to 250 people.

More than any other writer, O'Brien's career represents the phenomenal social change that has happened in Ireland since the 1960s. Her writing and career opened a path for the next generations of Irish women writers: Anne Enright, Eimear McBride, Nuala Ní Chonchúir, Claire Keegan.

18 MARCH

WOMEN OF THE RESISTANCE

'Without women's participation, many things would not have been possible. But more generally, women in the Resistance were never spoken of, and the silence and lack of acknowledgement lasted a very long time.'

Cécile Rol-Tanguy, Resistance fighter, 2014

• • • • • •

Cécile Rol-Tanguy (1919–2020) was a French Communist and Resistance fighter during the Second World War. After the occupation of Paris on 10 June 1940, Rol-Tanguy played an increasingly significant role in the Forces Françaises de l'Intérieure (the FFI; French Resistance fighters), first by typing pamphlets, later acting as a liaison officer. In the run-up to the liberation of Paris, she assisted her husband, Henri, the regional leader of the FFI, in setting up a command post. During this period, she gave birth to two of her four surviving children (her first child had died just before the Nazi occupation of Paris). She became Grand Officer of the Légion d'honneur in 2008.

The role of women in the war effort went unremarked for many years. Whether because of the secrecy surrounding their work, such as code-breaking at Bletchley Park, or because it happened on the domestic front in munitions, these contributions were more easily overlooked.

The national Monument to the Women of World War II, which stands on Whitehall next to the Cenotaph, was unveiled in 2005, and depicts clothing and uniforms representing the many roles that women undertook during the war.

19 MARCH

TICKET TO THE MOON

'I did want to be an astronaut from the time
I was little, and I just never grew out of it.
I discovered I loved science and engineering and
I discovered I loved exploration as well.
I just held onto that dream.'

Christina Koch, engineer and astronaut, 2023

· · · · · ·

The first woman in space was the Russian cosmonaut Valentina Tereshkova, who, in 1963, orbited the earth 48 times in Vostok 6. In 1983, as part of the Space Shuttle programme, Sally Ride became the first American woman in space. Helen Sharman was the first Briton to go to space (male or female) in 1991, part of a privately funded mission. By 2019, the percentage of women who have ever flown in space stood at around 12 per cent of the overall total.

Woman had always played an important part behind the scenes at NASA, not only in administrative posts, but in highly technical fields. Mathematician Katherine Johnson's work was critical to calculating flights from the early manned space missions (Project Mercury) up to the beginning of the Space Shuttle programme. But, as yet, no woman has set foot upon the Moon.

The Artemis programme, announced in 2017, is NASA's current Moon exploration programme. (The name was chosen as the counterpart to the Apollo programme, which landed the first men on the Moon.) The Artemis programme aims to return humans to the Moon, with the longer-term aim of building a base there that can subsequently be used as a springboard for the exploration of Mars.

In 2023, Christina Koch (b. 1979) was selected to be part of the crew of the Artemis II mission, which aims to fly around the Moon in 2025. One small step for a woman . . .

20 MARCH

CHILDHOOD DREAMS

'I wanted to become an archaeologist but became gradually put off by it, partly because it was increasingly difficult for Jews to go and work in some of the countries in the near East and partly because when I went and took part in digs in England, I found it was mainly just scraping bits of stone and wasn't fantastically interesting!'

Julia Neuberger, rabbi and politician, 1977

• • • • • •

In the late 1960s, Julia Neuberger (b. 1950), Baroness Neuberger of Primrose Hill, was studying Assyriology and Hebrew at Newnham College, Cambridge, with a view to becoming an archaeologist.

When she was unable to enter Turkey (on the grounds of being British) and Iraq (on the grounds of being Jewish), one of her Hebrew tutors suggested she instead consider becoming a rabbi. But women, Neuberger thought, didn't become rabbis.

Until they did. Neuberger switched her focus – and became the second woman ordained a rabbi in the UK, and the first to have her own synagogue.

Did your childhood ambitions come true? Or did you too have a lucky escape and find your true calling? Do you still harbour a secret wish, not yet fulfilled?

21 MARCH

GOING UNDERGROUND

'We didn't guess quite how much interest there was going to be. At that time we just lived in an ordinary London street ... We had to move and effectively go underground, which was rather a strange reverse when one had been trying to be more open.'

Stella Rimington, author and former Director General of MI5, 1999

• • • • • •

Dame Stella Rimington (b. 1935) was appointed Director General (DG) of MI5 in 1992, around the same time that the government of the day had committed to being more open about the security services. The following year, Rimington's photograph appeared in a brochure explaining the organisation's role and activities.

Being the first DG to be photographed, combined with the fact that she was a woman, meant that Rimington attracted a huge amount of press attention. A long-lens, out-of-focus press picture of her carrying shopping bags predictably earned her the tabloid nickname 'the housewife spy'.

Spies have a powerful hold on the popular imagination, as the continuing success of work by authors such as John le Carré shows. Rimington, too, has benefited from our fascination in her former profession, publishing a controversial memoir, *Open Secret*, and also writing spy novels, featuring a female intelligence officer, Liz Carlyle.

Still, even bearing in mind public interest in the spying fraternity, would the press coverage of Rimington have been as intense if she had not been a woman? Would a man ever be called 'the househusband spy'?

22 MARCH

BREAKING THE MOULD

'It made a huge difference ... More than anything
I gave myself permission to be different ... I stopped
trying to push myself and mould myself into a box
I just fundamentally didn't fit into and that
was a massive relief in itself.'

Caragh McMurtry, rower and Olympian, 2023

• • • • • •

In the past, the assumption was that people with autism were primarily men or boys, and that women, girls and non-binary people with autism were rare. More recently, however, research has been catching up with the reality – that many more women, girls and non-binary people have autistic traits, and that out-of-date stereotypes and assumptions may be preventing them from finding support.

Caragh McMurtry (b. 1991) is a retired British rower who represented Great Britain in the 2020 Tokyo Summer Olympics. A misdiagnosis of bipolar disorder in her teens led to a period of five years where she was prescribed anti-psychotic and mood-stabilising drugs which had a detrimental effect on her health. She was diagnosed in adulthood with autism.

Labelling our experiences can be constrictive, but when the right word is found, it can have a powerfully liberating effect, making sense of our experience of the world, and allowing us to reject the boxes into which we have been trying to fit. With a better understanding of who we are, we can become more ourselves.

23 MARCH

LOCKDOWN

'By the time you're my age or even – it should be way before – most things are like other things. This was like nothing I'd ever experienced in my life, and that is very unusual, to have such a new experience at this age.'

Fran Lebowitz, writer and essayist, 2021

• • • • • •

Even those who have not been directly and viscerally affected by the pandemic are nowhere near processing the impact of those months and years on us.

The missed family occasions; the inability to touch or to see loved ones; the online gatherings; the sense of helplessness. The need to move on – and quickly – is understandable. We may not yet be ready to think about and acknowledge everything that happened.

What will be the impact on those whose formative years were spent, in part, in lockdown? From children born in the early 2020s, to teenagers struggling with isolation during a time when they should have been enjoying independence, to college students stuck in small rooms in halls of residence – a generation made big sacrifices to keep others safe.

Fran Lebowitz, hardly known for pulling her punches, says straightforwardly what we all know: these were unprecedented times.

24 MARCH

WOMEN EARNED IT BY THEMSELVES

'In all important movements, women have featured in
a big way. In the French revolution, there were women;
in the Paris Commune there were women; in all the
revolutions of the nineteenth century, women
have played a big role. They say General de Gaulle
gave women the vote in 1945, but let me tell
you – women earned it by themselves.'

Cécile Rol-Tanguy, Resistance fighter, 2014

• • • • • •

Cécile Rol-Tanguy's involvement in the French Resistance during the
occupation of Paris speaks to the courage and commitment of women
in times of great crisis and terror. Rol-Tanguy was, at the time, a
mother of small children, and her father, also involved in the Resistance, was arrested and deported to Auschwitz, where he died.

Women are frequently erased from history, or treated as the victims of impersonal forces. We focus on the actions and decisions of
'great men', rather than placing these in a wider context.

But women, too, are the subjects of history, the protagonists, the
hands that make and move the world. Who do you think of when you
think of historical heroes? Do you tend towards great men of history,
or do other people and their achievements come to mind?

25 MARCH

ON GENIUS

'So many films have been made about male geniuses and people are tolerant if he's difficult: "Of course he's difficult! He's a genius!" If he's rude or abrupt, he's given a free pass. And now we come to make a film about a female genius and suddenly it seems that the same free rein isn't accorded her ... It's very revealing that we've looked so benevolently on the sort of tortured or difficult soul of somebody who is brilliant as long as he's male. If Marie Curie was sweet and lovely and kind, she would not have been Madame Curie.'

Rosamund Pike, actor and producer, 2020

• • • • • •

Rosamund Pike (b. 1979) has won Emmy and Golden Globe Awards, and received nominations for BAFTA and Academy Awards.

In the 2020 film *Radioactive*, Pike portrayed Marie Curie, twice recipient of the Nobel Prize, for physics and for chemistry. The film was directed by Marjane Satrapi, author of a graphic novel memoir of the Iranian Revolution, *Persepolis*.

Pike rightly points to the double standards that apply when driven men are compared to equally driven women. Compliance, and playing by the rules, does not necessarily lead to success. But where men's misbehaviour is seen as a necessary aspect of their talent and achievement, women are not given such freedom.

26 MARCH

COMMUNAL EXPERIENCE

'The audience was just so grateful and appreciative and wallowing in each other's company . . . We've all been swallowing television like there's no tomorrow, but sitting in a place where you could all react to something: it does something to your metabolism. The uniformed reaction of a group of people, whether it's at the theatre or a festival or whatever, a communal experience is vital.'

Imelda Staunton, actress and singer, 2021

• • • • • •

In the first months of lockdown, those of us not immediately affected by COVID learned a whole new lexicon: video meeting; screen sharing; 'put it in the chat'. We learned new ways of interacting via computer screen: 'you're on mute'; 'I'll change my background'; 'let me close the door to keep the dog/kids/partner out (no chance stopping the cat)'.

For the arts, particularly theatre, lockdown was a desperate time. Artists, producers and creators had to act swiftly and with imagination to be able to perform and earn a living. The actor Imelda Staunton (b. 1956) recalls returning to the stage at the Bridge Theatre before a socially distanced audience, and the deep relief of the audience at being able to go out again in company.

Many people with accessibility requirements reported that lockdown provided them access to many events for the first time that would previously have been impossible: concerts; theatre; talks and lectures. Much of this has now faded away. And some people are still vulnerable to COVID, and are shielding to this day.

We invested so much in putting our lives online. Have we maintained those structures? Or, in our rush to return to normality, have we left some people behind?

27 MARCH

WOMAN'S DESTINY

'When I became leader of the opposition it was very difficult, because as a woman I was trying to go for the top job in New Zealand public life ... and no one had done that before ... nothing [was] like what I ran into when I became leader of the opposition ... It really was all around the superficialities and trivialities that people bring out ... They commented on whether your voice was high or low. It really was quite pathetic.'

Helen Clark, politician and former prime minister of New Zealand, 2013

• • • • • •

In 1893, New Zealand's Electoral Act gave all women, including Māori women, the right to vote in parliamentary elections. This made New Zealand the first country in the world to give women the vote. (A handful of western US states had led the way: Wyoming in 1869, Utah in 1870 and Colorado in 1893.)

Like many other places in the world, this was only the beginning of women's parliamentary representation in New Zealand. Women could not stand for election until 1919, and the first woman MP was not elected until 1933.

In the late 1990s, New Zealand had two women prime ministers in quick succession. Jenny Shipley took over the post when the prime minister at the time resigned. And, in 1999, Helen Clark (b. 1950), leader of the opposition Labour Party, became the first woman to win a national election. She held the post until 2008.

28 MARCH

GET THE JOB DONE

'I very much hope that one day my political party
won't exist. I don't want [my grandson] to have
to listen to these same conversations when
he's an adult. Let's get the job done.'

*Sandi Toksvig, broadcaster, comedian,
writer and presenter, 2017*

• • • • • •

The Women's Equality Party was founded in 2015, after a conversation between journalist Catherine Mayer (b. 1961) and broadcaster Sandi Toksvig (b. 1958). Both had been attending the Women of the World Festival at London's Southbank Centre, and had separately come up with the idea of a national political party that would address itself specifically to the question of gender equality.

The party's launch meeting was held on 28 March 2015. It campaigns on a platform of equality in health, representation, pay and opportunity, parenting and caregiving, education, media treatment, and to end violence against women. The current leader, Mandu Reid (b. 1981), was appointed in 2019, the first Black leader of a national political party in the UK.

Building a national movement is hardly a small task. WE's successes have so far been at the local level, with a handful of local councillors elected. The prominent public profile of its founders has also ensured interest in the wider population.

But, as Toksvig states, the fact that the party needs to exist is part of the problem. When the question of gender equality is no longer on the table, when the political party can disband – that will be proof of its success.

29 MARCH

WIDER READING

'[Feminism has] become a much more intergenerational movement as well as a global movement . . . We have to co-learn and unlearn things. If you think about all the debates around trans and non-binary and how much we are learning, and how much work we're doing with each other, that makes me go back to people like Audre Lorde to bell hooks to Angela Davis to Maya Angelou so that I can understand more of what voices around the world have been writing about for years but we have not necessarily used.'

Jude Kelly, theatre director and producer, 2020

* * * * * *

Jude Kelly (b. 1954), primarily a theatre director and producer, is also the founder of the Women of the World (WOW) Festival. Kelly's career in theatre began in the mid-1970s. Since then she has moved between London and regional theatre, directing productions at the National Theatre, English National Opera and in the West End, and setting up Arts Council-funded grassroots projects outside of London.

In 2006, Kelly became artistic director of the Southbank Centre, the UK's largest arts centre. She stood down after 12 years to focus on WOW, which she had founded in 2010 to re-energise debates within the feminist movement. The WOW Foundation was formed in 2018 to urgently advance a gender-equal society.

WOW festivals are now held around the world, and include talks, debates, music, comedy and mentoring and networking opportunities. Kelly reminds us that, more than ever, feminism is both global and intergenerational, and that for it to thrive, we must expand our horizons, co-learn – and sometimes even unlearn – our feminism.

We are building a movement for the twenty-first century.

30 MARCH

NEVER SUCH DEVOTED SISTERS

'They both [Joan Fontaine and Olivia de Havilland] said that they got each other their most important roles. Joan Fontaine auditioned for *Gone with the Wind* for the role of Melanie Wilkes. The director said, "You're too chic," and she said, "Well, if you want a simple plain girl, what about my sister?" And Olivia said she got Joan the role of Rebecca.'

Alex von Tunzelmann, popular historian, screenwriter and author, 2024

• • • • • •

There are feuds and there are feuds – but the rivalry between sisters and film stars Joan Fontaine (1917–2013) and Olivia de Havilland (1916–2020) outstrips them all. Starting in childhood as they competed for the attention of their mother (Fontaine believed that their mother preferred her sister), they dealt in slaps, hair-pulling, torn clothes and a broken collarbone.

Olivia was the first to sign with a studio; when Joan followed her to Hollywood, Olivia forbade her from using her surname on the grounds that there was room for only one de Havilland. Both were nominated for the Best Actress Academy Award in 1942, with Joan edging out Olivia for her performance in Hitchcock's *Suspicion*. De Havilland would later win for *To Each His Own* (1946), making them the only sibling pair to win lead acting Oscars.

Gone With the Wind, *Rebecca*, *Suspicion*, *The Adventures of Robin Hood* and countless other films: one wonders, would either of them have achieved so much, without the other?

31 MARCH

I'D LIKE TO THANK MY AGENT

'[Orlando Bloom] made the choice to lift me, so he had to stay there till I was done . . . I remember knowing that I was talking for too long and I remember thinking that he was holding me and I remember this sort of conflict of "I know that he's uncomfortable but I'm not done, I'm not done. I'm sorry, but I'm not done!"'

Dakota Fanning, actor, 2016

• • • • • •

In 2001, at the age of seven, Dakota Fanning (b. 1994) won the Best Young Actor award from the Broadcast Film Critics Association for her performance in *I Am Sam* (2001), in which she starred alongside Sean Penn and Michelle Pfeiffer. Far too small to be able to speak directly into the microphone, Fanning was saved by Orlando Bloom, presenting the award, who lifted her up to speak.

Fanning – legs dangling – spoke, and spoke, and continued to speak until she had thanked everyone (in some cases, thanking them twice), including God, her parents and her agent.

Fanning's career has gone from strength to strength, shifting seamlessly into independent films – and Tarantino's *Once Upon a Time . . . in Hollywood* (2019); a rare example of a child actor breaking through successfully into adulthood stardom. Some people seem to know their exact plans in life from an early age.

APRIL

1 APRIL

WOMEN AREN'T FUNNY

'With every male-dominated genre – because the people that are commissioning work are men, because they come with a particular sensibility – it was one of those ideas that ingrained itself. Mainly because perhaps women being funny wasn't in the tastes of the men that were commissioning work initially or putting women on stage. They were always accepted as a foil, or as a grotesque, someone who was outside of the norm. But to actually be formidable enough to front your own show or be the centre of comedy, that was thought highly unlikely.'

Dick Fiddy, television historian and curator
at the British Film Institute, 2012

· · · · · ·

We've all heard it said – women just aren't funny. This despite all the evidence to the contrary: not just Woods, and French and Saunders, and Millican, and Christie, all the writers and performers, but the comic actors too – June Whitfield, Penelope Keith, Joyce Grenfell and thousands more.

Dick Fiddy, commenting on how this prejudice emerged, points to the limitations that come when the pool of people commissioning work is very small. If your comedy isn't to their taste, if you're covering material that they don't understand or which is beyond their comprehension, then you're hindered from the start.

These barriers and assumptions play out throughout hundreds of different professions. Women can't be leaders; women can't be bosses; women don't have what it takes. It's as untrue in these circumstances as it is in comedy.

2 APRIL

MEN AREN'T FUNNY EITHER

'One of the things that used to happen would be that we were never put on the same bill. So we all became friends, but it was never the idea that you'd have two women on the same bill. It was just that one woman representing women on the bill and then you had the trouble where if you weren't funny: 'Oh, women aren't funny.' The other three men, if one of them wasn't funny it didn't mean *all* men weren't funny suddenly.'

Brenda Gilhooly, comedian, 2012

• • • • • •

Brenda Gilhooly (b. 1964) describes some of the barriers she faced when breaking into stand-up as a female comedian. One woman would find herself on the bill, representing all women – and woe betide if she didn't make the punters laugh enough.

Studies have shown that as late as 2024, women make up around a third of appearances on UK panel shows. On some long-running shows – where regular panellists are male – the average drops dramatically.

Representation matters, but you can't put one woman there and call the job done. If a single person comes to stand in for the whole group, then that group is judged according to that person's ability or behaviour. That's stereotyping at best and prejudice at worst.

Putting a single woman on the line-up – not just in comedy, but in any professional panel in any work situation – does not count as diversity or equality. It's the bare minimum.

3 APRIL

NINETY-NINE PER CENT PERSPIRATION

'She composed her scripts and she didn't like it if people got it wrong. She said, if you write an F sharp and someone gives you an E flat, it's really annoying.'

Jasper Rees, writer, 2020

• • • • • •

Jasper Rees is the authorised biographer of Victoria Wood (1953–2016), arguably Britain's funniest woman. Describing Wood's writing process, Rees draws our attention to the meticulousness of her approach and the exactness of the scripts. Composed like a symphony, one wrong 'note' would sound completely out of place.

Those who excel at their chosen craft often make what they do look easy. Of course, the reality is that behind this panache and apparent effortlessness lies years of hard work and constant attention to detail. Talent is more about putting the hours in rather than having a knack.

In his book *Outliers*, Malcolm Gladwell (b. 1963) suggests that we need 10,000 hours of practice to excel at a skill. This adds up to around 90 minutes of practice a day across 20 years. Sound achievable? In fact, the psychologist on whose work this is based, Anders Ericsson (1947–2020), was making a more nuanced point. Hours of dedication and practice are needed if you want to excel, yes – but the point is that this practice should be deliberate and *intentional*.

Qualities of precision and attention to detail are ones that we can all adopt.

4 APRIL

MORE WORDS, MORE COLOURS

'Each new book is a new problem, and you're looking at a new set of difficulties. Writers are locked in the same kind of battle with language that painters are locked in with colours. You keep wanting there to be more colours; you keep wanting there to be more words.'

Margaret Atwood, writer, poet and critic, 1986

• • • • • •

Although she is perhaps best known for her dystopian novel *The Handmaid's Tale* (1985), Margaret Atwood (b. 1939) is the author of over 60 books. She has won multiple awards and seen her work adapted for film and television.

Many writers enjoy talking about the process of writing (it's better than having to write). Every artist has their own method and process, but many of their insights can be transferred to other forms of activity.

Atwood's reflections on writing hold good for all kinds of creative work, and all kinds of learning processes. We emerge from a sustained piece of work having learned how to do that particular piece of work. And while we can take a great deal of that over with us, the next task will most likely need new words, new colours – new ways of thinking.

And that's part of the fun.

5 APRIL

LOOKS CAN BE DECEPTIVE

'A review once said that I looked like a primary
school teacher but had the mouth of a biker.
I thought that was quite appropriate.'

Sarah Millican, comedian, 2017

• • • • • •

It remains outrageously true that women remain judged on their appearance as much as their ability. Even if our jobs or lines of work do not put us in the public eye, women's bodies are scrutinised and policed in very particular and judgemental ways. When we are young, we have to be beautiful; as we age, it has to be done gracefully – or not at all.

So when a woman who looks like they might be in charge of a class of Year 3s swears like a trooper, she can derive a great deal of power from that shock.

What assumptions do people make about us based on how we present ourselves? On how we look? And while we wait for society to change – how can we make those assumptions work in our favour?

6 APRIL

UNDER CONTRACT

'It was only when I was first locked in a padded cell in Paddington and told to write more I thought, "I think I'm a writer . . . I've got to be one anyway, because I've signed a contract!" You just do it and you have to do it.'

Carla Lane, television writer, 2006

• • • • • •

Carla Lane (1928–2016), queen of the sitcom, created some of the funniest and most memorable female characters on British television. From the cheeky Scouse flatmates of *The Liver Birds* (1969–78, 1996) to the family matriarch of *Bread* (1986–91), Lane's characters captured aspects of women's interior lives rarely seen before on television.

Ria Parkinson, the protagonist of *Butterflies* (1978–83), is a middle-class housewife who has become bored and unhappy after years of marriage. Played with gentle desperation by Wendy Craig, Ria knows that she wants something more from life, and begins to contemplate the unthinkable – an affair with her handsome and newly divorced friend, Leonard.

Lane's career in writing covered the heyday of British television. A young mother of two when she started out, Lane captures the realisation many of us have when we start on a new job: 'This is it, I really am doing this now.'

The reality of our lives is sometimes ahead of our realisation of what we're doing. Sometimes we surprise ourselves with what we've learned to do when we weren't looking; sometimes our dreams have come true while we were too busy to notice.

7 APRIL

A SILLY BOOK

'[*The Female Eunuch*] is a pretentious silly book.
What made that book was the readiness of women to
understand what it was striving to describe.'

Germaine Greer, writer, academic and public intellectual, 2016

• • • • • •

Germaine Greer (b. 1939) is perhaps the figure most associated in the public mind with second-wave feminism. Born in Melbourne, Greer studied English and French language and literature at the University of Melbourne. She came to the UK in 1964 to study for her PhD at Newnham College, Cambridge, joining Footlights, and making a startling appearance in Clive James's memoirs.

The Female Eunuch (1970) is Greer's most well-known book; published when she was 31, it became an international bestseller. The cover of the paperback edition – showing a female torso hanging from a washing line, with a handle on each hip – is unforgettable once seen, etched into one's consciousness forevermore.

The book was a call to arms, urging women to seize their liberation (since it would never be given by men or won by genteel ladies), to demand more and to question everything they had been told – about their nature, about their bodies, about sex, love, romance. And, above all, it was a call to women to *act*.

Polemical, eclectic and supercharged, Greer does her early work an injustice. Women were ready to hear what it had to say. And it changed lives.

8 APRIL

WE SEEK TO BE UNDERSTOOD

'One of the reasons that I write my books is to help people understand themselves. I think that is a good reason to write. To help people investigate their own motivations. My books seem to read the reader. The reader feels understood and therefore healed. Because what we all seek is to be understood.'

Erica Jong, novelist and poet, 2014

• • • • • •

Erica Jong's (b. 1942) debut *Fear of Flying* (1973) was one of the most influential novels to emerge from the second wave, putting women's sexuality at the heart of the book, with frank descriptions of sexual experiences and opinions on sex. The book spoke so honestly to its readership that it has sold over 20 million copies worldwide.

We read in part to enter into the minds and worlds of others – but we also read to help decipher ourselves, to understand the reasons why we have acted in a certain way, not to mention the justifications for our actions.

What are the books that have read us? The ones we have opened and seen ourselves so faithfully represented that it seems that the author has had access to our innermost thoughts?

9 APRIL

ON SOLITUDE

'Loneliness is a big deal. And it's a negative emotion. It's the way our bodies tell us that we're not getting enough social connection. Maybe we don't feel loved enough, we don't feel valued enough. Loneliness is about not having enough of something, about social connection . . . Solitude is something very different . . . Solitude is the neutral state of being alone. It's a whole different idea. We tend to confuse or conflate these ideas.'

Netta Weinstein, psychologist and professor, 2024

• • • • • •

The average adult spends a third of their time alone. How do we negotiate this time? Does being by ourselves leave us feeling disconnected and lonely? Or do we long for moments to ourselves, to recharge and be with our own thoughts.

Netta Weinstein is a professor of psychology whose research at the 'Solitude Lab' has focused on how we spend time alone, and how we can embrace it as an opportunity for reflection and creativity.

What would you do with a day by yourself? Would you find it easy to fill the time with projects or music or simply pottering about? Or would you text a friend and arrange to meet for lunch?

10 APRIL

THE GOOD FRIDAY AGREEMENT

'[Mo Mowlam] had huge courage and drive and guts and
she was someone who was going to get things done
. . . She knew deep inside what she was really brilliant
at and what she could do, and there was no way that
anyone was going to stop that . . . I don't think we'd have
got the Good Friday Agreement without her.'

Julie Walters, actress, 2010

* * * * * *

On 10 April 1998, the Belfast Agreement – the Good Friday Agreement
(GFA) – was signed, a political deal aimed at bringing to an end the
30-year violent conflict in Northern Ireland known as 'the Troubles'. The
agreement was ratified by public votes in both Ireland and Northern Ireland. It covered power-sharing, devolution, decommissioning of weapons
and early prisoner release, and it provided a framework to respect the
rights and identities of all communities in Northern Ireland.

One of the key people to negotiate the agreement, juggling the
claims, needs and grievances of the disparate parts of the community, was the new Labour Secretary of State for Northern Ireland, Mo
Mowlam (1949–2005).

In the years since her early death, Mowlam's contribution to the
signing of the GFA has been eclipsed by some of the more prominent
figures such as British Prime Minister Tony Blair, Irish Taoiseach Bertie
Ahern and US President Bill Clinton.

Julie Walters, who played Mo Mowlam in the television film *Mo*
(2010), saw Mowlam's essential qualities – her courage and willingness
to build bridges – as crucial to achieving the ceasefire.

Building – and maintaining – peace in Northern Ireland was, and
continues to be, the work of many people and communities. Mowlam's
contribution played its part.

11 APRIL

CHILD-FREE BY CHOICE

'The numbers are really quite remarkable: around 10 per cent across Europe as a whole, aged from 25 to 45, are saying they are voluntarily child-free.'

Catherine Hakim, professor and sociologist, 2010

• • • • • •

The days when motherhood was the defining aspect of womanhood are gone. The contraceptive pill, for the first time in human history, put reliable control of reproduction in the hands of women, to make the choices about their lives that they wanted to make.

Catherine Hakim (b. 1948) has studied the statistics on women who clearly and repeatedly state that they do not want, have never wanted and will not want to have children. She distinguishes this group from those who are ambivalent about having children, and those who are not yet decided.

Central to the battle for reproductive rights are issues of bodily autonomy, and the right to make choices about what happens to one's own body. Hakim's findings point to a consistent cohort who are clear about what they want and need from life. Their voices are unambiguous; their choice is clear.

We might not make the same choices as other people – but we can assume that they are making the best decisions for themselves.

12 APRIL

SPRING CLEANING

'My top tip is: just start with toiletries and food, eating and using things counts ... We've all got those moisturisers we've bought, and then we've got another one ... Put things in a beauty box from Boots, or a woman's charity, or a food bank. If you're doing it yourself, do it slowly.'

Jenn Jordan, professional organiser, 2024

• • • • • •

You could fill shelves to overflowing with books advising you on how to declutter your house, each one offering a sure-fire way to turn your home into an oasis of calm and yourself into an organisational machine. Keep only the items that 'spark joy'. Remove 30 items in 30 days – or, if you're feeling really ambitious, 100 items in 100 days.

More often than not, however, we start with good intentions, and then, as the size of the task becomes apparent and the busyness of everyday life intervenes, we abandon the effort.

Professional organiser Jenn Jordan advises small steps, and with an eye not simply to throwing away, but to making the removal of items meaningful in some way. Thirty items can go in much less than 30 days if it means clearing out unused cosmetics to donate to a woman's charity, or sorting through the stock cupboard for a food bank.

And try not to go online shopping in the meantime.

13 APRIL

CHALLENGING OUR CHOICES

'As you get older you challenge your own thinking
... I made a choice [about motherhood] but also I
challenged my own choices. The opportunity arose to
have children but I always come back to the
same conclusion: I have no maternal instinct.'

Julia Wallace, town planner and stepmother, 2010

• • • • • •

For some, choosing to become a mother comes naturally. For others, the question is fraught – will we be good enough? Can we afford it? What will be the impact on my health, my life, my career? And for some, there is no question – they have no maternal instinct.

When we make big choices about our lives, particularly those about which we feel ambivalent, we can sometimes fall into a trap of thinking that because other people have chosen differently, this somehow invalidates our decisions, or is intended to imply that we have made bad decisions.

Are we honest with ourselves when it comes to our choices, for example, about having children? Do we see different decisions as a rebuttal of the decisions we have made? How easily do we accept that others choose differently from us – and that's okay?

14 APRIL

CHOOSE YOUR BATTLES

'I do feel quite strongly that if you treat young adults with a bit of respect and assume that they have some gumption and [for example] let them stay up late sometimes, then on the nights when you say to them, "Look, you're clearly exhausted, you should go to sleep at eight tonight," I think they're more likely to agree.'

Sophie Hannah, poet and novelist, 2011

• • • • • •

Sometimes the teenage years can seem like a battleground, as the young person for whom you are legally responsible is learning to assert themselves and (rightly) take more control over their decisions. Sometimes you can see disasters in the making that you can't help but try to prevent.

But learning about consequences is part of becoming an adult. That too many late nights will lead to a crunch. That practice really does make perfect. That work doesn't miraculously do itself.

Not everything has to be a battle. Be clear about what is absolutely non-negotiable. And play the rest by ear.

15 APRIL

MOTHERING

'I wasn't mothered well. I know there are lots of people who weren't mothered well and that makes them have the desire to do it [well], but I never felt I could make up for not being mothered. I always felt that I don't know how to do that.'

Oprah Winfrey, talk-show host, television producer, actress, author and businesswoman, 1999

• • • • • •

Oprah Winfrey (b. 1954) is one of the world's most influential women. From her start in local radio, she went on to revitalise the talk-show format. Her ability to influence public opinion, dubbed the 'Oprah Effect', has exerted powerful sway on consumer choices, most notably through 'Oprah's Book Club', which would turn a book into a bestseller.

By 2007, Winfrey's influence was such that she has been credited with altering the course of the Democratic primary in favour of Barack Obama (whom she endorsed) and away from the front-runner Hillary Clinton. Some studies have claimed that her endorsement not only won Obama over a million votes in the primary, but also had a decisive effect on the election.

Winfrey has cited her own childhood experiences of poverty, abuse and teenage pregnancy (her baby son, Canaan, was born prematurely and died in infancy) as the reason behind her decision not to become a mother again. Through her philanthropy, she has donated millions to charitable causes with a focus on scholarships and education programmes, particularly her school for girls in South Africa.

16 APRIL

SPARKING JOY

'There are still boxes under my bed from when I was 22 or 23, of a playsuit from a fast fashion brand that cost about £10, that doesn't fit and didn't look nice at the time. But it's a love letter to the girl who bought that and did look all right in it, one day. And all of this stuff, every time I open it up, there's a story, there's a connection . . . They're like little passports back to a life I don't have any more.'

Rebecca Reid, journalist, 2024

• • • • • •

While the decluttering industry aims to persuade us to get rid of stuff (presumably to free up space to buy more stuff?), journalist Rebecca Reid points to the virtues of keeping stuff. Even after many house moves, the birth of her child and the break-up of a relationship, she has kept boxes from her early twenties, memories of the person that she was.

Marie Kondo (b. 1984), creator of the KonMari decluttering method, advises gathering together similar items in order to confront yourself with how much you have, then handling each in turn, keeping only those that 'spark joy'. The intent is to find those items that have real meaning for you, to hold on to them, and – with the space available from removing other items – be able to enjoy them in your everyday life.

And if it means keeping everything – that's okay too. You don't have to throw your life away.

17 APRIL

REASSESSING FRIENDSHIP

'I now cast my net further afield and I don't think that friends have to have a certain blueprint to be friends. I think, before, I imagined you had to have a shared background and a shared geography, but now I don't think so. Any human who wants to be a friend and proffers the hand of friendship is extremely welcome to be a friend of mine.'

Vanessa Feltz, author, journalist and television personality, 2024

• • • • • •

What assumptions do we make about the kind of people who are most likely to make good friends? Do we assume that we are more likely to be simpatico with people from similar backgrounds or who live nearby?

Changes in our lives might make us need something different from friendship. Becoming a parent, for example, inevitably brings involvement in parent and baby groups, and, eventually, the local school network, trading playdates and sleepovers. A new job will bring us a different set of colleagues with whom to socialise. Or perhaps losing a partner – whether through a relationship break-up or bereavement – takes us out again, not necessarily for romance, but for company.

Are we open to offers of friendship?

18 APRIL

MAMMA MIA!

'When we did the world tour for *Mamma Mia*, I [took] my four college roommates along with me on the trip and we did a lot of celebrating Dynamo-style, right around the world. Berlin, Stockholm, we left no bar closed.'

Meryl Streep, actress, 2009

• • • • • •

Take a handful of ABBA songs, throw them in the air and write a musical around them — what's not to like? And, indeed, the idea has been a huge success. The plot of *Mamma Mia!*, such as it is, concerns the attempts by 20-year-old Sophie to discover which of her mother's three old flames is her father, back from when her mother was part of girl group Donna and the Dynamos.

Mamma Mia! opened in the West End in 1999 and (barring lockdown closures) has been running ever since, making it one of the longest-running shows in West End history. Not to mention, there have also been two films: *Mamma Mia!* (2008) and *Mamma Mia! Here We Go Again* (2018). Feel-good and lightweight, the franchise is marketed as something to see with friends, and it's a joy to hear that the star of those two films, Meryl Streep (b. 1949), did exactly that with *her* girlfriends, Dynamo-style.

Who are your Dynamos? Who will always turn up to enjoy your company?

THROW A LOT OF GLITTER AROUND

'I knew I needed to pursue my creative abilities . . .
I knew I needed to be a different kind of mother, and
to follow my heart. To start with, just exploring my
creativity, because it had laid dormant for a long
time . . . For me, the creativity was about my healing.
So I made textile art, I upcycled furniture, I basically
threw a lot of paint around and a lot of glitter,
and enjoyed myself finding my style.'

Lucy Simm, artist with M/Others Who Make, 2018

• • • • • •

Motherhood disrupts. It disrupts the body and the mind, life at home and life at work, and for creators, it disrupts the process of creativity.

Art of any kind is produced through sustained attention and engagement, by entering and maintaining a state of flow. But motherhood – Lucy Simm suggests – is a state of being permanently interruptible.

How to square this circle? Not creating is one option – but what if that means too much surrender of the self? How might mothers of young children find the space to be able to create? How does anyone with intensive caring responsibilities create the space in which to be able to make art?

M/Others Who Make is an initiative aimed at connecting women and non-binary people to help them sustain their art alongside their caring responsibilities. Somewhere, in between these various roles we fulfil and the many identities we have, we can still call ourselves 'artist' and 'creator'.

20 APRIL

IT COMES FROM INSIDE

'I can only say, wherever I had lived, I would have
become a writer ... I think that if you really
are a writer, it comes from inside.'

Nadine Gordimer, writer, political activist and Nobel laureate, 2014

• • • • • •

South African writer Nadine Gordimer (1923–2014) received the
Nobel Prize in Literature in 1991. Her habit of writing began as a small
child, when she was frequently unwell and kept at home.

Writing can be a public performance, but at its heart remains the
need to express something – not necessarily to another person, but to
explain yourself to yourself. Some writers form the habit of keeping
'morning pages': sitting down as soon as they wake up and writing
uninhibitedly for a page or two, or for as long as inspiration lasts.

Journalling, diary-keeping, note-taking – what means do we have
to explain ourselves to ourselves? And can we find an opportunity to
take a moment out of the day to do so?

21 APRIL

A REALLY GOOD TEACHER

'I had a really good English teacher who told us a story about a pupil who copied out an entire Gerald Durrell story and passed it off as their own. Durrell got a B, and I used to get Bs and it made me think, maybe I could be a writer ... '

Sarah Millican, comedian, 2017

• • • • • •

What were you like at school? Were your talents obvious, or did they take a little coaxing out? Perhaps you only found your niche after your schooldays were long past?

There's an art – even alchemy – to teaching and mentorship. To helping people find their way towards a path in life. Sometimes people know exactly what they want to do, and need practical guidance. Sometimes people need directing down paths that they didn't even know existed.

Who were the teachers that inspired you? Who were the mentors that set you going in the right direction?

22 APRIL

ON TURNING 30

'I was at a friend's thirtieth quite recently and one girl
had been single for a long time. Now she's met the love
of her life and she was pregnant. She said to me, "Are
you seeing anyone?" I said, "No." She held my hand
and she went, "Ah, don't worry, I was the last one
in my group to settle down but it will happen!" And
I thought, "I never told you I'd got a problem?!"'

Amy Elizabeth, broadcaster and producer, 2020

• • • • • •

A survey carried out in 2022 by Relate, who provide relationship support for people in England and Wales, examined 'milestone anxiety', that is, the sense that one is missing out on reaching important milestones in life.

The differences were marked between the generations. 'Milestone anxiety' was reported by 77 per cent of millennials (born between 1981 and 1996) and 83 per cent of Gen Z (born between 1997 and 2012). This contrasted with 70 per cent of baby boomers and 66 per cent of over-75s reporting on how they felt when they were younger. A 'crunch point' seems to arrive in one's early thirties, when people look around and take stock of where they are in comparison to their peers.

Perhaps this partially reflects a sense, post-pandemic, of lost years of youth and early adulthood. Perhaps, as we age, we become more accepting of ourselves and our decisions. But perhaps, too, turning 30 is the moment when we have a first dim sense of ourselves as getting older, of even getting left behind.

But life is not a to-do list, where we tick off tasks, one by one. Nor is it about collecting trophies or unlocking achievements. We move at our own pace, and what works for others might not be right for us.

23 APRIL

LIVERPOOL BIRDS BEAT ALL THE REST

'We didn't realise it wasn't done. We thought everybody
did that ... I was in the BBC meeting people far
more talented than ever I would be, and wondering how I
was going to survive, and yet I'd go back
to this funny little room with a stray cat in it and a
gas fire that kept going out, and I wrote.'

Carla Lane, television writer, 2006

. . . . . .

When Carla Lane and her writing partner, Myra Taylor, were commissioned by the BBC to write a comedy about two young women sharing a flat, the result was *The Liver Birds* (1969–78), which broke new ground in showing the lives of young women.

The Liver Birds followed the trials, tribulations, lives and loves of two 'dolly birds' sharing a flat on Liverpool's Huskisson Street. Originally starring Pauline Collins as Dawn and Polly James as Beryl, Collins left after one season, replaced by Nerys Hughes as Sandra.

Beryl and Sandra captured something quintessential about the late sixties and early seventies. Two young Scouse women, single, leading independent lives and, crucially, working class – there had been nothing else like it on television.

But young women like these were everywhere at the time. And they weren't going anywhere.

24 APRIL

THE BIOLOGICAL CLOCK

'Fertility doesn't last forever and will decline as we get to our late thirties. [Fertility treatments] should not be seen as a substitute for normal conception. If you are at a stage in your life where you know you want to have children and you can, don't postpone it – do it, if you can.'

Mary Herbert, professor of reproductive biology, 2020

• • • • • •

What is the truth about the biological clock? Is it true that fertility in women declines catastrophically at a certain age? Or are we right to be wary about public pronouncements pushing us towards pregnancy, particularly when associated with expensive fertility treatments, such as egg freezing? How do we separate the scare stories from the facts?

Mary Herbert's research is aimed at advancing knowledge of early embryos with a view to improving our understanding of infertility and genetic diseases. She has been at the forefront of developing 'mitochondrial donation', a technique which replaces faulty mitochondria in eggs and zygotes with healthy mitochondria, preventing the transmission of genetic diseases.

Herbert's advice is grounded in expertise and pragmatism. If you want a child, and the conditions are right – go for it. And techniques such as egg freezing are better done in your early, rather than late, thirties, to maximise success.

There is no substitute for good information, the basis for informed choices about one's health and one's body.

25 APRIL

DIVAS

'[Diva] shouldn't be a negative term at all, because its origins are around goddesses, and strong creative women.'

Kate Bailey, museum curator, 2023

• • • • • •

In 2023, the Victoria and Albert Museum in London held an exhibition celebrating divas, iconic performers, their power and their creativity. From the nineteenth-century opera singer Adelina Patti, via Maria Callas to Elton John, Madonna, Whitney Houston and Lizzo, the exhibition looked at the history and style of the diva, how the idea developed in popular culture, and how it has been subverted.

Kate Bailey, who curated the exhibition, notes that the word 'diva' originally meant 'goddess'. Used to compliment the distinguished opera singers of the nineteenth century, the phrase became increasingly more pejorative throughout the twentieth century, taking on the connotations of being temperamental and difficult that we associate with the word today.

Bailey ties this to the demand for equal rights and recognition by creative women – but observes how it speaks in part, too, to our fascination with people's behaviour as much as their art.

And ultimately, divas – no matter their affinity with the divine – are only human, just like the rest of us.

26 APRIL

BLOWING A GASKET

'I have been known to blow a gasket now and then but I don't think I'm a diva. I've learned to control my temper now because I'm more mature. At least, I should be.'

Susan Boyle, singer, 2012

• • • • • •

Susan Boyle memorably burst into the public consciousness with her performance on *Britain's Got Talent* in 2009, singing 'I Dreamed a Dream' from *Les Misérables*. Despite placing second in the overall competition, Boyle went on to huge subsequent success with her albums and tours.

High-profile performances are stressful, and sometimes a loss of temper might happen. But it's too easy to stigmatise women's anger as uncontrolled and inappropriate, when a man's anger might be characterised as passion for the work.

Do we hold back on being angry if we feel we will be negatively received? When might expressing ourselves forcefully be not only appropriate, but effective?

27 APRIL

FINDING YOUR VOICE

'I should have been angry. I wish I was. I was
heartbroken. It was such a shock. Some nights I started
to sing and she was standing there. I was trying to
fight back tears. My voice just wouldn't work. I'd open
my mouth. Sometimes nothing came out. Sometimes I
managed a few croaks. I was lucky because
Martin Carthy was standing next to me and
he would help me out on the songs.'

Shirley Collins, folk singer, 2016

• • • • • •

Along with Linda Thompson, Sandy Denny, Vashti Bunyan and Anne Briggs, Shirley Collins (b. 1935) was one of a group of great women singers and songwriters who emerged during the English Folk Revival of the 1960s and 1970s.

In 1971, Collins married her second husband, Ashley Hutchings, formerly of Fairport Convention and Steeleye Span, and together they formed the Albion Country Band. The band enjoyed huge success, but, during a production at the National Theatre, Hutchings left Collins for one of the other performers. The stress resulted in Collins losing her voice – a condition known as dysphonia. Unable to perform, she retired from singing and turned to secretarial and administrative work.

Throughout the 1980s, her voice gradually began to return, and, in 2016, in her eighties, she recorded her first album in nearly 40 years, *Lodestar*. Two more albums have followed (*Heart's Ease* [2020] and *Archangel Hill* [2023]) and a documentary about her life, *The Ballad of Shirley Collins*, was released in 2017.

Some voices can't be silenced.

28 APRIL

STUCK WITH SUCCESS

'It's too late for me [to return to classical music].
I think I'm stuck with the success of "My Baby
Just Cares For Me" and songs like that.'

Nina Simone, singer–songwriter, composer,
pianist and civil rights activist, 1988

• • • • • •

Nina Simone (1933–2003) originally intended to become a concert pianist. In 1950, she spent a year at the Juilliard School in New York, in preparation for applying to the Curtis Institute of Music in Philadelphia. The family relocated to Philadelphia in anticipation of her acceptance at the Institute, but her application was rejected – a decision which she attributed to racism.

Turning to playing piano in nightclubs for a living, Simone began performing jazz and blues. In 1959, she released her first album, *Little Girl Blue*.

In 1963, Simone turned to political songwriting in the aftermath of the murder of four Black girls whose church was bombed by white supremacists while the girls were attending Sunday school in Birmingham, Alabama. Her song 'Mississippi Goddam' (1964), written in rage at the murders, also referenced the brutal murder of 14-year-old Emmett Till, abducted and lynched in Mississippi in 1955. The song was banned in several Southern states.

Simone always regretted the loss of her classical career, referring to her music as 'Black classical music'. The Curtis Institute awarded her an honorary degree in 2003, shortly before her death.

29 APRIL

LESS PRESSURE ON MY EGGS

'If you'd have spoken to me six months ago legit I didn't
feel any pressure . . . In my head I'm still 19 in
lots of ways. In my head I still want kids – when
I'm older. I'd really like to adopt, which puts a
little bit less pressure on my eggs.'

Amy Elizabeth, broadcaster and producer, 2020

· · · · · ·

Research carried out in 2022 by Relate into the milestones we feel we should have achieved by certain points in our life suggested that having children was at the top of the list, and that this pressure was stronger than ever.

Over a third of millennials (born between 1981 and 1996) felt the pressure to have children. This compared to only 17 per cent of baby boomers who reported feeling this pressure when they were younger.

Yet the picture that emerges is more complex. The survey reported that, on milestones that people felt should be better recognised and celebrated, adopting children was top of the list, and the decision not to have children also featured. So did paying off student debt.

Broadcaster and podcaster Amy Elizabeth voices some of this new perspective. The contraceptive pill was only the start of the reproduct-ive revolution. A reconfiguration of what family might mean seems also to be underway.

30 APRIL

TROOP LEADER CONRAN

'One of the advantages of being divorced is that you're not exactly a mother and you're not exactly a father, you're suddenly a sort of leader of the troop. And quite often, and certainly in my case, there's a whole new family relationship with far more family discussion. As a result of it, my sons have grown up to be far more responsible than I was at their age.'

Shirley Conran, author, journalist and campaigner, 1979

• • • • • •

Dame Shirley Conran (1932–2024) trained as a sculptor at the Southern College of Art, Portsmouth, and then as a painter at Chelsea Polytechnic. In 1955, she married designer Terence Conran (later Sir Terence Conran); they had two sons together before divorcing in 1962. After two subsequent and brief marriages, Conran turned to writing to support herself and her family.

In 1968, she created 'Femail', the women's section of the *Daily Mail*, where she pushed beyond the usual content of knitting, patterns and recipes; she later became women's editor for the *Observer*. In 1975, she published *Superwoman*, a practical and feminist guide to housekeeping, which launched the slogan: 'Life's too short to stuff a mushroom.'

Turning her hand to fiction, Conran published her first novel, *Lace* (1982), a legendary 'bonkbuster' that was required reading for any 1980s teen (as the 1984 miniseries was required viewing). Again, Conran delivered on quotable lines: 'Which one of you bitches is my mother?'

From her early thirties, Conran struggled with myalgic encephalomyelitis (chronic fatigue syndrome). In her later years, she lobbied for flexitime for men and women, and founded Maths Action, an organisation aiming to improve maths skills in Britain, and advised the Department for Education on getting girls to study mathematics. She died in 2024 aged 91.

MAY

1 MAY

MAY DAY

'I think the best advice is to outsource as many
domestic chores as you can afford. It's not always
possible for everyone, and it's not possible for me, but
it's very good advice. And avoid the rows.'

Lucy Mangan, journalist and author, 2009

• • • • • •

The first of May is May Day – International Workers' Day, a time to
reflect on patterns of work both inside and outside the home.

Outsourcing housework makes sense – if neither of you want to
do the job, then outsource it to someone who does. But who are the
people to whom we outsource our domestic tasks?

*Global Woman: Nannies, Maids, and Sex Workers in the New Global
Economy* (2003) was a landmark collection of essays edited by Barbara
Ehrenreich and Arlie Russell Hochschild that examined what the latter
called 'the global care chain', a pattern of migration for work where
women from the Global South migrate to take on domestic and caring
jobs in the Global North.

Both women have made peerless contributions to our understanding of the changing nature of women's work in a globalising
world. The nature of work changed profoundly in the move to the
post-industrial world. But certain jobs – such as care and cleaning –
remain the same. Who does this work in the global economy? Who do
we outsource it to?

2 MAY

WANTED CHILDREN

'Nowadays people do not have unwanted children ...
The children they have they really want and they really
love. It's a totally different affair from when I was a child.'

Marilyn French, feminist and writer, 2006

• • • • • •

The fiction and non-fiction of Marilyn French chronicles the rise of the
women's movement in the United States in the post-war period, most
famously in her debut and landmark novel *The Women's Room* (1977).

French's body of work delineates the reasons why women were
moved to organise, demonstrate and protest; chronicles the social and
political changes that were achieved; and scrutinises the rising backlash
against the women's movement.

Freedom from the inevitability of pregnancy and insistence on a
woman's right to choose what happens to her own body were central
to the women's movement, and brought about a fundamental shift in
childhood. Writing about people she observed in her own youth, French
movingly describes families of 12–14 children, many unwanted, whom
the parents could not afford to feed.

In the United States today, there are already significant barriers
to accessing healthcare among many socioeconomic groups. The backlash against women's reproductive rights threatens to return children
to this state of uncertainty, of being unplanned and not wanted. What
impact will this retrenchment have? What similar barriers exist in the
UK across socioeconomic groups?

How do we ensure that children are always wanted?

3 MAY

A SPIRIT OF KINDNESS

'When you're bringing up children and you want them
to be kind you have to start with yourself. Kids watch
everything you do; they pick up from your behaviour. So
you've got to start by being a kind person yourself, and
be kind to your children, which isn't always easy when
you're dealing with the day-to-day of parenting.
Just approach it with a spirit of kindness.'

Uju Asika, blogger, author, speaker and writing mentor, 2020

• • • • • •

Uju Asika's most recent book on parenting is *Raising Boys Who Do Better: A Hopeful Guide for a New Generation* (2023), written for anyone parenting boys, and those who care about the young men in their lives.

Sometimes children seem to know exactly which buttons to press, to have an uncanny instinct for what will make us see red. Sometimes we watch ourselves making the mistakes our own parents made with us, or hear ourselves saying things that we swore we would never say to children of our own – all of which can lead to some deeply despondent moments.

But parenting is not a competition sport. Certainly, there are no medals or trophies to be won. And knowing that can release us from a sense of failure. We can admit it when we go wrong, cut ourselves some slack and aim to handle ourselves better next time round.

If children see us admitting and learning from our mistakes, most likely they'll learn the behaviour that we're modelling.

4 MAY

ON BEING HEARD

'It's useful for women to act as allies to other women; the best thing of all is for men to act as allies, because what men say tends to carry more weight. Suppose you say something in a meeting and no one takes any notice until the man repeats it ten minutes later and it's treated like the second coming. Then one of your allies can say to the man, "Oh, I am so glad you agree with what [she] said earlier!"'

Mary Ann Sieghart, author, journalist and broadcaster, 2024

• • • • • •

'Girl Men Can't Hear' is a character from the comedy sketch show *The Fast Show* (1994–97). Played by Arabella Weir (b. 1957), the 'girl' puts forward ideas to a group of men who ignore her, only to congratulate one of their number when he later suggests the same idea. The sketches invariably end with the girl asking, in exasperation, 'Can any of you actually *hear* me?' (They don't hear that either.)

Mary Ann Sieghart's (b. 1961) book *The Authority Gap: Why Women Are Still Taken Less Seriously Than Men, and What We Can Do About It* (2021) addresses precisely this infuriating scenario, and others like it, and what women can do.

Allyship is, as ever, one strategy – and men need to step up and do this work. Putting forward expert women for high-profile jobs and opportunities. Refusing to participate in 'manels' (all-male panels at conferences). Giving credit where credit is due.

5 MAY

YOU ARE DESERVING OF BETTER

'[T]he younger me was very timid and insecure and was allowing other people to tell her who she was . . . You can get better, and the only way to get better is to believe that you are deserving of better. And that's what I had to do to reach that point.'

Chidera Eggerue, author and blogger, 2017

• • • • • •

Chidera Eggerue (b. 1994) is one of a new generation of feminists coming to prominence in the digital age. Blogging and posting as 'The Slumflower', referring to a flower that grows out of concrete, Eggerue focuses on issues of self-image and self-esteem, and fashion outside of the mainstream. Her first book, *What a Time to Be Alone* (2018), encourages young women to embrace single life to grow their own self-worth, and use this as a basis for adult relationships.

While there is general agreement that there is a mental health crisis among young people in Britain, there is no consensus as to the cause. A study carried out by researchers at King's College London in 2023 showed that there are generational divides over the reasons, with older generations tending to blame use of drugs or alcohol, and younger generations more likely to refer to financial difficulties preventing them from getting a start in life.

Whatever the causes – and they are likely to be many – there is no doubt that what's needed is better services and support; proper investment in the mental health of our young adults.

6 MAY

YOU ARE DESERVING OF BETTER

'To analyse prettiness, I also had to analyse how I exist in the body that I do – as a thin white cisgender woman – I have a lot more privilege, whether that's comfortable to acknowledge or not in so many interactions in my life. It reflects the beauty standard that has been set by racist patriarchy. And although women experience this pressure to perform prettiness to receive better treatment, marginalised women such as Black women and trans women and fat women experience this a lot more in society.'

Florence Given, author and illustrator, 2020

• • • • • •

Florence Given (b. 1998) rose to prominence in 2018 when she organised an online petition to cancel the Netflix comedy-drama series *Insatiable* (2018–19), in which an overweight teenager loses weight and takes her revenge on the people who bullied her over her size. The petition, which gained more than 200,000 signatures, complained that the show was fat-shaming. *Insatiable* was cancelled after two seasons.

Given's best-selling book *Women Don't Owe You Pretty* (2020), which she wrote and illustrated, was published when she was 21. It covers a wide variety of topics, including body positivity, internalised misogyny, rape culture and microaggressions, and considers the author's privilege as a white woman writing on these topics.

The book attracted controversy when Chidera Eggerue, whom Given cited as an influence, suggested that the style and content were sufficiently similar to her own work as to constitute a form of appropriation of work by a Black woman by the predominantly white publishing industry.

That books marketed to a similar young demographic have similar styles is perhaps no surprise, although Eggerue is correct that there are serious questions about appropriation. And how, too, do we persuade this readership to read on? What next steps will they take into feminism?

THE TALK

'I think my main thing is to explain to them that not everybody in the world feels that way and to really empower my kids. That's really important to affirm your child when they have experienced any kind of racial abuse or racist treatment. To just make them feel positive and powerful and to celebrate who they are.'

Uju Asika, blogger, author, speaker and writing mentor, 2020

• • • • • •

The Talk is the name given by Black parents to the conversation they must have with their children about race, and the impact that their skin colour might have upon the rest of their lives. The Talk was the subject of a documentary on Channel 4 in 2020, made in the wake of the murder of George Floyd.

George Floyd was a 46-year-old Black American man who was murdered in Minneapolis, Minnesota, on 25 May 2020 by police officer Derek Chauvin, who knelt on Floyd's neck for nine minutes. Chauvin was subsequently convicted of murder and sentenced to 22 years in prison.

Floyd's murder brought to global prominence the Black Lives Matter (BLM) movement, a campaign that aims to highlight racism, police brutality and racially motivated violence. BLM emerged in 2013 after the fatal shooting of Black teenager Trayvon Martin. The shooter, George Zimmerman, was acquitted of second-degree murder.

Uju Asika's book *Bringing Up Race: How to Raise a Kind Child in a Prejudiced World* (2020) aims to help parents open conversations with their children about race and prejudice, whatever their race or ethnicity. Honest conversations about racism are a necessary task for all parents if we are truly committed to seeing change in the world.

8 MAY

THEY NEED TO CATCH UP

'This is brand new theatre. Let's make it inclusive. Let's set it up. [The captions] are designed to integrate into the show. They're part of the show, not because I need access ... Some of the theatres are so old. They need to catch up!'

Rose Ayling-Ellis, actress and model, 2022

• • • • • •

Actor Rose Ayling-Ellis (b. 1994) made her West End debut as Celia in *As You Like It* in 2022 at Soho Place.

Ayling-Ellis has described her frustrations with many West End productions as a Deaf member of the audience. There may be only a limited number of signed or captioned performances, and, with the stage at the front, captions can be awkwardly positioned, leaving a Deaf audience member turning to read the words rather than being able to watch the actors.

Soho Place, which opened in October 2022, is the West End's first new theatre in 50 years. With the stage constructed in the round, the production was able to take an entirely new approach to integrating sign language and captions. They became part of the production, rather than added to meet accessibility requirements.

There are moments when the way we usually do things is suddenly revealed not only to be inadequate, but outdated and backward-facing. People have innovated, and the world has moved on. Do we let ourselves be disorientated? How quickly can we catch up?

9 MAY

NOBODY ASKED

'I want to just enjoy the job I do. But part of me,
I can't just enjoy it. I still have to make changes ...
It can be exhausting sometimes ... I am political without
asking to be political.'

Rose Ayling-Ellis, actress and model, 2022

• • • • • •

Deaf Awareness Week, usually held in the first half of May, is an annual event which aims to raise awareness about the Deaf community, and Deaf language, culture and history.

Sign languages are fully functional languages that differ in profound ways from spoken language, making use of their own distinctive grammar based on gestures, facial expression, body language and how the hands are shaped. British Sign Language became a recognised language of England, Scotland and Wales in 2022.

The British Deaf Association states that British Sign Language (BSL) is the preferred language of over 87,000 people in the UK. English may be a second or even third language. The total number of users of BSL in the UK is around 150,000 people (this does not include professional BSL users, unless they use BSL at home).

Rose Ayling-Ellis, who has been Deaf since birth, is a British Sign Language user. After appearing in *EastEnders*, Ayling-Ellis won *Strictly Come Dancing* in 2021 with her partner Giovanni Pernice; their 'silent dance', in which a portion of the dance was performed without music, replicating Ayling-Ellis's experience, won the 'Must-See Moment' BAFTA (an award voted on by the public) in 2022.

Sometimes, simply by being present, people can be politicised in ways that they have not chosen, and are asked to perform work by teaching us about their experience in the world. How might we take on this work ourselves? How might we educate ourselves better?

10 MAY

FEAR AND LOATHING

'Why is popular culture full of this kind of stuff and
nobody is talking about it? Nobody is noticing it? ...
The wider context is that there is this current of fear
of and loathing of women ... I was aware of this as
something that had existed for thousands of years.
At the time nobody knew what misogyny was: people
would say, "What are you writing next?" "A book about
misogyny." [And] people would say, "What's that?"'

Joan Smith, journalist, crime novelist and activist, 2014

• • • • • •

In May 1981, Peter Sutcliffe, nicknamed by the press the 'Yorkshire Ripper', was put on trial for the murder of 13 women and the
attempted murder of seven more. Sutcliffe was convicted on all counts,
and sentenced to 20 concurrent life sentences. West Yorkshire Police,
who interviewed Sutcliffe multiple times throughout their years-long
investigation into the crimes, faced severe criticism of their handling
of the case.

Joan Smith (b. 1953) was a young journalist at the time of Sutcliffe's arrest, and covered his trial. Her recognition that Sutcliffe's
actions arose from the wider context in which misogyny was not only
accepted, but normalised, led, in 1989, to the publication of *Misogynies*,
an electric collection of essays covering the fear, loathing and objec-
tification of women that permeates society, from Page 3 to violence
on screen, to the institutional sexism that failed to capture Sutcliffe
sooner.

Smith's analysis in *Misogynies* continues to be desperately relevant,
providing us with the tools we need to put the blame on the perpe-
trators of violent crime – rather than their victims – and the social
structures that enable them to operate.

11 MAY

RECLAIM THE NIGHT

'I'm not saying we should go around being terrified that bad things are going to happen to us, but we should be aware ... It's at the back of most women's minds. Because as we grow up, we get the messages that the world is a dangerous place.'

Val McDermid, crime writer, 2013

• • • • • •

Reclaim the Night was a protest movement that began in Leeds in 1977 in response to the Yorkshire Ripper murders. When police instructed women to stay at home after dark, marches took place across several British cities in protest. One slogan of the movement was: 'No curfew on women: curfew on men.'

Val McDermid (b. 1955) is the author of more than 30 crime novels. A journalist for many years, McDermid published her first novel, *Report for Murder*, in 1987. Her novels regularly feature female detectives, both amateur and professional, including police officer Karen Pirie, private investigator Kate Brannigan and investigative journalist Allie Burns.

A radical feminist, McDermid's novels engage seriously with the question of the use of violence within her chosen genre. Crime fiction can easily fall into gratuitous and exploitative violence against women; in McDermid's hands, the crime novel becomes a means to interrogate how and why violence occurs, or how and why it is allowed to occur.

From childhood, the subliminal message is sent out to girls that the world is full of hidden dangers. McDermid's point is not that girls and women should move about the world in fear, but that awareness of our immediate environment might help to keep us safe. In lieu of a curfew on men, this seems pragmatic advice.

12 MAY

STRENGTH THROUGH SELF-KNOWLEDGE

'I think it's a very mixed time for women. Some of the difficulties are having things in extremis, that everything has to be awesome or absolutely terrible and there's not enough complexity in our emotional lives. I think a way to have resilience is not only through friendship and community but also to dare to know what you feel, to dare to accept your vulnerabilities and your difficulties. Allowing those vulnerabilities to exist inside of you gives you enormous strength.'

Susie Orbach, psychotherapist and social critic, 2016

• • • • • •

Susie Orbach (b. 1946) brought the insights of second-wave feminism to the practice of psychotherapy and psychoanalysis. After co-founding the Women's Therapy Centre (established in London in 1976), Orbach produced her most famous book, *Fat Is a Feminist Issue* (1978), a robust attack on the harm done to women and girls by the food and diet industries and the corporatisation of self-image in the pursuit of profit.

Do we refuse to admit when we are struggling? Do we tend to say that we are fine when in fact what we require is a little support or sympathy? As well as reaching out to friends and networks, we must also be honest with ourselves, and realise when we need to ask for help, rather than soldiering on.

Orbach reminds us that complexity and nuance are at the heart of a full and resilient emotional life. Acceptance of one's vulnerabilities and self-knowledge are a truer and more robust source of personal strength.

13 MAY

FEELING RIGID AND STUCK

'A lot of my anxiety manifests from a loss of belonging or a sense of being so isolated and on my own. A lot of my suffering comes from feeling totally rigid and stuck, like I can't move for fear of collapsing or breaking.'

Laura Mvula, singer-songwriter, 2017

• • • • • •

Research carried out by the Mental Health Foundation in 2023 reported that 60 per cent of UK adults experienced symptoms of anxiety that interfered with their daily life across the previous fortnight.

Anxiety can express itself in the most distressing of symptoms, such as shortness of breath or tightness in the chest, which can seriously disrupt day-to-day life. Perhaps you have found yourself struggling at work; perhaps you've had to avoid using public transport; perhaps it has been even too difficult to leave the house.

Laura Mvula (b. 1986) is an Ivor Novello award-winning singer-songwriter who has spoken about her own experiences with anxiety and, more generally, the impact of anxiety upon the millennial generation (those born between 1981 and 1996). Her description of her sense of isolation and fragility captures the awful fearfulness that anxiety can induce.

Would we notice if a friend or colleague was suffering from anxiety? How might we be able to help, or react?

14 MAY

BUILDING SELF-ESTEEM

'[I]t's never too early to start building self-esteem, but in terms of when the awareness of the problems comes in, I would always have said that it was around Year 8 when they start to have an awareness of things like eating disordered behaviour or body dysmorphic–type thoughts, or comparing themselves to their peers. That has got younger and younger and younger, and now it's Year 4 and 5, which is in the middle of primary school.'

Natasha Devon, writer, campaigner and broadcaster, 2017

• • • • • •

Natasha Devon (b. 1981) has worked with schools and colleges throughout the UK to raise awareness of mental health issues among young people, particularly in relation to body image, mental wellbeing and self-esteem.

Devon's anxiety, which she began to experience in secondary school, developed in her late teens into bulimia, from which she recovered in her twenties. She has campaigned extensively for media awareness and sensitivity in reporting on mental health issues and, between 2015 and 2016, was the government's Mental Health Champion for Schools.

Devon is clear that loss of self-esteem can start young – and younger than it has in the past, with children as young as eight or nine making comparisons with their peers, and judging their own self-worth accordingly.

When much of our media presents impossible achievements, how do we give children the skills to navigate this world? How do we communicate self-worth? What behaviours do we model ourselves? What messages do we send?

15 MAY

COMPETITIVE SELF-CURATION

'Research tends to show a correlation: the more people use social media, the worse [their] self-esteem, body image and things like that.'

Phillippa Diedrichs, professor of health psychology, 2017

• • • • • •

We've all done a little curation at times. Posted a picture from a café with a great cup of coffee and an impressive book. Fiddled with the filters on an image. Watched the number of 'likes' creep up.

It's often the inverse that's true, too: maybe we've spent too long on Instagram or Facebook, seeing what other people are doing, and feeling – more and more, as we scroll through – that we are most definitely missing out.

Perhaps we've even considered deleting our social media accounts; leaving that heightened world behind. But that's not always a practical choice. We may have professional networks that couldn't exist otherwise, or communication channels with distant friends and family that would suffer.

Social media cannot be un-invented. But can we think more mindfully, as we skim and post? Is there a middle ground, between the little hit of dopamine that we receive from a like, and the hollow feeling that comes from doomscrolling? How might we achieve this?

16 MAY

WHAT NOT TO SAY

'Those phrases – like "had a good innings" or "lived to a ripe old age" – the intention is not to diminish what you're feeling but the impact of it can be quite different.'

Helen Bullough, journalist and producer, 2023

• • • • • •

Helen Bullough lost both of her parents late in life, and has found that, in trying to offer consolation, people reach for phrases that try to express the sentiment of a long life well lived, but instead feel like they're diminishing her grief.

Losing parents is a blow at any age: something foundational has been taken away. Losing them later in life brings its own complications: these are the people who have been present through every stage of one's life, from childhood to making one's own way as an adult, through relationships and (potentially) children – even, perhaps, a shared retirement.

The loss of such long-established presences in one's life brings its own particular kind of adjustment. When you have been someone's child for most of your life, becoming an orphan casts a huge shadow. As the generations before us live longer, as we live longer, we may need to find ways to speak to each other about this experience, to offer real comfort.

17 MAY

A TRUE PICTURE

'So many people come up to me and they think they know me because they've read about me, but they haven't really got what I think is a true picture of me.'

Cherie Blair, barrister and writer, 2008

• • • • • •

Cherie, Lady Blair (b. 1954) became a barrister in 1976 and Queen's Counsel in 1995. In 2000, she became a founding member of Matrix Chambers, which specialises in human rights law. Between 1997 and 2007, she was in the public eye as the wife of then Prime Minister Tony Blair. During that time, their fourth child was born, the first baby born to a serving prime minister in 150 years, attracting significant press attention.

Cherie Blair has been portrayed on stage and screen on many occasions, notably in *The Queen* (2006) and in later seasons of the television series *The Crown* (2016–23). In 2008, Blair published her memoirs, *Speaking For Myself: The Autobiography*, in which she reflects upon the challenge of maintaining her own career alongside that of her husband, and living family life with public scrutiny.

What face do we habitually present to other people? Are we expected to be a certain way? The responsible one, the thoughtful one, the resourceful one? Are we content with these assumptions, and leaving aspects of ourselves private? Or are there facets to us that we wish others knew better or understood more?

18 MAY

KEEPING PERSPECTIVE

'My father is a radiation oncologist and we've all, in my family, reminded ourselves almost every day in this past year that what we're going through is not more difficult than someone who's facing a terminal illness.'

Monica Lewinsky, activist, 1998

• • • • • •

In the late 1990s, Monica Lewinsky (b. 1973), still only in her twenties, became internationally famous when details of her affair with then President Bill Clinton were made public. Such was the media attention that in later years Lewinsky referred to herself as the 'patient zero' of online harassment.

After more than a decade out of the spotlight, during which Lewinsky studied for an advanced degree in social psychology at the London School of Economics, she re-emerged to speak about cyberbullying, public shaming, #MeToo and the personal cost of her early brush with fame. Her social media accounts have been noted for their humour and self-deprecation.

To be embarrassed or humiliated must count as one of life's most painful experiences. Keeping perspective – that you and your loved ones remain in good health, or that this too shall pass – can be a first step towards restoring one's sense of wellbeing and agency.

Lewinsky's experiences remind us too that while it's easy to fall into simplistic narratives of heroes and villains, passing quick judgements, real people exist behind the news stories that we consume in our everyday lives.

19 MAY

MOVE THROUGH TOGETHER

'This is something that doesn't have to be a prison
for me, for other people. Because the more it's spoken
about, the more we can figure out how to move through
it together, rather than on your own ... Speaking
through things, making them tangible, has
been really important for me.'

Laura Mvula, singer-songwriter, 2017

· · · · · ·

Laura Mvula's courageous account of her experience with anxiety
offers hope that there is a way through. Mvula has used her platform to
reach out and speak out, which, in turn, has brought her into contact
with others who are struggling in the same way.

The act of opening up is not only a way of caring for yourself, but
of caring for others who may hear your words and take counsel and
comfort from them.

What platforms do we have in our day-to-day lives that can help
make these differences?

20 MAY

DISENGAGE

'I heard that thing so many times that you are not your thoughts and I thought that was total codswallop ... What else am I other than my thoughts? Meditation helped me see that there is a truth in that. You can see the thoughts that you're having and you don't have to always engage with them.'

Monica Ali, novelist, 2022

• • • • • •

After instant and huge success with her first novel, *Brick Lane* (2003), Monica Ali (b. 1967) published three more works of fiction. By the early 2010s, she was burned out, depressed and unable to write. It was a decade until her next novel, *Love Marriage*, was published, in 2022. Part of Ali's recovery process involved mantra-based meditation.

Sometimes we find ourselves paralysed by our own thoughts, locked in circular thinking that reinforces itself. Are there ways that we can 'circuit-break' these thought processes. Can we somehow step outside of them, and remind ourselves that we think differently? How might this help?

21 MAY

PUTTING YOURSELF FIRST

'In order to live in any kind of balanced way emotionally, you have to put yourself first, then you do everything else. But it's very difficult to do that!'

Emma Thompson, actor and screenwriter, 2018

• • • • • •

Anyone who has boarded an aeroplane and listened to the safety routine will have heard the instructions to parents to put on their own oxygen mask first before turning to those of their children. This seems counter-intuitive – our instinct is to protect those dependent on us – but in fact makes practical sense. We can't look after those around us if we're not fit ourselves.

Self-care amounts to the same thing. Whether that means making sure you are rested and have eaten and exercised, or checking in on your emotional state. Self-care is finding the time to connect with friends, or doing something that is important to you and brings you joy.

Self-care is not self-centredness. It's a matter of making sure that you don't stop functioning.

Take a deep breath. What do you need to do for yourself today before dealing with everybody else?

22 MAY

RADICAL SELF-CARE

'Self-care is radical in the sense that in the world we are taught to accept the bare minimum as women . . . And it's actually showing yourself the love that you know you deserve, and giving the love that you give to other people to yourself.'

Tanya Compas, youth worker and LGBTQ+ rights activist, 2017

• • • • • •

The concept of radical self-care originates in the writings of Audre Lorde (1934–92), professor, philosopher and civil rights activist – or, in her own words, 'Black, lesbian, feminist, socialist, mother, warrior, poet.'

In Lorde's writing, self-care goes well beyond the version we see more commonly today, where it has become synonymous with lighting some scented candles or treating yourself. For Lorde, self-care was a radical act – in a world that was politically aligned against her, often violently, and in the face of illness, to care for herself was 'not self-indulgence, it is self-preservation, and that is an act of political warfare'.

We are often offered up ideas from radical, intersectional and Black feminism repackaged, with the originators of these ideas erased, and the revolutionary agenda neutralised. In the case of radical self-care, what is meant to be a political challenge to society to reconfigure itself is subverted into private acts that do not challenge the status quo.

Do we know the sources of the ideas that we have adopted? Where, and from whom, might they have been appropriated? Have we lost touch with the radical heart that beats within them?

23 MAY

ON GUILT

'When you're doing something you shouldn't do, a lot of times we trick ourselves into believing certain things. Certainly, for me, I always felt, well, they would never find out ... I can only imagine how painful this has been for [Chelsea Clinton]. I have a lot of guilt about that.'

Monica Lewinsky, activist, 1998

• • • • • •

It's bad enough to be caught doing something that we shouldn't, but to be found out on a global scale, as Monica Lewinsky given only a few pages back, on p. 168 was, after her affair with President Clinton became public knowledge, is surely excruciating, and made worse by the knowledge of how others – such as Clinton's daughter, Chelsea – must have been affected.

We can be very good at justifying our own actions, for finding reasons to explain why we've chosen to act in certain ways. But what do we do when we're confronted with the fact of our own bad behaviour? Do we continue to rationalise? Or refuse to face up to the truth?

And what about the people we have harmed? They owe us nothing – but what do we owe to them? What if an apology is not welcome? What if forgiveness is not – and will not – be forthcoming? How do we come to terms with the consequences of our own actions?

24 MAY

ON FORGIVENESS

'Forgiveness is a journey. It's not an event, it's a process [that] begins with telling the story. What is it that happened, and describing the story of what happened to you as fully as you possibly can. And then naming the hurt, actually saying how the injury has landed with you: "The words you used made me feel ashamed. I felt that my dignity was rubbed in the dust. I felt afraid. I felt enraged." ... Forgiveness is a gift that you give to yourself.'

Mpho Tutu, Anglican priest, author and activist, 2014

• • • • • •

In 2012, Mpho Tutu (b. 1963) returned to her family home to discover the body of her housekeeper, Angela. She had been brutally murdered.

In the years that followed, Tutu embarked upon a long process of attempting to forgive the murderer, who was known to both her and Angela, and has spoken about that process, and what is has entailed. With her father, Desmond Tutu, she co-wrote *The Book of Forgiving*, on the art of healing from injury.

What counts most, Tutu says, is being able to describe and narrate the harm done – to be able to say what it is that has happened, and to give oneself the gift of healing. Forgiveness may follow in time.

What might we be called upon to forgive in our lives? Do we even want to forgive? How might this process begin when we turn the narrative away from the person who has harmed us, and towards ourselves, and what we need?

25 MAY

NO WRONG FEELINGS

'There is nothing wrong with any feeling. It's what we do with the feelings that becomes problematic.'

Mpho Tutu, Anglican priest, author and activist, 2014

● ● ● ● ● ●

How often have we caught ourselves feeling angry, or envious, or bitter – and then tried to suppress that emotion? How often have we told ourselves that it's wrong to feel in a certain way.

There are no wrong feelings. The choice we have is whether or not to act on them. Whether to take these feelings out on someone else, to turn them over inside until we cannot move past them, or to acknowledge them, and understand the source of them.

26 MAY

ON ANGER

'I call it a particular disease of privileged white people that they think that they can get through life without anger ... How can I not be angry? I absolutely and wholeheartedly embrace anger. It is insane to be a sentient being right now and not be angry.'

Mona Eltahawy, journalist and activist, 2018

• • • • • •

There's a politics to politeness. To being told that in order to be heard, you have to play nice. It's a racialised politics, too, as Mona Eltahawy points out.

But what if anger is the correct response when faced with systemic injustice? How can it be used productively – to make your voice heard, to insist that some injustices cannot be massaged away?

And how do we respond to the righteous anger of others? Do we focus on the tone of voice rather than the content – the challenges – of their speech? Are we deflecting, when we complain about the anger of others?

27 MAY

SETBACKS

'What I learned at a young age was you can have natural talent, but actually it's about working really hard and being focused and clear in your goals. And every time you have a setback, you learn from it and you move on.'

Tanni Grey-Thompson, wheelchair racer
and television presenter, 2013

• • • • • •

Tanni Grey-Thompson (b. 1969), Baroness Grey-Thompson of Eaglescliffe is a former wheelchair racer and life peeress. She won 16 medals across five Paralympic Games, and six London Marathons.

Sometimes natural talent can be its own drawback. If we do something easily, then we're not always equipped to deal with the occasions when everything goes wrong. We might think we've lost our knack. We don't have strategies in place for when things don't go to plan.

How well equipped are we to deal with setbacks? Do we meet them with resignation and a sense of defeat? Or are we equipped to take a deep breath, step back, work out what happened, and put plans in place for next time round?

Focus, clarity in your goals, a plan for how to reach them and, above all, hard work are talents in their own right.

28 MAY

DISRUPTING THE SYSTEM

'[T]here are some experimental studies which have tried to look at cause and effect and increasingly what we're understanding is a more nuanced perspective on social media ... [W]omen have amazing social media accounts and are using them to disrupt the system ... There is a lot of panic about [social media] and it can be problematic, but it can also be something that's for good.'

Phillippa Diedrichs, professor of health psychology, 2017

• • • • • •

Phillippa Diedrichs's research focuses on the connections between body image and mental health. Her particular interests are in how mass media and advertising affects body image, and how schools can intervene to promote positive health image.

Diedrichs leads a team of researchers at the Centre for Appearance Research (CAR) at the University of the West of England who have carried out research into the use of social media. Alongside the negative effects, there are powerfully positive impacts for women countering negativity surrounding body image, showing that there are multiple and diverse ways of interacting with social media.

The ways in which we use social media are complex, but even those of us who have been online since our youth don't always use these tools wisely.

Do we have a nuanced understanding of our own use of social media? Are we self-aware when it comes to our behaviour? Do we use it constructively or to criticise?

Do we stop and think before we post?

29 MAY

BEING PRESENT

'People can tell when you're not paying attention . . . You focus on those kids and you really listen and, boy, do they open up. That's the trick to teenagers. You don't have to see them all day, just be present when they're there . . . If you can hold your ground and be really present, they'll open their hearts.'

Ruby Wax, actor, comedian, author, presenter and mental health campaigner, 2017

. . . . . .

A classically trained actress (she was with the Royal Shakespeare Company for five years), Ruby Wax (b. 1953) became known throughout the 1990s for her comic interviews. Across her various series, she interviewed figures as diverse as Imelda Marcos, Hugh Hefner, Pamela Anderson – and Donald Trump, who threw her off his plane. (Wax laughed at his ambition to enter the White House.)

She became particularly friendly with one of her interviewees, Carrie Fisher: both women were open about their struggles with mental health (Wax has been diagnosed with bipolar disorder and depression), and Wax went on to study for a diploma in psychotherapy and counselling. She is the mother of three children.

A skilful interviewer is always present and engaged with what their interviewee is saying. Where some of Wax's subjects have clearly found this disconcerting, it's a talent that serves well in parenting. Listening, being there, paying attention.

30 MAY

ROAST OR QUICHE

'You can't just be in your own little bubble, cos it's a wide world. When you live in your house every Sunday you have a roast and you think, "Ah, that's how everybody lives every Sunday, they have a roast." And then you meet a friend and you go to their house and on that Sunday they're having a quiche.'

Joan Armatrading, singer-songwriter, 2022

· · · · · ·

Joan Armatrading (b. 1950) was born in Basseterre, the capital of St. Kitts, and came to Britain when she was seven years old. She began performing in her mid-teens – first cover songs and then her own compositions – and has been recording and performing ever since.

Armatrading released her debut album, *Whatever's For Us*, in 1972, after which she was a regular on John Peel's influential sessions show. Her breakthrough came with her third and fourth albums, *Joan Armatrading* (1976) and *Show Some Emotion* (1977), and she became the first Black British female singer-songwriter to enjoy international success.

Her songs are about love and affection and how people connect; her lyrics derive from watching the world around her, observing not only what people do, but what they do differently.

31 MAY

ORDER! ORDER!

'The job of the Speaker lies somewhere between being a bungee jumper and a trainspotter. Sometimes it's very dull and you think about what you are doing at the weekend or the weekend shopping list, and you take your eye off the ball for a moment. That's when all sorts of things break loose. Then of course there's the bungee jumping – you never know if you are going to jump into difficulties or not, so every word has to be guarded.'

Betty Boothroyd, parliamentarian and
Speaker of the House of Commons, 1987

• • • • • •

From 1992 to 2000, Betty Boothroyd, Baroness Boothroyd of Sandwell (1929–2023) reigned supreme as Speaker of the House of Commons. The Speaker's role is to preside over debates in the lower house, deciding who will speak and which amendments will be brought forward for consideration, and to maintain order during debates.

To date, Boothroyd is the only woman to have held the post, over a chamber which is not always renowned for its decorum. Boothroyd disliked the 'ya-hoo' behaviour often exhibited in the Commons, and was at pains to suppress it as much as possible. It was, she said, a frequent topic of letters she was sent and complaints made to her in person by members of the house.

Prior to entering politics, Boothroyd was a dancer and, famously, a member of the Tiller Girls – a dancing troupe renowned for their high kicks. Universally respected, she entered the House of Lords in 2001, serving as a crossbench peer, and died in 2023 at the age of 93.

JUNE

1 JUNE

INTERNATIONAL CHILDREN'S DAY

'I remember vividly what it was like to be ten. Ask me
what I was doing, what I was feeling last year, and my
mind goes blank. I remember being ten, and I remember
the feelings, and although today's ten-year-olds
experience different things, inside I think we're all the
same: "Have I got a best friend?", "I'm getting scared
because my mum and dad are having a quarrel." You fuss
about the way you look, you get absorbed in whichever
book you're reading. I know what it's like to be ten.'

Jacqueline Wilson, writer, 2015

• • • • • •

1 June is International Children's Day. The date was first designated
in 1925 during the World Conference on Child Welfare in Geneva,
and is predominantly recognised in post-Communist countries. World
Children's Day falls on 20 November, to celebrate the UN General
Assembly's Declaration of the Rights of the Child, 20 November 1959.

The author of over a hundred books, Dame Jacqueline Wilson (b.
1945) is one of the UK's best-known and best-selling children's writers.
Her breakthrough book, *The Story of Tracy Beaker* (1991), narrated by
a lonely and frustrated ten-year-old living in care, exemplifies Wilson's
genius for entering the mind of children. Her books, with a kind but
realistic touch, cover issues such as adoption, divorce and unhappiness.

Between 2005 and 2007, Wilson held the post of Children's Laureate, campaigning to encourage children and parents to read out loud
together. Do we remember what it was like to be a child? Do we see
differences in the children around us that we know, or do we in fact
have much in common?

2 JUNE

YOU'LL NEVER WORK AGAIN

'[W]hen the press made a big deal of me coming
out and my children ... I was told categorically
by everybody that I would never work
again ... Especially at the BBC.'

Sandi Toksvig, broadcaster, comedian, writer and presenter, 2009

• • • • • •

National treasure Sandi Toksvig began her career presenting children's programmes. She is now one of the most recognisable faces on television, co-presenting *The Great British Bake Off* (2010–) from 2017 to 2020, hosting the panel quiz show *QI* since 2016 and being a regular radio broadcaster.

In 1994, Toksvig came out publicly as gay, and the mother of three children with her partner. She was, to her recollection, at the time the only gay woman in British public life. After coming out, she and her young family received death threats, and had to go into hiding for several weeks.

Toksvig draws our attention to the history of gay people at the BBC. Hilda Matheson (1888–1940) was the first Director of Talks for BBC Radio, playing a pivotal role in the establishment of the nascent organisation's news section. She was also Vita Sackville-West's lover.

Pride Month, celebrated throughout June, reminds us not only of the long history of LGBTQI+ people in British public and intellectual life, but how hidden this history has been, how recently we have moved to public acceptance, and how much it took to get here.

3 JUNE

THERE ARE PEOPLE OUT THERE

'I was able to find a community of people that assured me that I'm okay. And that my existence is okay ... Find a community ... There are other people out there that are waiting for you with open arms.'

Tanya Compas, youth worker and LGBTQ+ rights activist, 2017

• • • • • •

Tanya Compas (b. 1991) is a London-based youth worker and LGBTQ+ rights activist who works with young Black queer people, particularly those made homeless as a result of coming out.

Adolescence can be lonely enough, and it's often a time when young people are hiding their differences in order to fit in. Sometimes, families are not able to give the support and acknowledgement that people need; sometimes they are not willing, and outright reject the person that an adolescent is becoming.

Compas points to the importance of finding community beyond the family elsewhere; people with whom we can identify, who are able to tell us that it's fine for us to be exactly who we are.

The opening line to Tolstoy's *Anna Karenina* famously states that 'All happy families resemble one another; every unhappy family is unhappy in its own way.' And while our idea of what happiness is might not have changed much, our understanding of what we call family has broadened.

Who might we choose to be our family?

4 JUNE

I KNOW EXACTLY HOW I'M SEEN

'I know exactly how I'm seen and how the community is seen . . . Stereotypes are stronger today than they ever have been. Even as a child there were all the sort of issues of dirty Irish, no Blacks, no dogs. It has got worse because the country has become more racist and more unkind. We've become so vilified it's perfectly acceptable to make racist comments.'

Candy Sheridan, campaigner, 2013

• • • • • •

The Gypsy, Roma and Traveller communities are one of Britain's most overlooked and misunderstood communities.

In the 2021 census, just over 71,000 people identified as Gypsy or Irish Traveller, which accounts for 0.12 per cent of the population of England and Wales. Of these, 21.6 per cent reported living in mobile or temporary structures (compared to the 0.3 per cent average for England and Wales). Those who identified as Gypsy or Irish Traveller reported higher instances of bad health than average.

Candy Sheridan, a member of the Irish Traveller community, who served as vice-chair of the Gypsy Council during the Dale Farm evictions, speaks eloquently of the stereotypes and racism faced by members of these communities, and how this situation has worsened in recent years.

A common refrain made in a 2022 report conducted by the Office for National Statistics on Gypsies' and Travellers' lived experiences was that their traditional nomadic lifestyle was a 'dying way of life'.

What do we owe the various communities that live in this country? How impossible is life made for people to lead their lives without constraint or interference?

5 JUNE

WORK

'I hate working. I realised by the time I was in my middle twenties and I kept switching these bad jobs I had, I finally realised, "Fran, you don't like to work. It's as simple as that. You, Fran, you would've made a fantastic heiress."'

Fran Lebowitz, writer and essayist, 2021

• • • • • •

Work for women means financial independence, autonomy, agency. It can also mean the exhaustion of coming home to face the 'second shift' of housework; the knowledge of structural inequalities that lead to disparities in pay; the struggle to break through those barriers that prevent women from reaching positions of power and seniority.

Imagine what we could do with limitless time and money . . .

Fran Lebowitz puts her finger on the truth. We have, all of us, missed our true vocation. We would all make fantastic heiresses.

6 JUNE

SECOND-CLASS CITIZENS

'There were quite a lot of women working at MI5 but they were regarded as second-class citizens ... Women were not regarded as suitable to do the sharp end of intelligence work, to go out on the streets and try to recruit and run the human sources of information. That was regarded as men's work.'

Stella Rimington, author and former Director General of MI5, 1999

• • • • • •

Stella Rimington was recruited to MI5 in 1969. At the time, she had recently given up her job as an archivist to follow her husband when he was posted to the British High Commission in New Delhi. Bored with no longer being at work, she received a 'tap on the shoulder' from the local MI5 representative, and agreed to come and 'help out' with some typing.

Rimington recalled that throughout the early part of her career at MI5, in the 1960s and 1970s, there were two distinct career paths for men and women. Women were unlikely ever to rise above being in supporting roles, and were not seen as suitable for the jobs at the 'sharp end'.

Rimington's description of working her way up through MI5 would surely be familiar to anyone who entered the workplace around the same time that she did. And, to some extent, these divisions of labour endure. Men and women often gravitate – or are directed – to different functions within organisations.

During her career in the Service, Rimington was Director of each of the operational branches: counter-subversion, counter-espionage and counter-terrorism. In 1992, she was appointed Director General of MI5, the first woman to hold the post, and was made a Dame Commander of the Order of the Bath (DCB) in 1996. Judi Dench's 'M' often bears a striking resemblance to her – a professional accolade that would surely delight any of us.

7 JUNE

THE RIGHT STUFF

'There's a very specific formula [to becoming an astronaut]! ... I used to go to space camp ... and there was a class you could take about how to become an astronaut, and they literally wrote these things on the board ... A lot of the skills that they're looking for were around teamwork and being comfortable in different environments and taking care of the people around you.'

Christina Koch, engineer and astronaut, 2023

• • • • • •

American astronaut Christina Koch became a NASA astronaut in 2013. She has been a flight engineer on three separate expeditions on the International Space Station, participated in the first all-female space walks, and holds the record for the longest single space flight for a woman (328 days).

In 2023, Koch was selected to be part of the crew of the Artemis II mission, which aims to fly around the Moon in 2025.

Speaking about her path to becoming an astronaut, Koch demystifies the process, explaining how NASA runs programmes for children and young adults, throwing light on exactly what they need to do to stand a chance of going into space. She downplays the popular image of the astronaut as heroic, instead emphasising the qualities that will allow you to live for days and weeks on end in a deeply claustrophobic and hostile environment.

Astronauts, it turns out, are not risk-takers and daredevils like *Star Trek*'s Captain Kirk (William Shatner went into space in 2021, aged 90). The qualities that help people survive are collaboration, trust and expertise, and caring about those who are around you. Step forward, Captain Picard.

8 JUNE

PHOTOGRAPH 51

'I would weep every night as her [Rosalind Franklin], for her. It's difficult for an actor emotionally to walk through those things, but that, for some reason, that role and [playing] Rosalind was so emotional for me.'

Nicole Kidman, actress and producer, 2017

• • • • • •

Rosalind Franklin (1920–58) was a chemist whose work provided critical steps in revealing the structure of DNA. The importance of Franklin's work was largely overlooked in her lifetime; in recent years, her profile has been significantly raised through concerted efforts to understand the contribution of women in science.

Francis Crick, James Watson and Maurice Wilkins shared the Nobel Prize in Physiology or Medicine for the discovery of the DNA double helix in 1962; the rules at the time did not allow the prize to be given posthumously, and as Franklin had passed away four years earlier, her contributions became obscured by her male counterparts.

In 2015, Nicole Kidman played Rosalind Franklin in *Photograph 51*, a stage play by Anna Ziegler based on Franklin's life, at the Noël Coward Theatre in London. 'Photograph 51' is the diffraction image taken by Franklin that provided the critical evidence that revealed the structure of DNA. Kidman's portrayal was very well-received; it was her first stage performance in nearly two decades.

In 1995, Newnham College, Cambridge, where Franklin studied, named its new graduate residence after her; a bust of Franklin stands in the garden.

9 JUNE

THOSE OGRES

'There came a time when I naturally wanted to marry and have children. "You cannot marry and have a career," they said. Those ogres. I thought, naively, "Men marry, work, and have children." Truly they said, "But you are not a man, you must choose." What ghastly tyranny, this choice between the work that one loves and the natural, normal life for a woman, which usually means a man, children and home. Well, I did marry, I've had my children . . . and I continued working at music, by day and by night if necessary. [For me] this combination of composing and running a home has become quite normal, and I hope it will for my daughters too.'

Elisabeth Lutyens, composer, 1949

· · · · · ·

Elisabeth Lutyens (1906–1983) decided at an early age that she was going to be a composer. The daughter of architect Sir Edwin Lutyens, she studied music in Paris, where she met Stravinsky, before returning to London to the Royal Academy of Music, where her spare and avant-garde style put her at odds with the prevailing taste for pastoralism. Throughout the 1960s, however, her music moved back into fashion, with numerous commissions and performances at the Proms.

The presence of women at the Proms has transformed in the past decade, but there is still some way to go. The annual repertoire report conducted by the Women's Philharmonic Advocacy group shows that the percentage of women composers has improved vastly – but there remains huge gendered imbalance in the average length of individual works, and, therefore, the actual airtime given to women's music.

Can you name your five favourite female composers?

10 JUNE

LIVING WITH DEMENTIA

'I really want to stress that every single person with dementia is on a different journey, so what happened to [my wife] doesn't necessarily happen to everyone ... As carers know, you behave as if the person you're caring for has died. You are grieving. You are in mourning ... You are behaving exactly as you would if the person you loved had died, and yet you go to see her in the afternoon and in a situation like that, as I learned, you need help.'

John Suchet, author, journalist and classical music presenter, 2010

• • • • • •

Dementia is an umbrella term for a range of conditions that affect brain cells, impacting people's ability to think, speak and remember. The national charity Dementia UK estimates that by 2025, more than 1 million people in the UK will be affected by dementia, and almost everyone in the country will know somebody with dementia.

In 2006, John Suchet's (b. 1944) second wife, Bonnie, was diagnosed with Alzheimer's disease. Suchet subsequently made many appearances on national broadcasting outlets to promote understanding and awareness of dementia, and in support of Admiral Nurses, specialist dementia nurses. In particular, he has spoken of the painful loss of the person he once knew, and the difficult decision to place Bonnie in a care home.

His book, *My Bonnie: How Dementia Stole the Love of My Life* (2011), is a record of their meeting, marriage and her illness. Bonnie died in 2015.

What do we know about this condition, which affects so many of us in some way? Are there ways that we can help those around us living with dementia?

11 JUNE

SPARE RIB

'[Our audience was] women all around the country. The Women's Liberation Movement at the time was very much ridiculed and misunderstood in the national press ... I'd worked on *OZ* magazine in Australia back in the early sixties. Reading it for the first time opened my eyes ... And I thought, well, a magazine just out there on the newsstands for any woman, no matter what small village or isolated place that she would live in ...'

Marsha Rowe, journalist, writer and editor, 2022

• • • • • •

Spare Rib, the monthly feminist magazine, was launched in June 1972. Intended as an 'alternative' to traditional women's magazines, *Spare Rib* – in its first issue alone – featured pieces on the suffragette movement, Chiswick Women's Aid (now the domestic violence charity Refuge), the novels of Georgette Heyer and Barbara Cartland, the BPAS service in Liverpool, and a short cultural history of breasts.

Spare Rib was co-founded by journalists Rosie Boycott (b. 1951) and Marsha Rowe (b. 1944). Australian-born Rowe had been part of the Sydney-based editorial team of *OZ*, the underground counter-culture magazine whose creators were prosecuted (and ultimately acquitted) for obscenity in both Australia and the United Kingdom.

From *OZ*, *Spare Rib* adopted an ethos of subversion, wit and taboo-busting – but its commitment to women's liberation and its presence on the newsstands made it one of the critical venues for second-wave feminism.

Spare Rib ceased publication in 1993, but looking back through its pages one can see the vitality – not to mention the urgency – of the women's movement at this time. We recall that feminism is not simply an intellectual exercise, but one grounded in the nitty-gritty of all women's lives.

12 JUNE

FAME

'I hated [being famous]! I went to [theatre school,
Juilliard] because I wanted to be a theatre actress.
It shocked me that somebody hired me for a
movie ... I had a great time making the
movies – don't get me wrong! It's just the fame
part of it that I don't get along with so well.'

Kelly McGillis, actress, 2010

• • • • • •

At the height of her fame, Kelly McGillis (b. 1957) was one of
Hollywood's most recognisable actresses, acting alongside some its
best-known stars, appearing opposite Tom Cruise in *Top Gun* (1986)
and Jodie Foster in *The Accused* (1988). Most heart-stoppingly, she and
Harrison Ford played star-crossed lovers in *Witness* (1985) – McGillis
the Amish widow Rachel Lapp; Ford the detective on the run, John
Book.

Increasingly disillusioned with Hollywood, McGillis took time out
in the 1990s, when she married and had two children. Intrusive press
coverage about her personal life, including vicious comments on her
weight gain, coupled with problems with alcohol, made for a deeply
unhappy period. She returned to the stage in the late 1980s, performing with the Shakespeare Theatre Company in Washington, DC.

When a sequel to *Top Gun* was announced (*Top Gun: Maverick*
[2022]), McGillis was not invited to reprise her role. But – now teaching acting, and an out lesbian – McGillis seems to have understood
early that acting is not the same as Hollywood, and stardom is not life.

13 JUNE

THEY HADN'T READ
THE BOOKS WE'D READ

'[I] worked with the paperback publishers of my
generation, the great ones. They were all men and
they hadn't read the books that I had read, that my
mother had read ... Every single friend I knew who got
pregnant had to get a second-hand copy of [Rosamond
Lehmann's *The Weather in the Streets*]. It was about
an abortion and that particular book went all round
my circle of friends who got themselves into tricky
situations before the abortion laws changed.'

Carmen Callil, publisher, writer and critic, 2022

• • • • • •

The rapid success of *Spare Rib* magazine led to the launch, in 1973, of
a new publishing imprint – Spare Rib Books – dedicated to publishing,
promoting and celebrating women's voices. We know it now as Virago
Books, founded by Dame Carmen Callil (1938–2022).

From the outset, Virago drew on two different types of books:
new work by feminist writers, and bringing back into print neglected
works by forgotten women writers. Their dark green spines – with
iconic bitten apple logo – have a distinctive presence on the bookshelf.

Callil's genius was in seeing that the books that women read by
no means overlapped with the books that her male colleagues were
publishing, and that a whole sphere of human experience was being
passed by word-of-mouth, or below the counter. Virago's list asserts the
literary quality of women's writing, and that the lives of women are not
ancillary or secondary, but can form the subject matter of literature.

14 JUNE

IT'S ALL RIGHT FOR THEM, BUT NOT FOR US

'Many men, when I was first in family planning, would hide their wives' caps or throw them in the fire. All sorts of horrors you can hardly believe civilised people would think of ... Men have very funny minds when it comes to that sort of thing. It's all right for them, but not for us.'

Helen Brook, family planning campaigner and organiser, 1989

• • • • • •

Helen Brook (1907–97) was a pioneer of family planning services, and the founder of the Brook Advisory Service. The first Brook clinic opened in 1964, controversially providing free contraception and sexual health advice to young unmarried women. The service expanded rapidly throughout major cities in Britain; now known as 'Brook', the organisation continues to provide advice on sexual health and wellbeing, with a focus on young people.

Helen Brook reminds us of the precarious position in which women found themselves throughout the 1950s and 1960s, and the double standards that existed when it came to men's and women's sexual activity.

Open conversation and good information – these are at the heart of assisting people to make the decisions that are best for them.

15 JUNE

BREAKING BARRIERS

'I don't want to be in a place surrounded by glass. I want to bring the edifice down. Because when . . . you're having to break the ceiling, it is a very lonely place to be. I want to see women in my lifetime surpass what I did. I want to remove the hurdles. I want that generation coming after me not even to see the hurdles I hit.'

Asma Khan, restaurateur and cookbook author, 2021

• • • • • •

Born in Calcutta in 1969, Asma Khan moved with her husband to the UK in 1991. Arriving in the middle of January, during a particularly freezing winter, Khan's homesickness — particularly for food — drove her to learn to cook. After earning a PhD in law, Khan began to organise supper clubs at home. Their reputation spread, and her restaurant, Darjeeling Express, opened in London in 2017.

Darjeeling Express is run by an all-women team, several of them grandmothers, and with an average age in their fifties. Part of the restaurant's profits goes to Khan's charity, the Second Daughters Foundation, which advocates for the rights of girls and women in South Asian culture, particularly those who are second daughters.

One of the UK's most prominent restaurateurs, Khan was the first British chef to be profiled on Netflix's *Chef's Table* (2015–24).

In a world where we are told that only competition and self-interest will bring success, Khan's ethos represents the very opposite. She epitomises the spirit of 'uplifting', using one's position and power to facilitate the advancement of those who come after.

16 JUNE

CUTE AND BLONDE

'I started competing in the small festivals that went through town. It kind of took off from there. A dumb Saskatchewan girl who was eleven singing, "I don't love him!" She whipped me and I was singing an original. She was cute and blonde though. I think I was wearing my volleyball outfit.'

k.d. lang, singer-songwriter, 2016

● ● ● ● ● ●

k.d. lang (b. 1961) is the winner of multiple industry and other awards, including eight Grammy Awards, eight Juno Awards, a BRIT, four awards from GLAAD, and the Order of Canada, Canada's highest civilian honour. She has performed with legendary artists such as Elton John, Tony Bennett, Loretta Lynn and Roy Orbison.

Born in Edmonton, Alberta, lang answered a classified ad in a local paper in 1983 looking for a singer, and was part of The Reclines until 1989. After going solo in the late 1980s, lang's public profile was raised when she recorded a duet with Roy Orbison of his song 'Crying', which won a Grammy for Best Country Collaboration with vocals.

In 1992, lang's album *Ingénue* broke her through into the mainstream; she came out publicly later that year, on 16 June 1992, in a cover interview for *The Advocate*, an American LGBTQ magazine.

Coming second place at a local music festival when she was a young girl doesn't seem to have held lang back. She teaches us to stick to your guns; success will come your way in time.

17 JUNE

RUNNING UP THAT HILL

'I thought that the track would get some attention but I never imagined that it would be anything like this . . . The whole world's gone mad! . . . Music is very special. It's different from all other art forms. All art forms have their own space but music has a way of touching people.'

Kate Bush, singer-songwriter, 2022

• • • • • •

On 17 June 2022, Kate Bush's song 'Running Up That Hill' (1985) reached No. 1 in the UK charts, propelled there after it was popularised by the TV series *Stranger Things* (2016–25) . A new generation had discovered Bush's music. Bush (b. 1958) was nearly 64 years old, and this was her second No. 1 hit. Forty-four years earlier, in 1978, 'Wuthering Heights' reached the top of the charts. Bush was 18 years old.

Bush's career trajectory has always followed a unique path. Success came very early, and continued throughout the 1980s and early 1990s. Her success was through her studio albums – after one gruelling tour, in 1979, Bush gave up live performance . . . until 2014, when she toured again, this time with her teenage son at her side.

Women's careers weave throughout the life course, sometimes following very different trajectories. Creativity is not the sole property of the young.

18 JUNE

KNEES KNOCKING

'The first time [my mother] saw me perform I was seven, singing, and she could see my knees knocking together, and you know that fear of performance has never really left me ... I've come to a point where I realised that I'm a lot more calm, but the focus is still very particular. I don't like to talk much to anybody before I perform because I'm still very keenly aware of what I'm doing.'

Annie Lennox, singer-songwriter and activist, 2010

• • • • • •

Annie Lennox (b. 1954) is the possessor of a singing voice of extraordinary range and power. Starting out in the short-lived but successful new wave band The Tourists, Lennox and her bandmate Dave Stewart went on to form Eurythmics.

Eurythmics broke through to global stardom in 1983 with the title track from their second album, *Sweet Dreams (Are Made of This)*, a perfectly formed piece of synth-pop that was accompanied by a legendary music video. Lennox was iconic in business suit and short, dyed orange hair. A string of hits followed throughout the 1980s and 1990s; in 2004, Lennox won an Academy Award for Best Song for 'Into the West' from *The Lord of the Rings: The Return of the King* (2003).

As well as touring with Eurythmics and as a solo artist, Lennox has performed live at many high-profile events, including the Nobel Prize ceremony, the Academy Awards and Live 8, and on behalf of the many charities and human rights groups that she supports.

Even the most experienced of us can find public performance nerve-wracking. How do we cope with the anxiety, and turn it into the energy we need while we're speaking or presenting or performing?

19 JUNE

A FABULOUS DEAL

'Being in the underground press was meant to be a
wonderful alternative life ... women still did the
typing, still made the coffee, with the added bonus of
being expected to be sexually available 24/7 ...
For the blokes it was a fabulous deal.'

Rosie Boycott, journalist and editor, 2022

• • • • • •

Rosie Boycott, Baroness Boycott of Whitefield (b. 1951) was one of
a cohort of women journalists – including Eve Pollard, Wendy Henry
and Janet Street-Porter – who broke through in the 1980s to become
editors of national newspapers.

Starting a career in journalism in the 1960s was to enter an almost
entirely male-dominated world, one of hard drinking and rampant
misogyny, and the countercultural movement was no exception. Ostensi-
bly part of a liberation movement, whose members espoused alternative
ways of living, the reality for the women involved a different kind of trap,
in which the domestic tasks were delegated to them – and their sexual
availability was assumed. One of the driving forces behind *Spare Rib* was
to create a magazine owned and operated entirely by women.

But how far has the contemporary workplace really come? Rose
Hackman, in her book *Emotional Labor* (2023), examines the invisible
work done in the workplace – from remembering birthdays to giving
service with a smile and making small talk – work that provides the
social 'glue' that keeps people together. It's work that falls predominantly on women.

Liberation that offers freedom only to a few is no real freedom
at all.

20 JUNE

NO LACK OF TALENT OR AMBITION

'It was difficult for women [to enter professions in the 1970s] and it was difficult for Black women to enter any profession. If you look at journalism, any profession you like, and then you ask a very similar question, how many of us are there. And, regrettably, the number is still quite few. It's not because Black women lack talent and lack ambition. Sometimes, it's the opportunities that aren't easily obtainable.'

Patricia Scotland, diplomat, barrister and politician, 2004

• • • • • •

Patricia Scotland, Baroness Scotland of Asthal (b. 1955) was the first Black woman to be made a Queen's Counsel, in 1991. Scotland is also the first woman to hold the post of Attorney General since its foundation in 1315.

Born in Dominica, Scotland's family emigrated to London when she was two years old. Called to the Bar in 1977, she specialised in family law. In 1997, she received a life peerage and entered the House of Lords as a working peer, and served in variety of ministerial roles. Since 2016, she has been the sixth Secretary-General of the Commonwealth of Nations – again, the first woman to hold the post.

By 2022, only five more Black women had been appointed to QC.

21 JUNE

SOUNDS AND SWEET AIRS
THAT GIVE DELIGHT

'It's the best thing I'm involved in . . . I love my job, I'm
very, very lucky, but nothing comes close to what I get
from working with people that are doing things to help
other people. And that might sound a little "do-gooder",
but if anybody volunteers, or has to help somebody,
you do get something back from that.'

Vicky McClure, actress, model and presenter, 2024

• • • • • •

Vicky McClure (b. 1983) is best known for her performances as DI
Kate Fleming in the crime series *Line of Duty* (2012–21).

In 2018, McClure participated in a BBC documentary, *Our Dementia Choir*, which took her back to her home town of Nottingham, where
she helped form a choir made up of people living with dementia.
McClure's grandmother, who died in 2015, had lived with dementia,
and McClure had observed at first hand not only the calming effects of
music on her grandmother, but the occasional glimpses of her old self
that it facilitated. Members of the choir have continued to meet.

Music therapy has demonstrable effects not only on people
living with dementia, but in rehabilitation after neuro-injuries such
as strokes, and for those with mental health issues. And, as McClure
points out, the benefits go both ways. Her volunteering gave back to
her at least as much as she put in.

22 JUNE

WINDRUSH DAY

*'I wanted to go back, but when I think about my
family – my 7 children, my 25 grandchildren, and my 19
great-grands and twins on the way – I just couldn't face
going back and leaving my family here.'*

Roma Taylor, founder and chair of Windrush Cymru Elders, 2023

• • • • • •

Roma Taylor (b. 1943) came to Britain from Antigua in 1959, aged
15. She went out to Cardiff, settling in Tiger Bay, where she trained
as a nurse and got married. Aged 26, she joined the Territorial Army,
serving for 25 years. Windrush Day has been celebrated on 22 June
since 2018. It honours the contribution of the post-war generation
of migrants to the UK, particularly the Afro-Caribbeans who began
arriving on HMT *Empire Windrush* from 1948.

After the Second World War, the British government, facing labour
shortages, encouraged mass immigration. The British Nationality Act
(1948) gave citizenship of the UK to all people living in the colonies,
as well as the right of entry to and settlement in the UK. This was
an attractive proposition for many West Indians, who commonly per-
ceived the UK as the mother country.

The *Empire Windrush* arrived at the Port of Tilbury on 22 June
1948, with 802 migrants from the West Indies. It is estimated that
about half a million people migrated to Britain from the Caribbean
between 1948 and 1971, when restrictions were put upon entry and
citizenship.

The National Windrush Monument, a bronze sculpture by Basil
Watson, was unveiled in Waterloo station in June 2022.

23 JUNE

HOSTILE ENVIRONMENT

'I thought we would be welcomed with open arms, and it
was the beginning of a good future. The reality was very
different ... My nightmare started when I went out on
the wards after six months in the classroom ... I suffered
a lot of racism. That was quite new to me because
we had so many different types of people, all different
colours and races and religions in Trinidad, and I never
experienced any such behaviour. But there was even
physical abuse. My hands were slapped away countless
times ... After six months, I said, "Oh,
Mum, I can't stand these people here, they're
so rude and they're so ignorant."'

Allyson Williams, midwife, 2023

. . . . . .

Allyson Williams arrived in London in May 1969 from Trinidad to train
as a nurse. In London, she met her husband, Vernon, who was one of
the founding members of the Notting Hill Carnival.

In the 1980s, Vernon and Allyson founded the Genesis Mas Band. Mas
Bands are one of the key arts of the Carnival. In 'mas' (short for masquer-
ade), participants dress in costumes and masks to dance along the parade
route, telling stories through costume. Mas originated in the Caribbean
in the 1800s, after the emancipation of slaves, and continues to evolve – a
fusion of African, European and, increasingly, Brazilian samba traditions.

Williams, recollecting her early days in Britain, writes of house
parties in Brixton, Croydon, Wood Green and Tottenham; dancing at
the Hammersmith Palais; concerts at Ronnie Scott's. And she recalls,
also, the racism she faced, on this small damp island.

The Windrush scandal, which began in 2018, concerned people
who had been wrongfully detained, threatened with deportation and,

in some cases, deported from the UK, and particularly affected members of the Windrush generation. The scandal led to the resignation of the then Home Secretary, Amber Rudd.

24 JUNE

DIVERSITY NIRVANA

'People like myself stand on the shoulders of giants.
My mum came here because her aunt came around
1962, so a crucial part of that post-war reconstruction
era for the United Kingdom. She worked on the buses.
She was a bus conductress, doing the Route 12 when
they still had the change bucket. Her husband
Keith worked as a driver in the NHS.'

Amina Taylor, journalist and broadcaster, 2023

• • • • • •

The 2024 summer riots, which lasted for six days across various towns and cities in the UK, fuelled by false claims from the far right about asylum seekers, involved indiscriminate racial attacks and riots throughout the country.

These were only the latest in a long and ugly history of racially motivated riots in the UK. From the Notting Hill riots of 1958, to the summer of 2024, there is a subset of British society unable to accept the reality of the country's multicultural history.

In her speech at the unveiling of the Windrush Monument, Baroness Floella Benjamin (b. 1949) spoke of the possibility for what she calls 'diversity nirvana': a vision of Britain that not only accepts the multicultural nature of British society, but celebrates it.

25 JUNE

DEGREE BY DEGREE

'I did an interview with somebody and the lady said, "I tried to get a degree ... three times and I didn't get it." And she said, "What's the secret?" And I said, "The secret is to start it and then finish it."'

Joan Armatrading, singer-songwriter, 2022

· · · · · ·

Joan Armatrading left school at 15. In 2001, after years of study, she earned a BA degree in history from the Open University – and did so all the while she was touring (she took the final exam the day after the last date of her 2000 tour).

Armatrading has received honorary degrees from Aston University, the Royal Scottish Academy of Music and Drama and the University of the West Indies, and she is an honorary fellow of Newnham College, Cambridge.

Asked about how she went about achieving her degree, Armatrading is refreshingly matter-of-fact about her process. She started it; she finished it – but she has called it one of her biggest achievements so far. And this alongside a recording career that has stretched over 50 years and more than 20 albums.

26 JUNE

ON COMING OUT

'It's a difficult thing and it's always an intensely individual and personal choice. And I don't think there's a right or wrong, or should or a must ... And unfortunately it's very difficult to test the waters. Once you [come out you] cannot really very easily take it back.'

Tim Franks, LGBT+ campaigner, 2008

• • • • • •

We would like to think that we are becoming a tolerant society. Figures from the Office for National Statistics published in 2023 indicate that the number of police-recorded sexual orientation hate crimes fell by 6 per cent over the previous year. However, transgender hate crimes rose by 11 per cent over the same timescale. The figures might be much higher, still: a Stonewall survey from 2017 suggests that up to 80 per cent of LGBT hate crimes are not reported to the police, and that one in five LGBT people had experienced a hate crime in the year before the survey.

The decision to come out to one's family can be fraught, and some people may decide never to come out to elderly relatives. Even in cases where the family is supportive, family members might not fully understand what coming out entails, or what kinds of support might be welcome.

Curiosity, interest, asking questions about the experience and what it means – these all go a long way. But, before everything else, a background of tolerance and acceptance is required, within the family and beyond.

27 JUNE

SETTING THE RECORD STRAIGHT

'It's a terrible thing – for women who are hearing this –
to be the object of someone's obsession that you're
not interested in in that manner. And it became very
obsessive ... I got to the point where ... I just said I have
to get out of this. It was a tragic thing because, you
know, [Hitchcock] had given me a wonderful education
in film-making, and I thought what a cruel thing to
do ... to hand me this and work with me and then to lay
this on me. What a cruel thing to do.'

Tippi Hedren, actor, 2012

• • • • • •

Tippi Hedren (b. 1930) was working as a fashion model, featuring on
the cover of magazines such as *Life*, when she came to the attention of
Alfred Hitchcock. She appeared in two back-to-back films directed by
him, *The Birds* (1963) and *Marnie* (1964). That, however, marked the
end of their partnership.

In her memoir, *Tippi: A Memoir* (2016), Hedren recounted how
during the filming of *Marnie*, Hitchcock became increasingly obsessive
towards her, culminating in a sexual assault. Under contract to Hitchcock for two more films, Hedren was unable to work for two years
after *Marnie*, until her contract ran out.

Hedren continued to act well into her eighties. If Hitchcock's
intention was to ruin her career, he failed.

28 JUNE

SHE GROUNDS ME

'[My partner] has her own professional world and I
have my own professional world; they're very different
worlds because she's an academic and I'm very caught
up in my world ... but I long for her presence all
the time ... I love and respect her and she
keeps me steady. She grounds me.'

Miriam Margolyes, actor, 2017

• • • • • •

Miriam Margolyes (b. 1941) and her partner, Heather Sutherland, have been together for over 55 years. Sutherland is a retired academic, specialising in the history of Indonesia. They have split their time between the UK, the Netherlands and Australia, mostly living in separate houses – with lockdown, Margolyes has said, being exactly as difficult as might be imagined.

The practicalities of couples living together don't change, but the ability to be open about relationships has altered immeasurably in those decades.

29 JUNE

ICONS

'Jane Cholmeley was a total hero. She was
as much a social worker as a bookseller.'

Sandi Toksvig, broadcaster, comedian, writer and presenter, 2009

· · · · · ·

The Gay Icons exhibition at the National Portrait Gallery, which ran
from 2 July to 18 October 2009, was an exploration of gay social and
cultural history through 60 photographic portraits. Each selected
icon – who may or may not have been gay themselves – was significant
in some way to the life of the person who selected them.

Icons included Benjamin Brittain and Pyotr Tchaikovsky; k.d. lang
and Will Young; Martina Navratilova and Ian Roberts; Patricia High-
smith and Ellen DeGeneres.

Sandi Toksvig, who chaired the selection committee, draws our
attention to one of the quieter icons in the selection, the bookseller
Jane Cholmeley, who, with Sue Butterworth, co-founded and ran the
feminist Silver Moon Bookshop.

Established in 1984, the bookshop was a fixture on Charing Cross
Road in London until its closure in 2001, providing not only a venue
for literary events, but a safe space where people could receive advice
and information on, for example, sexual abuse, or get the number of
the nearest women's refuge.

Toksvig's choice reminds us of those people whose life's work
is building community, and that icons may be quiet and unsung. As
George Eliot wrote in *Middlemarch*, 'the growing good of the world is
partly dependent on unhistoric acts; and that things are not so ill with
you and me as they might have been, is half owing to the number who
lived faithfully a hidden life.'

30 JUNE

A RESPONSIBILITY

'I took on [the role of spokesperson for the LGBT community] and it got a little tiring at some point. I want the focus to be on my music but at the same time I realised that I had a responsibility . . . I have tried to answer the questions as openly and as directly as possible . . . It's wonderful, the evolution of the LGBT culture. It's very inspiring.'

k.d. lang, singer-songwriter, 2016

. . . . . .

In March 1992, k.d. lang released her second solo album, *Ingénue*. The album was her breakthrough, multi-platinum-selling, and nominated for six Grammies. The single 'Constant Craving' won lang the Grammy for Best Female Pop Vocal Performance.

Three months later, lang came out as gay, in an interview with *The Advocate*, making her the entertainment industry's – and possibly the world's – most prominent lesbian.

American singer-songwriter Melissa Etheridge came out shortly afterwards, in 1993. In 1997, Ellen DeGeneres, then at the height of fame with her sitcom *Ellen* (1994–98) , appeared on the cover of *Time* magazine, under the headline, 'Yes, I'm gay.'

Speaking about her role as a spokesperson for the LGBT community, lang expresses the frustration that often the focus was more on her sexuality than on her music. However, more than 30 years since she came out, it's remarkable to see how far society has come, and how much is owed to this generation of visible gay people.

JULY

1 JULY

BETTER OFF

'On an everyday basis, disabled people are dealing with a lower expectation, and people are actually saying to their faces, "Gosh, surely it's better to be dead than be you." That happens. It's shocking.'

Liz Carr, actress, broadcaster and disability rights activist, 2024

· · · · · ·

Disability Pride Month, most commonly celebrated in July, originated in the United States in the 1990s. It has become a worldwide celebration of people with disabilities and their contribution to society, as well as an opportunity to raise awareness of the stigmas and structural obstacles faced by many people with disabilities.

The event arose from the disability rights movement, which asks us to reconsider our ideas of disability, moving away from outdated ideas of disability as a deviation from theoretical norms, to focus instead on a 'social model'. This aims to identify and remove the social barriers that make it difficult or impossible for people with disabilities to function.

Olivier Award-winning actress Liz Carr (b. 1972) is best known for playing the part of forensic expert Clarissa Mullery in the crime drama series *Silent Witness*. Carr is also an advocate and activist for disability rights, and has, in recent years, spoken out against assisted suicide and the devaluation of certain groups within society, including those with disabilities.

What assumptions do we make, about the capacities of others? What unnecessary barriers are placed in the way of people who simply want to go about their daily lives? What do we take for granted, in terms of ease of access, in living in a world that does not constrain or limit us?

2 JULY

THE PRAM IN THE HALL

'Real life does have to come first because writing isn't life. If [the children] don't come first, I really don't think you would have much to say. It does seem to me that is one of the advantages women have over men when they're writing. Men have wives who look after everything and I think this is a great pity.'

Fay Weldon, writer, 1974

• • • • • •

Fay Weldon (1931–2023) combined a 55-year writing career with raising four sons (the first as a single mother in the 1950s). The author of more than 30 novels, she was also an award-winning writer for television, including the first episode of *Upstairs, Downstairs* (1971) and an adaptation of *Pride and Prejudice* (1980).

Robustly feminist, Weldon's most famous novel, *The Life and Loves of a She-Devil* (1983), concerns the gloriously baroque revenge taken by a plain and unloved wife on discovering her husband's affair with a younger and more attractive woman. Memorably dramatised for television in 1986, it also became a film starring Roseanne Barr and Meryl Streep in 1989.

The author Cyril Connolly (1903–74) once wrote that the 'pram in the hall' was the enemy of good art: that domestic responsibilities are incompatible with creative work. Weldon's life and career demonstrate the opposite.

Caregiving responsibilities and domestic life do not have to be the antithesis of meaningful creative work. Rather, as Weldon suggests, the living of life is the truest source of art, giving us something meaningful to say about the world.

3 JULY

I CAN DO WHAT I WANT

'It's such an exhilarating feeling. You're in control. I can do what I want to do. And it's brought out the best in me. My confidence, of being able to negotiate airports and public transport by my own self, has not just helped me with confidence travelling, but outside of life as well, meeting new people. It's made me see the world and see so many cultures.'

Ellie Simmonds, Paralympian and swimmer, 2017

• • • • • •

Ellie Simmonds (b. 1994) was 13 years old when she represented Great Britain at the Beijing Paralympics in 2008. She won two gold medals there, in 100m and 400m freestyle events, and followed this with further gold medals in London, 2012, and Rio de Janeiro, 2018.

Since retiring from swimming in 2021, Simmonds has combined a career in television, with ambassadorial roles for organisations such as the Prince's Trust and the Scouts Association.

Alistair Duggin, head of accessibility at GDS, writes that at the heart of the idea of accessibility is the principle that 'people can do what they need to do in a similar amount of time and effort as someone that does not have a disability'.

Too often we think of accessibility in simplistic terms, such as adding wheelchair ramps, but a proper approach to accessibility puts the range of human experience and ability at the heart of design. We have a vast range of abilities; we may experience temporary disability through illness and injury, and, after the age of 65, more than half of us experience a form of disability.

Simmonds expresses the sheer joy of the liberty and confidence that comes from travelling alone, at your own pace – embarking on a voyage of one's own.

4 JULY

LET'S TALK ABOUT SEX

'They have no sense of humour. Life is too short for those people, those flat-footed, boring, dreary, ancient, dry-as-dust people who think that men are allowed to write about sex but women aren't. That men are allowed to have sex, but women . . . [gasps!]'

Erica Jong, writer, 2014

• • • • • •

Erica Jong's first novel, *Fear of Flying* (1973), was one of the most controversial and groundbreaking novels of the second wave, a no-holds-barred account of the life of Isadora Wing, and her sexual experiences. The book was a bestseller and hugely influential – you might say that Isadora Wing walked so that *Sex and the City* (1998–2004) and *Girls* (2012–17) could fly.

The frank descriptions of sex – and the lead character's opinions on the subject – led to criticisms that the book was pornographic. Responding to these criticisms, Jong rightly points out the double standards at work.

The backlash against the second wave formed the subject of Jong's introduction for the fortieth-anniversary edition of the novel in 2013. Since then, the United States Supreme Court has significantly rolled back reproductive rights, in a ruling most commonly known as the 'Dobbs decision' (2022), which overturned the constitutional right to an abortion established in Roe vs. Wade (1973) and Planned Parenthood vs. Casey (1992).

We've come a long way – but we can still fall back.

5 JULY

I COULD DO ANYTHING

'It has been written that I had the best women's serve in tennis history, and I believed it! ... Once I got experienced and felt comfortable on the tennis court and knew exactly what I was doing – that was the key. I'll brag about myself on that! I had all the equipment with that tennis ball and that racket. I could do anything with that ball during those years.'

Althea Gibson, tennis champion and golfer, 1989

• • • • • •

In 1956, Althea Gibson (1927–2003) became the first African American tennis player to win a Grand Slam title (the French Championships). She followed this with her first Wimbledon single's title, in 1957, defending the title the following year.

Although Gibson was not technically banned from playing tennis in the United States on the grounds of race, ranking events frequently took on all-white courts, effectively disbarring her from the necessary competitive play. When she won Wimbledon, she received the Venus Rosewater dish from Queen Elizabeth II. The queen shook Gibson's hand – an incredibly powerful image during segregation.

Gibson titled her autobiography *I Always Wanted to Be Somebody* (1958). Her belief in herself was absolute – and absolutely justified.

6 JULY

YOUR INTERPRETATION IS VALID

'The songs always said to me: "We need to make relationships and friends with people all over the world, and however people envision us," the songs would say to me, "it's valid." Their interpretation is valid.'

Tori Amos, singer-songwriter, 2012

· · · · · ·

Tori Amos's (b. 1963) songs and lyrics have provided a soundtrack for many young women, identifying with her personal and confessional stories ranging from heartbreak in relationships, pregnancy fears and her experience of rape.

Too often, the story of popular music seems to be a mostly male affair. But the women have always been there, writing their songs, singing their stories, pioneering sounds – and kicking down doors.

In their edited book *This Woman's Work: Essays on Music* (2022), Sinéad Gleeson and Kim Gordon collect a series of essays on artists and styles from the well known, such as Lucinda Williams and Laurie Anderson, through excursions into drill and Communist propaganda songs, as well as bringing attention to musicians at risk of being forgotten, such as Wendy Carlos and Lhasa de Sela. The range is extraordinary – not that that should come as any surprise.

Who are the women whose songs you have made your own? That have provided the soundtrack to your life?

7 JULY

A STRONG WILL

'I am a frightened person, I am fearful of many things, but I have a strong will, and I had a will to write from the moment almost that I was born.'

Edna O'Brien, novelist, short story writer, playwright, poet and critic, 2019

• • • • • •

Edna O'Brien's first novel, *The Country Girls* (1960), so shocked Ireland that it was added to the list of banned books compiled by the Irish censorship board, and was the subject of several book burnings, including in O'Brien's home town in County Clare.

To speak openly and frankly as a woman has been fraught with peril in many times and many places, and continues to be the case.

Are there occasions when we wish that we had spoken our mind, but felt afraid of what the consequences might be? How do we summon the courage to speak up? What might the impact be if we did?

8 JULY

YOU HAVE NO IDEA

'I became a wheelchair user when I was seven. Loads of people around my parents told them about all the things I would never do in my life ... You have no idea what a seven-year-old is going to achieve.'

Tanni Grey-Thompson, wheelchair racer and television presenter, 2013

• • • • • •

Tanni Grey-Thompson is one of Britain's most successful Paralympians, and a crossbench peer in the House of Lords. She has spina bifida and is a wheelchair user.

There are many times in life when we find people who insist on defining us, who are eager to tell us what we can't do, or quick to tell us what we're not allowed to do. Grey-Thompson reminds us that it is better to focus on discovering what we are good at, what we enjoy, and working hard to be the best that we can be.

Constructive criticism can be helpful. But when the opinions and definitions of others constrain rather than encourage, we are within our rights to be wary, and within our rights not to listen if their advice does not ring true. Sometimes we will astonish others with what we're capable of doing.

9 JULY

ONE VOICE

'Change hasn't happened yet, has it? ... When you see
so many beautiful women, one after the other, all being
treated like pieces of meat, it's so un-discriminatory
... When I was younger, I thought maybe I was being
singled out because I was attractive ... You almost felt
flattered at the same time as horribly harassed.
Now we realise – this is just a common experience, and
every woman is walking through it. And the women
are sensing the change – but I don't think the men
have really woken up to the reality yet.'

Sarah Baxter, journalist, 2017

• • • • • •

Sarah Baxter (b. 1959) began her professional career in publishing as a
copywriter for Penguin Books, and a press officer at Virago. She moved
into the editorial side when she joined *Time Out*, and progressed rapidly throughout the 1990s and 2000s, becoming deputy editor of the
Sunday Times in 2013. She held that position until 2021.

Print journalism has long had a reputation for machismo; the
expectation was that women would play the game and take the joke.
Baxter, talking about the #MeToo movement, speaks frankly about her
naivety at the start of her career, believing that expressions of sexual
interest were in part because of her attractiveness.

She describes her realisation that this was a form of false consciousness: a misunderstanding of women's real position within her
industry – and within wider society – and her recognition of the reality of the harassment and abuse rife within our institutions.

Change can only start when we begin to understand the true
nature of oppression; when we swap our false consciousness for raised
consciousness.

10 JULY

I'VE BEEN TO LONDON TO VISIT THE KING

'The day [when McClure received an MBE] was surreal! Everywhere you looked, you were flabbergasted at being in a castle, and at Windsor. When we got there, my mum said to somebody, "Do you know who it is? Who's giving them out?" And they went, "It's the King." And she went, "Yes!"'

Vicky McClure, actress, model and presenter, 2024

• • • • • •

Vicky McClure grew up in a working-class household. Her career in acting was almost stalled at the start – aged 11, she auditioned for the Central Junior Television Workshop (now the Television Workshop), a scheme launched by Central Television to act as a casting pool for young talent. Unsuccessful at first, she gained a place when another child dropped out.

Supporting herself at the start of her career with office jobs and stints at H. Samuel and Dorothy Perkins, McClure's breakthrough part came when she was cast in *This Is England* (2006), a raw drama focused on skinhead subculture in the early 1980s. A series of television dramas followed, extending the narrative throughout the 1980s and early 1990s, and earning McClure a BAFTA in 2019. McClure is now best known for playing Detective Inspector Kate Fleming in the crime series *Line of Duty* (2012–21).

It's a long way from Dorothy Perkins to Windsor Castle – and it's delightful to know how much McClure's mum enjoyed her day.

11 JULY

ONE VOICE

'For the first time we were all together. It changed
our world for all time. And we had one voice.
We never said we were better [than the men].
We said we were as entertaining.'

Billie Jean King, tennis champion and activist, 2013

· · · · · ·

When tennis moved into its 'Open Era' in 1968, allowing professional players to compete against amateurs, the question of disparity in prize money between men's and women's tournaments became a burning issue. By 1970, the disparity was 12:1 in favour of the men.

In 1970, a group of nine women tennis players broke away to set up an all-woman tournament, the 'Virginia Slims' Invitation, in protest against unequal pay. In 1973, the Women's Tennis Association (WTA) was founded by Billie Jean King.

The US Open offered equal pay in 1973, but the other Grand Slam events were much slower to fall into line, with Wimbledon only agreeing to equal pay in 2007.

The story of equal pay in tennis is a triumph of women's self-organisation and solidarity – and canniness in keeping the message clear. The women's players did not dispute men's comparative strength. Their point was that tennis was – in the Open Era – as much about the theatre as about the sport.

12 JULY

ON BEING CHEATED

'The question I'm fundamentally asking is why isn't [Gibson] remembered and who writes history, who decides who's remembered and who decides who is erased.'

Kemi-Bo Jacobs, actor and writer, 2022

• • • • • •

Althea Gibson was the first African American woman to appear on the cover of *Time* magazine, on 26 August 1957. She had just become the first African American to win a Wimbledon title.

When Kemi-Bo Jacobs learned of the life of Gibson, she reports feeling a sense of being cheated; that the exceptional achievements of a Black woman had faded from view. She describes this as being like discovering you have sat an exam where everyone else has been given information that you have not.

These questions – of how certain stories become erased; of what it means to go through life knowing that one's story is more likely to be excised or forgotten because of race and gender – form the subject of her one-woman play about Althea Gibson, *All White Everything But Me*, which premiered in 2022.

Who gets forgotten? How do we bring their stories back to life?

13 JULY

GOOD PRACTICE

'Sylvia Plath used to say the short story was like the
toothbrush and the novel was like the whole house ... The
short story's spatial; as a form it moves out from a
central point, like a poem, like music ... The novel has
to be in some ways chronological, in some ways about
social things in a way that short stories can escape from.'

Ali Smith, writer, academic and journalist, 2008

• • • • • •

Ali Smith offers us here a glimpse into her working practice, the kinds of choices that writers make when choosing the form that suits the characters and the subject matter.

Smith has published a dozen novels and five collections of short stories. Here she considers the differences in those two forms. The short story catches a moment in time, a snapshot of life through the eyes of a single character, usually someone on the periphery – the 'lonely voice', as Frank O'Connor called it in his study of the form.

The novel is expansive, it moves through time when the short story hesitates or lingers, and is more suited to representing the multiplicity of voices that make up a society. Smith's own 'seasonal quartet' novels do exactly this, capturing the mood of Britain as it passed through the paroxysm of Brexit, and into the COVID years.

Any craft is a process of making decisions about how to go about doing the work, and choosing the right tools for the job. But when we work at something for a long time, we sometimes fall into a rut of perspective or practice.

Stopping to think about our process can be productive; mixing things up can have a positive impact.

14 JULY

STEP-PARENTING

'I think you're in a very fortunate position as a stepparent. You don't need to rely on maternal instincts. You can treat the children as real people and deal with that in that context. I think I have a good relationship with them on that basis that is quite different from one of their own parents.'

Julia Wallace, town planner and stepmother, 2010

· · · · · ·

The 2021 census reported that just under 1 in 10 children lives in a stepfamily.

Stepfamilies form for many different reasons: there might be a divorce, a separation, a bereavement. There can be complications – the children might not want this new adult in their life – and unexpected legal ramifications, too; for example, if a child is hurt or injured, and neither parent is readily available to make decisions about medical care. Is the stepparent in a position to decide?

Vice President and presidential nominee Kamala Harris (b. 1964) is part of the most high-profile stepfamily in the world, stepmother ('Momala') to her husband Doug Emhoff's two children. He has spoken about their 'big, beautiful, blended family' – and his ex-wife, Kerstin, has a close friendship with Harris. 'We sometimes joke,' Harris has written, 'that our modern family is almost a little too functional.'

Any relationship between an adult and a child – including between parents and their children – is a process. Trust doesn't happen overnight, but can – with time, and patience.

15 JULY

JUST CHECK IN

'When I say accommodated, [it's] a case of coaches understanding that [neurodiverse] people exist and you might need to tweak the way you say something or just check in with them in a different way. It's really simple. Yet at the moment there's absolutely no understanding at all.'

Caragh McMurtry, rower and Olympian, 2023

• • • • • •

Caragh McMurtry's experience of being misdiagnosed with bipolar disorder, and subsequently correctly diagnosed with autism, has led to her work to promote awareness of neurodiversity, particularly within sports.

Neurodiversity has no categories in parasport. Neurodiverse athletes might want to compete in intellectual impairment sport, or else want to compete in non-disabled sport. Neurodiversity exists across sport – and life – which McMurtry asks people to recognise and accommodate.

McMurtry calls for us to be sympathetic, to show understanding, to be willing to do the small amount of work to accommodate diversity.

Are we aware of the diversity that exists around us? What simple things might we do that level the playing field?

16 JULY

GLUING IT ALL TOGETHER

'Somebody has to take responsibility for keeping in touch with other relations. Somebody has to take responsibility for gluing it altogether.'

Helen Bullough, journalist and producer, 2023

· · · · · ·

The shock of losing parents doesn't lessen with age. While we might anticipate grief and loss, and prepare coping strategies, we might not have considered what the impact might be upon the structure of our relationships with siblings.

Parents, particularly as they become elderly, provide a focus for a family. But, as Helen Bullough — who lost both parents later in life — points out, when that focus goes, something structural is lost. Siblings who were sharing responsibilities for care, and are now sharing their grief, may find that the whole family needs time to resettle.

It's a hard thing to think about, and an even harder conversation to have. But who will take the lead and keep the family together, when the older generation has gone?

17 JULY

COMPASSION NOT PASSION

'This government needs more compassion, not passion . . . I've got a reputation for being a party girl, but in this situation the answer is no. No. You set an example, and you live by that example.'

Tracey Emin, artist, 2022

• • • • • •

Dame Tracey Emin, once the 'enfant terrible' of British art, is now a member of the Royal Academy.

In 2022, following revelations about parties at Downing Street during lockdown, Emin requested that an artwork she had donated to the government collection be taken down from display in No. 10. The neon art, titled *More Passion*, had been installed in 2011. For Emin, a royalist who voted Conservative in 2010, the idea of parties taking place under her neon sign while others watched the funerals of loved ones on their laptops was unacceptable.

Context is everything. The meaning and message of art can be as much about where it is, and who can experience it, as about the physical piece itself.

18 JULY

THREE RULES TO LIVE BY

'Life goes by so fast, there's hardly any time to think:
"What should I do? What should I think? Is it getting
better? Is it getting worse?" We [Anderson and her
husband, Lou Reed] were interested in how to act
quickly [and devised] three rules to live by. No. 1: Don't
be afraid of anybody. You can imagine your life in which
you are not afraid of anybody. Second, get a good
bullshit detector and learn how to *use* that. Don't just
get one. No. 3: Be really tender. With those three things,
you're set. You don't have to even think about all of
these baffling questions. Just try to do your best.'

Laurie Anderson, musician, filmmaker and artist, 2015

• • • • • •

Part of the New York avant-garde, Laurie Anderson (b. 1947) has,
through her work, experimented extensively with technological innovations. A pioneer of electronic music, her song 'O Superman' was an
unexpected hit, reaching No. 2 in the UK charts in 1981. Anderson
was married to musician Lou Reed until his death in 2013.

Anderson's rules are based on the assumption that life moves very
quickly, that we don't always have time to ponder the best course of
action, and that we can become paralysed by over-thinking.

Be unafraid, trust but verify – and act tenderly. This is wisdom.

19 JULY

LOOKING OUT FOR EACH OTHER

'What I love about it is that [women] now have a community there and they're looking out for each other ... [They] speak up and also have a sounding board. You know: "What do you do in this situation? Could I get some advice?" or "How does this work?" Not just about music but about interpersonal interactions and all those things because they're very complex. The conductor's job is not just about the music. It's about managing one hundred egos that have very different viewpoints on everything.'

Marin Alsop, conductor, 2019

• • • • • •

Marin Alsop's (b. 1956) many achievements include being the first woman to be awarded the Koussevitzky Prize for outstanding student conductor – and, of course, the first woman to conduct at The Last Night of the Proms. (Astonishingly, this was as late as 2013.)

Alsop's description of conducting as being not simply about the music but about the complex management of interpersonal interactions reminds us that art takes place within social and institutional contexts. Trailblazing women smash through glass ceilings – but once that barrier has been shattered, there are the quotidian questions of how to go about managing both the work and the professional relationships.

What networks and communities do we need to form to support each other? What conversations must we have with each other, to ensure that the first woman isn't the only woman? How do we have each other's backs?

20 JULY

WE AIM TO (DIS)PLEASE

'Reject the idea of likeability. I think we teach girls
constantly to mould themselves into shapes to make
themselves likeable, to think about what other people
think about them ... It's so important to teach
a child, particularly a girl, that your job is not to
be likeable, your job is to be your fullest self.'

Chimamanda Ngozi Adichie, writer, 2016

· · · · · ·

The idea that girls, and women, were made to please men — that our role in life was primarily to support male ambitions, to be pleasant and likeable company — has historically run deep.

Our education systems, too, reflected this for longer than we might care to admit. Girls' education focused on the domestic: giving a girl the skills she needed to enable her to create a peaceful home for her husband (always assumed) to do his life's work.

When insisting that girls also have the right to be the fullest people that they can possibly be, Adichie is echoing Mary Wollstonecraft (1759–97), who dedicated a section of *A Vindication of the Rights of Woman* (1792) to refuting the idea that girls' education should be focused on making her a good companion for men. Girls and women are rational beings in their own right and should be educated to their fullest potential — without reference to men.

You're not here to please. Neither are our daughters.

21 JULY

THE QUEEN OF LATIN

'There's no difference at all [with same-sex dance partnerships]. A heel is a heel and a toe is a toe. I didn't have tall men, I danced with two men that were 5'6'! People come in all shapes and sizes and everyone can dance. We have a guide, a technique book, and it shares with you what kind of foot placements you have to make, heels, toes.'

Shirley Ballas, ballroom dancer, dance teacher and dance adjudicator, 2019

• • • • • •

Shirley Ballas (b. 1960) began dancing at the age of seven, taking up competitive dancing not long after. At the age of 15, she moved away from home to live with the family of her then dance partner; she broke up the partnership after two years to form another dance partnership, marrying her new partner at the age of 18. Specialising in Latin dance, she was a multiple championship winner by the age of 21.

After moving to the United States to compete there, Ballas's television career began in 2004 with appearances and commentary on *Dancing With the Stars*. In 2017, she joined the judging panel on *Strictly Come Dancing* as head judge.

In 2020, boxer and Olympian Nicola Adams and dancer Katya Jones were the first same-sex couple to appear on the programme to a brief press flurry. Same-sex couples appeared in subsequent years from 2021 to 2023.

Ballas points out that there are no technical reasons for same-sex couples not to dance together. What matters is the dance itself.

22 JULY

TALKING TO YOURSELF

'Some people mean speaking out loud, and others mean
rehearsing imaginary conversations in the future. We
constantly imagine the future and try to think about
how we might change our present circumstances ... We
are unique in the animal kingdom in being able to
imagine. Far from it being a source of madness, it gives
us the ability to think about other possible worlds, and
so it is critical to what it means to be human.'

Molly Andrews, psychologist and professor, 2017

• • • • • •

Do you talk to yourself? Have you wondered whether this might mean
that perhaps, just possibly, you could be turning a little eccentric? Or
is the best conversation you get the one that you have with yourself?

Psychologist Molly Andrews's specialism is in narrative research:
the stories people tell themselves about their lives and their world-
views. Her particular interest is in how people narrate their political
views, and which stories have the capacity to be more tell-able than
others.

Far from being an eccentricity, Andrews suggests that talking out
loud is one way in which we imagine what the future might be like.
We rehearse future conversations – perhaps we develop 'scripts' for
how these conversations go – in order to shape in advance the actual
encounters. And imagination, Andrews points out, is a critical means
by which we bring the future, with all its possibilities, into being.

Keep talking. You're doing some of your best work.

23 JULY

UNREPRESENTED

'I'm from an age group that actually don't feel represented by government and by Parliament ... When we look at democracy and we look at the avenues that people have to have their say, I think sometimes I feel excluded from that, and it means that I want to get out onto the streets and actually make some change happen.'

Tamsin Omond, writer and environmental activist, 2010

• • • • • •

Age has been a key dividing line in voting patterns for several general elections now. In the 2024 UK general election, according to a YouGov post-election survey, the median age of a Labour voter was 46 and the median age of a Conservative voter was 63. The median age for a Green Party voter was 39.

But the youth vote is not a party vote. Again, according to the survey, fewer than half of under-30s voted for one of the two main parties, and their vote fractured across several parties (although votes for the Greens and the Liberal Democrats accounted for just under a third of the under-30 vote).

As for turnout, the survey showed that it was lower among the under-30 demographic, particularly young people from poorer households. This is a particular matter of concern because voting habits tend to be formed in one's twenties, and a person who does not vote when they are younger is increasingly likely to continue to abstain.

What does it mean for a democracy when the younger generation shows disillusionment with its institutions? Is it time for our political system to catch up?

24 JULY

A MORE-THAN-OKAY BOOMER

'I wanted to spend my retirement campaigning for the environment, and I did some Open University modules for information. And then I found I was giving money to environmental charities, but not doing anything. A local campaign was something I could get a grasp on and take part in, and feel that I was part of reversing the damage to the planet.'

Sarah Evans, environmental campaigner, 2010

• • • • • •

The challenge that the climate crisis poses for us as a species can often seem like too much to comprehend. We can become paralysed in the face of its enormity, or slip into defeatism, believing that there is nothing that we can do that can make any difference.

Sarah Evans turned to campaigning for the environment during her retirement, showing that it's never too late to start thinking – and acting – seriously about climate change.

We have to start somewhere. And if not now, when?

25 JULY

REFRAMING

'I was messy in my delivery at times in ways that I now regret, but can recognise that just like a man is allowed to grow from his mistakes, so are women. And so I'm learning in real-time, in front of my audience on my podcast ... reframing the way that I talk to someone with whom I disagree. And learning non-violent communication. Because I find I don't learn when I'm being shamed and maimed, and therefore why should anyone else learn from me in that way?'

Jameela Jamil, actress, activist and presenter, 2024

• • • • • •

Jameela Jamil (b. 1986) rose to international prominence for her performance as self-centred socialite Tahani Al-Jamil in the fantasy comedy-drama *The Good Place* (2016–20). A savvy user of social media, Jamil has used her platform to raise awareness about eating disorders and promote regulation on the advertising of dieting products online, particularly aimed at teenagers.

She has not shied away from expressing her opinions forcefully, and has had spats with a variety of other prominent online figures, but has, more recently, been reflecting on her use of social media and the 'outrage economy', whereby money and public profiles are made from generating conflict. It's not just sex that sells these days — it's outrage.

Jamil's reflection on her online activity has led her to step back from this cycle. If your purpose is to persuade someone of your point of view and change their mind, she suggests, you're unlikely to succeed if you deal in blame and shame.

26 JULY

CAREFUL WHAT YOU WISH FOR

'Daydreaming – that's just a hazy indefinite imagining,
no good at all. You've got to work at it. But I must
warn you, it may not be exactly as you dreamed. It
may be like my dream of the wonderful house,
standing in its own grounds. I got it. But I forgot
to dream up the servants and the gardener.'

Catherine Cookson, author, 1950

• • • • • •

Dame Catherine Cookson's personal story saw her leave behind a childhood of deprivation in the north-east to become one of Britain's best-selling and most loved popular novelists.

It's the kind of success we might all envy – but Cookson sounds a gentle note of caution about having your dreams come true. What we want – what we *think* we want – might turn out to have unanticipated consequences, and unexpected downsides. Yet Cookson's fame and fortune allowed her to set up a charitable trust which has benefited her home region of the north-east immensely.

Perhaps dreams coming true isn't *all* bad.

27 JULY

ME AND A GUN

'I did get kicked out [of the Peabody]. They were really down on pop music. They weren't open to the Beatles. They said, "This will be over in 30 years." I said, "It will not be over in 30 years." I won that one . . . I was ten.'

Tori Amos, singer-songwriter, 2012

• • • • • •

Tori Amos taught herself to play piano and was already composing music when she won a prestigious scholarship to the Peabody Institute in Baltimore. She was five years old – the youngest student ever admitted to their preparatory school. Creative differences ensued, and Amos's scholarship was rescinded for what *Rolling Stone* described as 'musical insubordination' (she was 11). Aged 13, Amos began playing in gay bars and piano clubs, chaperoned by her father – a Methodist preacher.

Amos's breakthrough came in 1992 with the release of her first solo album, *Little Earthquakes*. The album showcased her virtuoso piano-playing, with personal and confessional lyrics that centred on the female experience. The first single from the album, 'Me and a Gun', performed a cappella, starkly recounts Amos's experience of being raped in her early twenties.

In 2019, Amos won the George Peabody Medal for Outstanding Contributions to Music – a medal given by her alma mater.

28 JULY

LOSING YOUR VOICE

'I had a major loss of confidence. I stopped writing and
when I wasn't writing I got depressed – and that, of
course, makes you even less confident, so I fell into a
vicious downward spiral. But I came out of it . . .
I need to be writing, no matter what.'

Monica Ali, novelist, 2022

• • • • • •

Monica Ali's debut novel, *Brick Lane* (2003), follows the life of Nazneen, a Bangladeshi woman who moves to London aged 18, exploring the community in which she lives. The book propelled Ali to rapid literary stardom. Ali was named one of Granta's 'Best of Young British Novelists'; the novel was shortlisted for the Booker Prize in 2003, and made into a film in 2007.

Two more novels and a collection of short stories followed but, by the early 2010s, Ali was in the grip of serious writer's block. A lack of confidence, compounded by depression, meant that she did not publish again for over a decade. In 2022, she published *Love Marriage*, which earned excellent reviews, and was shortlisted for the Comedy Women in Print Prize.

American feminist writer Tillie Olsen (1912–2007), in her book *Silences* (1978), examined the many reasons why women writers – particularly working-class women – have periods of extended silence. Shortage of time or resources or confidence or energy – the reasons are many, and the blockages are not always overcome.

We tend to think of success as linear, an arrow on an ever-upward trajectory. But perhaps our creativity needs to follow a different course; one that allows for fallow periods; one that recognises the many ways in which we may leave our mind simply to be for a while.

29 JULY

PUSH AND PULL

'We're driven to be competitive. It's natural to be competitive. It's a survivor mechanism, to be able to fight for limited resources . . . We're allowed to be competitive. But sometimes, especially with women, this has been squeezed out of us . . . We see brothers being competitive, but for sisters it's also amazing.'

Jennifer Gledhill, psychologist, 2024

• • • • • •

Are you in competition with your sister? Are you an older one, your nose pushed out of joint by the arrival of a new and demanding baby? Or a younger one, always chasing to catch up and, perhaps, the recipient of hand-me-down clothes and games? And were there expectations that – as girls – you'll play nicely with each other? Perhaps you're too similar in temperament – or too far apart.

Research into sibling relationships carried out by psychologists Laurie Kramer and Megan Gilligan suggests that sister–sister relationships tend to be closer – but tend to have more conflict.

Jennifer Gledhill reframes competitiveness between siblings as a potentially positive aspect of their relationship. A survey of 2,000 adults in the UK in 2021 (carried out as part of a promotional campaign for the television programme *Succession*) showed that more than half of respondents felt they were still in competition with their siblings. But two in ten said that this competition was healthy, and had pushed them to achieve more in life. When the relationship is based on love – on the shared experience of growing up together – then the possibilities for mutual support, and challenge, are boundless.

30 JULY

THE QUIET ONE

'[The Brontë sisters] challenged each other in a really useful way. They almost had a writers' workshop. Even as children they would swap work, they would rewrite each other's characters. They explored writing together. They were allowed to read whatever they wanted and they read voraciously . . . Not many clergymen's daughters were allowed to do that.'

Samantha Ellis, playwright and author, 2017

• • • • • •

Most of us have a favourite Brontë sister, and for Samantha Ellis (b. 1975) it's the quiet one – Anne Brontë (1820–49). Usually overlooked when set against the authors of *Wuthering Heights* and *Jane Eyre*, Anne was no less part of the imaginative games that were the crucible of the sisters' creative output. She published two novels in her lifetime – *Agnes Grey* (1847) and *The Tenant of Wildfell Hall* (1848).

Ellis's biography of Anne, *Take Courage: Anne Brontë and the Art of Life* (2017), charts how the youngest sister's reputation was carefully curated after her early death at 29. Charlotte, who would not allow *The Tenant of Wildfell Hall* to be reprinted, portrayed Anne as a somewhat passive and full figure in her writings about her sister.

But the two novels, as one would expect of a Brontë, are no less subversive than her elder sisters'. As Ellis notes, Anne was a governess – she worked out in the world longer than either Charlotte or Emily – and *Agnes Grey* is a bitter fictionalisation of her experiences. And in *The Tenant of Wildfell Hall*, Anne portrays with sympathy a woman who has left her abusive husband, who seeks to keep her child and who reaches out for happiness beyond that marriage.

It is often the quiet ones.

31 JULY

DOUBLES

'I missed out on Tokyo and watched my sister go to Tokyo. It was hard for her to enjoy it without that guilt complex of leaving one behind. To make Paris together was amazing . . . something we've dreamed of since we volunteered at 2012 together.'

Lina Nielsen, sprinter, hurdler and Olympian, 2024

• • • • • •

'We [my sister and I] started the sport together, and I think we've always known that we could be on the podium together. There's been moments where one of us has made it and one of us hasn't, and that's been really tough, and being there together felt like a combination of all those highs and lows . . . Finally we were able to put an Olympic medal around our necks together.'

Laviai Nielsen, sprinter and Olympian, 2024

• • • • • •

The path to the Olympic Games is never easy, and for twin sisters and athletes Lina and Laviai Nielsen (b. 1996), the journey there has been harder than for most.

Aged 13, Lina experienced a sudden weakness in her left arm. Originally diagnosed as a stroke, it was not until a more serious flare-up of symptoms when Lina was 17 that she was diagnosed with relapsing-remitting multiple sclerosis (MS).

After struggling with depression – and watching Laviai's career go from strength to strength – Lina found her form again, only to relapse the day before her World Championship debut in 2022, missing out on the bronze medal won by the women's 4x400m relay team. She went public with her diagnosis shortly afterwards.

Two weeks prior to the Tokyo Olympics, in 2021, Laviai, too, was diagnosed with multiple sclerosis. She was able to compete, but missed out on a medal in the 4x400m relay. Lina, meanwhile, was unable to go to Tokyo.

Relapsing-remitting MS means that symptoms may be mild, or disappear entirely before flaring up again. Both athletes were part of Team GB for the Paris Olympics in 2024 – and shared the podium, part of the team that won the bronze medal in the women's 4x400m relay. Theirs is an extraordinary story of sisterly love, courage and solidarity.

AUGUST

1 AUGUST

WHO'S BOSS

'Taking on labels and putting on labels makes me very uncomfortable, because I think that it definitely excludes me – accented, in my fifties. I see myself as successful. I would never call myself a "girl". Or a "boss".'

Asma Khan, restaurateur and cookbook author, 2021

• • • • • •

The word 'girlboss' dates from 2014, with the publication of entrepreneur Sophia Amoruso's autobiography, *#GIRLBOSS*, which chronicles the founding of her fashion retail company Nasty Gal.

The term caught a zeitgeist, the media latching onto the image of the young female entrepreneur leading her own business, the very opposite of how we imagine masculine corporate culture. For others, however, the term has pejorative undertones, as best implying women's complicity in toxic corporate structures; at worst, infantilising the very women it is supposed to empower.

Asma Khan, one of Britain's most successful restaurateurs, has built a brand that represents the exact opposite. For her restaurant Darjeeling Express, which is staffed by women mostly in their fifties, the style of leadership she adopts is inclusive and warm.

Leadership is not about being the 'boss'. It's about inspiring people to do their best, and showing that you are invested in them and the work that you're all doing. It's about creating circumstances in which people can create something special together.

2 AUGUST

OBSERVER, PARTICIPANT

'Performance really only works if you are doing something for the public. It's not work in your private house. Performance is a dialogue with the public and together with the public you have to complete the work. This performance is super simple. You have the chair and sit on the chair as long as you want.'

Marina Abramović, performance artist, 2016

• • • • • •

In 1976, Marina Abramović (b. 1946) performed the piece 'Rhythm 0', in which she stood still for six hours and invited the audience to use any of a number of objects laid out to do whatever they chose to her. These objects included razors and a gun. As the hours progressed, the actions escalated into physical assaults; a fight broke out when the gun was put to the artist's head. After six hours, Abramović began to walk towards the audience; she recalled that they ran away to avoid confrontation.

Between March and May 2010, Abramović performed 'The Artist Is Present' at the Museum of Modern Art in New York, in which she sat still on a chair while people took turns to sit opposite her. Some sat for a few moments; others for most of a day. Over 1,500 people participated, including Lou Reed and Björk.

What makes a performance, and who are the performers? Is there a difference between you or I sitting opposite Abramović, and Björk taking the chair? Performance art is radical, confrontational and rarely easy.

Do we stop and look, or do we turn away?

3 AUGUST

SIBLING RIVALRY

'It's been to Andy's advantage to be the younger brother because Jamie was always better and bigger at everything from a young age. Andy always had somebody to aspire to and somebody to try to beat.'

Judy Murray, tennis coach, 2012

· · · · · ·

Not all of us find ourselves tasked with parenting two Wimbledon champions in the making. Judy Murray's (b. 1959) two sons – Andy and Jamie – between them hold ten Grand Slam titles.

How do parents manage competitiveness between siblings? A healthy sense of competition can push one to stretch themselves to catch up, while the other pushes themselves to stay ahead. But how does a parent prevent this from corroding the relationship? How can this be balanced?

Equality is of course central – but also diffusing the competition wherever possible. Making it clear that it's not about who is better, but about being the best each one can be.

4 AUGUST

THE CLEVER ONE

'My mother was very scathing of people that label their children – "the clever one", "the singer", etc. – because that doesn't give you any freedom to be anything else at all. I had that as a watchword with my children and they then constantly surprise me with what they want to do.'

Janet Ellis, television presenter, actress and writer, 2016

. . . . . .

Janet Ellis (b. 1955) is best known to children who grew up in the 1970s and 1980s as one of the team of presenters of *Blue Peter*. With a presenting style somewhere between a youthful aunt or a favourite older cousin, she was a calm and warm on-screen presence. A mother of three, one of her children is singer-songwriter Sophie Ellis-Bextor (b. 1979).

It can be tempting, sometimes, particularly with larger families, to have labels for each child. Sometimes the children themselves may like the labels, if it gives them a sense of identity and place within the wider family group.

But labels can also constrain; we may feel that we have to live up to these expectations, that we don't have room to manoeuvre. And, if we were one of a number of siblings, we may find these labels long outlasting their welcome: nobody in their fifties wants to be referred to as 'the baby', just as no one in their sixties wants to be referred to as 'the naughty one'.

Meeting our adult siblings on adult terms might take some readjustment – but the effort will be worthwhile.

5 AUGUST

ON NOT BEING FRIENDS

'We have lots of communication, we have lots of fun,
we spend lots of time together – probably a sickening
amount – but I also like the fact that we have a clear
dynamic in that my mum never wanted to be my best
buddy. She wanted to be my mum.'

Sophie Ellis-Bextor, singer-songwriter, 2016

• • • • • •

Sophie Ellis-Bextor started her career as lead vocalist for indie band Theaudience; after a successful first album, they were axed by their label before the release of a second.

Ellis-Bextor moved on to a hugely successful solo career; her first solo album went double platinum; she followed this with a series of irresistibly catchy dance tracks, including 'Groovejet (If This Ain't Love)' and 'Murder on the Dancefloor'.

We may love our mothers, speak to them daily, enjoy spending time with them, and share habits of thought and a sense of humour – but, as Ellis-Bextor says, mothers are not our best friends. Parenting is about love, affection, attention (and laundry) – but also about security, making clear where the lines are drawn, being the safety net when things go wrong or when consequences catch up.

Friends are for friendship. Parents are for parenting. They're not the same.

6 AUGUST

FAMOUS FATHERS

'In the 1960s, in Liverpool especially, my dad was an extraordinarily well-known person. "The Scouse Git" in *Till Death Us Do Part*. I experienced there myself what it was like to be the child of a famous father and the pluses and minuses of that . . . My children were obviously going to be children of a famous father [and] I was determined that [they] wouldn't feel that this was something that was done to them.'

Cherie Blair, barrister and writer, 2008

. . . . . .

Family life inevitably has its ups and downs, and there can be hard times. To be a member of a family that is in the public eye must exacerbate these stresses enormously.

Cherie Blair is in the unusual position of having experienced being in the spotlight as both the daughter and the spouse of a famous person. As a child, her father, the actor Tony Booth, appeared in the sitcom *Till Death Us Do Part* as Mike, son-in-law of loud-mouthed and prejudiced Alf Garnett (played by Warren Mitchell). Garnett's nickname for the character was 'the Scouse Git', which must have played well in the playgrounds of Sefton.

Blair's husband (another Tony) was prime minister from 1997 to 2007. When they entered Downing Street, the Blairs had three children, the eldest of whom was 13 years old. In 2000, the Blairs had a fourth child; the first child to be born to a serving prime minister in more than 150 years.

Social media has made us all more exposed to the public eye than ever before. Are we cautious about what we share about our families? Do we know, exactly, what information about them exists online?

7 AUGUST

SORORITY

'If we think about women's relationships, they're so rich – we connect, we tell stories when we feel safe and vulnerable together. Put that with someone who has known you probably all your life. [Our relationship with sisters] is the biggest relationship possibly you will ever have. Your parents will die before you, you won't have met a partner yet, or had children.'

Jennifer Gledhill, psychologist, 2024

• • • • • •

As well as our parents, siblings (if we have them) are the first people with whom we form relationships, and (since our parents are most likely to predecease us) the people with whom we have the longest relationships. Confidantes, playmates, rivals – these have the potential to be among the richest relationships of our lives.

But sisterhood isn't limited only to direct family relationships. Families have become more complex, for one thing, and with them our idea of what constitutes kinship. And some bonds of friendship can feel as close as that of siblings.

Where do we feel sisterhood? Who are the women with whom we feel most deeply connected, with whom we know we are safe?

8 AUGUST

YOU ARE NOT ALONE

'As anyone who has ever suffered from mental illness will know, what all mental illnesses have in common is that they lie to you and tell you that you're a freak and they tell you that no one will understand what you're going through and they tell you that you're the only person who's ever thought this. And that is rubbish. There is someone down the road who has probably experienced the same things as you have. So the very act of speaking out about it – people come to you and they tell you and you feel less alone … And mental illness loses its power over you.'

Bryony Gordon, journalist, author, podcaster and mental health campaigner, 2017

• • • • • •

In 2016, Bryony Gordon (b. 1980) was struggling with her mental health, when, while out trying to 'outrun' her OCD, as she describes it, she decided to reach out and find people who shared her experience. She issued an invitation on social media for anyone who wanted to talk about their mental health to join her in Hyde Park to walk and talk.

Twenty people showed up, strangers who had come to walk and talk and connect. From this first meeting emerged 'Mental Health Mates', a national network of walking groups aimed at helping people to get out for a walk, and talk with sympathetic people about their experiences of mental illness. Entirely volunteer-led, there are now over 100 walks throughout the UK and Ireland.

Opening up about one's mental health is often terrifying. Sometimes it might be easier to talk to a kindly stranger, in an unfamiliar space or side by side, rather than face to face.

9 AUGUST

CALL THE MIDWIFE

'Midwife means "with woman". [*Call the Midwife*] has given us a chance to explore the dimensions of that very personal form of caregiving. Often it's as much a pastoral job as a medical or scientific job ... It's a great shame that in the present day women are statistically safer in childbirth than they have ever been, but they don't feel safe. That to my mind is the issue that needs to be addressed and I'm hugely pleased it's coming out into the open for discussion.'

Heidi Thomas, screenwriter and playwright, 2017

• • • • • •

Heidi Thomas's (b. 1962) adaptations for screen have focused almost exclusively on books by women, from Dodie Smith's *I Capture the Castle* (2003) to Elizabeth Gaskell's *Cranford* (2007) and Noel Streatfeild's *Ballet Shoes* (2007).

Her most enduring success has been with *Call the Midwife* (2012–), which has run for over a decade, with more than a hundred episodes. The series is adapted from a trilogy of memoirs by Jennifer Worth (1935–2011), who worked as a district nurse and midwife in London's East End in the 1950s. The programme has dealt frankly with a wide range of issues, not exclusively linked to pregnancy and childbirth, including epidemics, incest, intersex people and the effects of thalidomide.

At the heart of the series, as well as its focus on the social history of caregiving, lies a vivid account of the early years of the NHS. In this the programme has a very contemporary purpose – a reminder of what we built, and what we stand to lose.

10 AUGUST

EDUCATION OF A LIFETIME

'I thought I was a very sussed 18-year-old who knew it
all. And I got there and I suddenly realised – arriving at
Yellow Gate and talking to the women there – I realised
I knew absolutely nothing ... It was the start of my
education as to the place that women have in the world,
and learning that actually I could say no. We're not
going to do this and we're not going to have violence
and we are going to look after each other and we are
going to look after our planet.'

Sue Ray, Greenham Woman, 2021

* * * * * *

Sue Ray was 18 years old when she decided to join the Women's Peace
Camp at Greenham Common. The camp, which lasted in various forms
from 1981 to 2000, was set up to around RAF Greenham Common, to
protest the stationing there of nuclear weapons.

The protest was centred on nine smaller encampments; Yellow
Gate was the earliest of these. Other camps had a religious or New Age
focus, but all were marked by the solidarity shown between women,
who also created iconic art in the form of banners and songs.

Pictures of women forming human chains to encircle the base,
chaining themselves or cutting through the fences, or being forcibly
evicted by police, are some of the most enduring protest images of the
1980s.

For the women who were at Greenham, this was one of the most
memorable experiences of their lives; a sense of the power that can be
achieved through solidarity and community.

11 AUGUST

ON TURNING SIXTY

'I've lost so many people. So my first feeling is to be grateful to be alive. And that is very helpful, because it immediately expunges any worries about the state of one's thighs.'

Emma Thompson, actress and screenwriter, 2018

· · · · · ·

What are our impressions of turning 60? Are we considering retirement? Are we expecting – or have we already welcomed – grandchildren? Are our children – if we have them – adults themselves now, with their own lives and families? Are we looking forward to more freedom? Are we worried about ageing family members? Or anxious about ageing ourselves, and how life might change?

We may be conscious of the people that we have lost, and how we are likely to have that happen to us more, as friends grow older.

From a glamorous shoot in *Vogue*, to taking on grand dame villainesses such as Baroness von Hellman in *Cruella* (2021, opposite Emma Stone in the title role) and Miss Trunchbull in *Matilda: The Musical* (2022), Dame Emma Thompson is navigating her seventh decade with consummate style. Her mindset seems to be simultaneously aware of the passing of time, and delighting in the present moment.

Do we remember everything that makes us glad to be alive?

12 AUGUST

AS GOOD AS THE PILL

'Reaching my sixties, the thing was the bus pass, being able to travel all over Scotland on the bus. That was fantastic. I go everywhere. I don't drive, I've never driven, so the bus pass has been as good for me as the Pill was in the sixties!'

Liz Lochhead, poet and playwright, 2016

• • • • • •

Between 2011 and 2016, Liz Lochhead (b. 1947) held the post of Makar, the Scottish National Poet, the second person appointed to the post. Prior to that, she was the Poet Laureate for Glasgow, 2005–11. Her poetry is feminist, political, vernacular and unpretentious.

We hear a great deal about the freedoms enjoyed by women in the 1960s; some of us might even remember them!

Lochhead, reaching her sixties in the 2010s, receives that most treasured honour of increasing age: the free bus pass.

A working public transport system and free passage to wherever you like. You've never had it so good.

13 AUGUST

WHY WEREN'T THESE STORIES BEING TOLD?

'Victim of arranged marriage, woman in corner shop, caring but committed social worker with two lines ... Very limited, and not at all reflective of the dynamic matriarchs that I grew up surrounded by. I couldn't understand why these stories weren't being told.'

Meera Syal, actor, comedian and writer, 2023

• • • • • •

Meera Syal (b. 1961) was part of the team that created the sketch comedy *Goodness Gracious Me*, which explored British Indian life, and appeared in the sitcom *The Kumars at No. 42*. The latter was a success both in Britain and internationally, and won a Peabody Award in 2004.

Syal speaks about the frustration she felt at the stereotypical parts for Asian women that were on offer when she started out on her acting career, that did not represent the women that she knew, and which drove her to write the scripts that she wanted to see.

Bhaji on the Beach (1993), written by Syal and directed by Gurinder Chadha, tells the story of a group of British women, mostly Punjabi, who take a day trip to see the Blackpool Illuminations. The different generations pull between tradition and modernity, have different takes on love and life, and the trip away brings these tensions to the fore. In representing a group of women in all their complexity, the film breaks down the stereotypes that so frustrated Syal.

Syal was awarded the BAFTA Fellowship, its highest accolade, in 2023.

14 AUGUST

GREENHAM WOMEN EVERYWHERE

'Greenham brought women together . . . and taught them their primary relationship did not have to come from men. You can never go back to that. It's magical.'

Rebecca Mordan, actor, writer and activist, 2021

. . . . . .

The Peace Camp outside RAF Greenham Common was the largest women's protest movement since the suffrage movement.

Rebecca Mordan was a child at Greenham Common. She has spearheaded numerous projects to document and commemorate the camp and the women who were there. These include organising a fortieth-anniversary march and co-editing an anthology of recollections of members of the Peace Camp, *Out of the Darkness: Greenham Voices 1981–2000*.

Mordan also manages the 'Greenham Women Everywhere' project, an online archive of visual, audio and written material related to the encampments. The project was inspired when Mordan learned that a younger generation of women had no idea the encampment had happened, which she considered a form of cultural robbery.

From middle-aged mothers to pacifist churchwomen, radical lesbian separatists and New Age witches to children whose future was at stake who were brought along – there was no standard profile of a Greenham woman. What united them was their belief that the world deserved a better future than the one on offer.

15 AUGUST

A VISION OF A FAMILY

'I had a vision and I just wanted to, and I had that vision when I was very young, and I just felt that was going to be a part of my life, which I think a lot of adoptive parents say.'

Nicole Kidman, actress and producer, 2017

• • • • • •

Nicole Kidman (b. 1967) has four children: an adopted son and daughter with her first husband, Tom Cruise, and two daughters, one conceived through in vitro fertilisation (IVF) and the other through gestational surrogacy, with her second husband, Keith Urban.

The Human Fertilisation and Embryology Authority (HFEA) licenses, monitors and inspects fertility clinics in the UK, and collects statistics on fertility treatments. Their figures show that in 2022, 52,500 patients had IVF and 3,000 had donor insemination (DI) treatment at clinics licensed by the HFEA. Between 1991 and 2001, there were more than 390,000 births as a result of fertility treatments.

Today, our families are created in ways that our ancestors could barely have imagined.

16 AUGUST

SAGGY BOOBS

'I created a hashtag #SaggyBoobsMatter, where I talk about the importance of women adoring their body for what it looks like right now. I received a lot of abuse online from men who are telling me that my boobs shouldn't look the way they look for a young age and I'm like: "Thanks for policing my body, you were probably breastfed on saggy boobs as well."'

Chidera Eggerue, author and blogger, 2017

• • • • • •

Chidera Eggerue, who blogs as 'The Slumflower', came to prominence in 2017 when her hashtag #SaggyBoobsMatter went viral. Eggerue posted pictures of herself without a bra, describing her personal journey from feeling shame about having large breasts and considering reduction surgery to becoming positive about her own body.

The online conversation that followed, which was intended to encourage young women to become positive about the shape of their own breasts, inevitably attracted the usual online trolling. But Eggerue was also contacted by many young women who told her that her posts had given them the self-confidence to cancel breast reduction or augmentation surgery.

Bodily autonomy is a key principle of contemporary feminism, and Eggerue is clear that no judgement is implied towards anyone who ultimately decides on surgery. Her point is that there are no shortcuts to self-acceptance – and your body can be beautiful on its own terms.

17 AUGUST

GROOVE IS IN THE HEART

'People are wired to dance. We make music, we also dance. That's across the world. There are different cultures, they may have very different styles of dancing, and that's the wonderful thing – dance comes in myriad forms, just like people do, and there's a dance out there for you, whether it's hip hop, or Morris dancing, or Kathak, there's something out there for you.'

Theresa Buckland, emeritus professor of dance history and ethnography, 2019

. . . . . .

Are you a dancer? Or, somewhere along the way, did you lose your confidence? Perhaps it was childhood ballet lessons taking the joy away. Or an adolescent self-consciousness preventing you from taking the floor.

You might not be ready to put on your tap shoes, jingle with the Morris or revel in the rumba, but it's never too late to start again.

Is the house empty? Close the curtains. Turn on the music. Dance like nobody's watching.

18 AUGUST

WRONG VOWELS

'Emma Thompson came over and played Hillary Clinton
in *Primary Colours* ... and nobody raised a peep.
Because she was great! And so I thought, "Well, if I do
the job right [playing Margaret Thatcher] they'll forgive
me for whatever vowels I get wrong."'

Meryl Streep, actress, 2012

• • • • • •

Meryl Streep is one of the most acclaimed actresses of her generation. Establishing her dominance on screen during the 1970s and 1980s, she won Academy Awards for Best Supporting Actress in *Kramer vs. Kramer* (1979) and for Best Actress in *Sophie's Choice* (1982), and acquired a reputation for skill in replicating a variety of accents, most notably as Danish writer Karen Blixen in *Out of Africa* (1985).

Streep played Margaret Thatcher in *The Iron Lady* (2011), with a screenplay by Abi Morgan and directed by Phyllida Lloyd (who had previously directed *Mamma Mia!*). The film controversially showed Thatcher experiencing symptoms of dementia, but Streep's performance was praised, and won her the Academy Award for Best Actress.

Early parts, such as union organiser and whistleblower Karen Silkwood in *Silkwood* (1983), proved her dramatic ability; her switch to comedies in the 1990s was less well-received, but, more recently, her guest appearances in the TV comedy-drama series *Only Murders in the Building* (2021–) have proven her versatility and longevity.

What's your favourite performance by Meryl Streep?

19 AUGUST

SLOW LIVING

'We have human limits. We can't keep on giving and over-giving . . . I ended up taking a year out . . . I had to do the mundane, which I had never done before because I was obsessed with work . . . I looked after a friend's dog, and I spent ages hanging out the washing, and I watched reality TV for the first time . . . [T]opping up those energy levels that had been so depleted, like a bank account being in debt.'

Emma Gannon, writer, broadcaster and podcaster, 2024

. . . . . .

In 2022, Emma Gannon (b. 1949) found that she was suffering from a variety of distressing symptoms: confusion, headaches, lack of focus and feelings of fragility. She was diagnosed with extreme chronic burn-out, and was forced to take a year off from work.

Gannon's account of that year is documented in her book *A Year of Nothing* (2024). She spends the time in the moment – bird-watching, napping, swimming, walking a friend's dog, gaining a new appreciation for children's television.

Gannon's book describes a kind of 'slow living', moving at a leisurely pace, being more aware of the present and the everyday aspects of life. And while a year off is not a practical option for very many of us, perhaps there are some simple pleasures that we have forgotten – staying in tune with the seasons, going for a walk, breathing deeply.

Are there spaces in your life where you could live more slowly, and take time to recoup?

20 AUGUST

BEND IT LIKE BECKHAM

'We've had these conversations for so many years now about this bonus structure or facilities or a number of different issues ... I'm really proud of this group for speaking out. It's not just for this group collectively, it's for the whole legacy of women's football ... I hope these conversations continue after the World Cup because these girls deserve so much. What they're achieving – they deserve to get what they deserve.'

Ellen White, footballer and Lioness, 2023

· · · · · ·

Ellen White (b. 1989) retired from professional football in 2022 as the record goal scorer for the England women's team, the Lionesses.

In 2023, the Lionesses reached the final of the FIFA Women's World Cup. The match, played between England and Spain on 20 August in Sydney, was a historic occasion for many reasons: both national teams were finalists for the first time; both teams were hoping to become only the second country to complete a 'double' World Cup success for both men's and women's teams. In the event, Spain won 1–0.

The success of the Spanish women's team should not be over-shadowed by the behaviour of the president of the Spanish Football Federation after the match. But the fact remains that women's football remains structurally disadvantaged compared to the men's game – even when, as is the case of the Lionesses, their international success has surpassed the men's team.

Equal pay, equal access, not to mention respect, and acknowledge-ment of their achievements: White's comments remind us that in many professional fields it is still the case that these remain women's due, more than half a century after feminism's second wave.

21 AUGUST

YOU ARE THE WEAKEST LINK

'I was trained from kindergarten not to be a team player.'

Anne Robinson, journalist and television presenter, 2016

• • • • • •

Anne Robinson (b. 1944) began her career in the cut-throat world of print journalism, before moving into television. She presented the consumer affairs programme *Watchdog* (1985–2019) for many years, before taking on the job for which she is most recognised: the sardonic and pitiless host of the quiz show *The Weakest Link* (2000–12).

Organisational citizenship refers to behaviours in which people take on tasks that are not formally part of one's job description, but which contribute to the overall functioning of the organisation. Research into the subject seems to suggest that women perform more 'altruistic' tasks, that is, assisting colleagues, where men tend to 'sportsmanlike' behaviour, that is, tolerating less-than-ideal situations for the benefit of the team.

Feminist critiques of the concept, however, point out that the terms used to frame the research are already deeply implicated in gender normativity, and may be serving to reproduce the behaviours observed, rather than dismantling them.

Do we make too many assumptions about women in the workplace? Surely we can compete as well as men – given the opportunity?

22 AUGUST

AMBIVALENCE ABOUT MOTHERHOOD

'Right now, I'm trying to live with "what is", rather than
"what if" ... My goal is to feel entirely happy with
where I am. That's what we need to talk about. That's
what mothers need to talk about ... some of my
friends ... have children, and they still feel ambivalent
about it. And they really struggle, and they wonder
what it would be like not to have them. That's the
conversation we all need to have.'

Katherine Baldwin, relationships coach, 2017

· · · · · ·

Sheila Heti's semi-fictional novel *Motherhood* (2018) follows several
years in the life of her narrator as she considers the emotional, practical, moral and philosophical decisions of her life — whether or not
to become a mother, which is, in the end, a choice about how to live.

The discussion about whether or not to have children can quickly
become fraught, sometimes freighted with moral judgements in both
directions. But what if we stepped beyond this and recognised the
complexity, accepting that while the decision is hugely consequential
either way, there is, ultimately, no right or wrong choice.

Our conversation could then turn to more honest reflection on
our choices (not least the ambivalence that many women feel about
motherhood — not the children, but the impact upon their life and
their career), and, like Katherine Baldwin says, find happiness with our
lives as they are, rather than how they might have been.

23 AUGUST

REFLECTED IMAGINATIVELY

'You can't really see who you want to be unless you can see yourself reflected imaginatively, whether that be in theatre or in literature or in poetry ... [Recently] there's been an explosion of different voices which has just been so welcome because for years you would be lucky if you came across one Black poet on the curriculum.'

Jackie Kay, novelist and poet, 2020

• • • • • •

Jackie Kay (b. 1961) was born in Edinburgh to a Scottish mother and Nigerian father, and was adopted at birth by a white couple who lived in Glasgow. Between 2016 and 2021, Kay was the Makar, or National Poet – Scotland's poet laureate.

Much of Kay's work explores themes of identity, arising from her experiences of being biracial in Britain, being adopted and coming out as gay. Her debut novel, *Trumpet* (1998), chronicles the life of famous jazz trumpeter Joss Moody, who, upon his death, is revealed to be transgender. The novel's intricate construction, using multiple points of view, formally represents the complexities of our lives and identities that Kay is asking us to consider.

In speaking about representation, Kay invites us to think about the impact of being, in essence, invisible when it comes to the arts. What effect does it have never to see oneself in books or plays, or on screen? What messages does that send about what lives are considered worthy of being the subject of art?

24 AUGUST

THE BECHDEL TEST

'I will not go see a movie that doesn't have at least one female character, and you'd be surprised how many movies I don't see because – seriously? There's not a single woman in this? I can't stand it!'

Julianne Moore, actor and author, 2010

• • • • • •

The cartoonist Alison Bechdel (b. 1960), in her comic strip *Dykes to Watch Out For* (1993–2008), described a test – created by her friend Susan Wallace – which can be applied to all media to check how well women are represented: does the work contain at least two women who have a conversation about something other than a man?

It's surprising how frequently media fails to pass this bare minimum. Keep an eye on the media that you consume. Is there a woman character? Are there two women characters? What, exactly, are they talking about?

And then, when the credits roll – don't leave the cinema or switch the channel. Take a closer look at what's going on behind the scenes. How many films directed by women did you see last year? Written by women? Produced by women?

Where are our stories?

25 AUGUST

THE ACCUSED

'I got a lot of letters [after the release of *The Accused*] from women thanking me and talking about their own experiences ... In some ways it was very healing for some people ... It seems to be something that we go back to our default mode of what our assumptions are as a culture and I think we need to continually address those and question those and have a dialogue about them.'

Kelly McGillis, actress, 2010

• • • • • •

The Accused (1988) starred Jodie Foster (b. 1962) as Sarah Tobias, a young woman raped by three men in a bar. Kelly McGillis plays the attorney who prosecutes the men. Foster won the Academy Award for Best Actress for her performance.

The film's frank and graphic treatment of the rape provoked both controversy and outrage (on behalf of the victim); it was also one of the first films to highlight the devasting impact of rape upon the victim, and the extent to which women are judged as to whether or not they will appear credible and sympathetic to a jury.

The film was both directed and written by men (Jonathan Kaplan and Tom Topor, respectively) but women played their part in getting the film made. Studio executive Dawn Steel at Paramount Pictures encouraged Topor to write the screenplay, which was based on a real case. (Steel was later president of Columbia Pictures, and one of the first women to run a major Hollywood studio.) Sherry Lansing (later CEO of Paramount) co-produced with Stanley Jaffe.

The Accused concerns two women attempting to navigate a system stacked against them in an attempt to find justice. No man comes to their rescue or saves the day. Hollywood can do it, if it wants, and when it tries.

26 AUGUST

LEGACY

'[This] is the last period of my life. I want to cut
the bullshit and concentrate on the things that are
important, and the important thing for me first is
legacy, to have the situation that performance
art has become mainstream art.'

Marina Abramović, performance artist, 2016

• • • • • •

Why is women's art more likely to be neglected after their deaths? Why
are women artists more quickly forgotten, and fail to enter the canon?
The question of legacy is one to which women artists now give conscious and considered attention.

In 1971, art historian Linda Nochlin addressed these questions in
her essay 'Why Have There Been No Great Women Artists?' Nochlin
examined the institutional barriers to women's art entering the 'canon'
of the visual arts: lack of access to education was of course one significant factor; barriers to networks of mentorship and patronage; as well
as questions about what constitutes a proper subject for art, or who
gets to be called a genius.

Similar questions form the subject matter of comedian Hannah
Gadsby's shows *Nanette* (2018) and *Douglas* (2020).

Who curates the galleries? What are the grounds upon which this
curation is made?

27 AUGUST

FATHERS AND DAUGHTERS

'There's some fascinating work that has been done by novelists like Sarah Mawson and Sophie Mackintosh, and filmmakers like Sally Potter and Deborah Granik, really putting to the fore the perspectives of the daughter, and the daughter having to reckon with failures of parenting, with the ways in which their own fathers have been driven mad by grief, by war, by the constraints of masculinity itself, and individuation having to happen through a kind of empathy, but also disillusionment with the father. I think that's a really fruitful place for us to think culturally.'

Katherine Angel, writer and academic, 2021

· · · · · ·

Katherine Angel has a PhD in the history of psychiatry and sexuality from the University of Cambridge. She is a senior lecturer in creative writing at Queen Mary University of London.

Angel's long essay, *Daddy Issues* (2019), argues that while contemporary feminism has addressed its concerns about men towards partners, colleagues and friends, relationships between fathers and daughters have remained primarily within the domain of psychotherapy. Angel contends that the father–daughter relationship, too, should be subject to political – rather than simply personal – analysis.

In anthropology, after all, patriarchy does refer to the rule of families or kinship groups by fathers, or the eldest males. We scrutinise in detail our relationships with our mothers; do we give as much attention to our relationships with our fathers? How does masculinity under patriarchy affect those who will be parenting children?

28 AUGUST

DADDY-MUMMY

'Mummy got very ill very suddenly . . . and it seemed
within seconds she was dead. And I remember my father
coming out of the room, taking all three of us in his arms
and simply saying, "She's died." And from that moment
onwards he came into focus. He became Mummy-Daddy.
And that's how I see him and I think that's very much
how my siblings see him as well . . . I call him
Daddy but he is Mummy-Daddy, no doubt.
He took on both roles immediately.'

Fay Ballard, artist, 2012

· · · · · ·

Fay Ballard (b. 1957), who works particularly in pencil and water-
colour, trained at Central Saint Martins College of Art, London. Her
2015 exhibition *House Clearance* comprised a series of autobiographi-
cal drawings made after her father's death in 2009, and was based on
the personal belongings of both her parents found while emptying her
father's home.

Fay Ballard's father was the writer J. G. Ballard (1930–2009),
whose novels and stories are typically centred on dystopian modern
environments, bleak and derelict landscapes, and the psychological and
alienating effects of technology. His novel *Crash* was adapted for film by
David Cronenberg in 1996, *High-Rise*, directed by Ben Wheatley, was
released in 2015, and Ballard's semi-autobiographical novel *Empire of
the Sun*, about a young boy held in an internment camp in Japan, was
made into a film by Stephen Spielberg in 1987.

In 1965, when Fay was eight years old, her mother Helen died
suddenly while the family was on holiday. She, her brother and her
sister were brought up by their father, and their mother was rarely

mentioned. *House Clearance* gave Fay the opportunity to write her mother back into the family history, while remembering her father.

The sudden death of a parent tears the heart out of a family, and the surviving parent may find that all their energy is turned to the day-to-day task of looking after the children, with very little capacity left for the hard work of grieving.

But we all must come to grief, in time, however long it takes us.

29 AUGUST

ABSENCES

'I have many brides who have lost their father or for whatever reason don't speak to them, and it's either a sibling or their mum [who] gives them away. I think when you're a little girl when you think of your wedding, you always think of your father giving you away, so it's quite sad for many reasons.'

Lucy Wright, wedding planner, 2018

• • • • • •

When we plan for special occasions – graduation, festivals, weddings, the arrival of children – we often have in our mind an image or an idea of how those occasions should go, of what constitutes a perfect day. Often these are ideas that we have had in mind from childhood, perhaps built up from what we have read in books, or seen on screen, or involving family traditions.

The absence of a family member completely alters the nature of these occasions. Sometimes the absence might be as a result of estrangement; at others, a result of that person's death. The emotions that these absences bring up can be very painful and, in many cases, may never be resolved.

Are we aware of people in our lives for whom an absence may be causing them particular sadness? How might we help? Is there such an absence in our own life? Do anniversaries of a loss cause us pain? How might we like our friends to reach out to us?

30 AUGUST

TIME OUT

'Sometimes you have to take a time-out from people in life. I don't think you should beat yourself up too much for that ... As I grow and get older, I maintain the relationships of my life, and that includes my mother.'

Drew Barrymore, actor, producer, talk-show host and author, 2007

• • • • • •

At the age of 14, Drew Barrymore 'divorced' her parents; more accurately, she was emancipated from them, becoming legally an adult four years early. The decision was taken after a turbulent childhood (her father was an alcoholic; her mother unable to cope).

Before her teens, Barrymore had her own drink and drugs problems, and her mother institutionalised her. Staff at the hospital suggested that she legally separate from her mother, believing she would cope better on her own. Latterly, she paid for her father's hospice care, and supports her mother financially.

Breaking off family ties is not a decision taken lightly, but sometimes it is essential for survival, until the time comes (if it comes) when the relationship can be renegotiated on terms that will not cause harm.

31 AUGUST

SOLD OUT

'This is the first [Paralympic] games that will have been a sell-out. Two-and-a-half million people have bought tickets to come and watch. That's never happened before ... It's important that the athletes know that people have paid a fiver or whatever it is to come and watch.'

Tanni Grey-Thompson, wheelchair racer and television presenter, 2012

. . . . . .

The 2012 Summer Paralympics were held in London between 29 August and 9 September 2012. While previous Paralympic Games had given away tickets for free to ensure full stadiums, the London Paralympics broke all expectations when it came to ticket sales and demonstrated that there was indeed an audience for parasports.

If we don't contribute to the upkeep of things that we value, they tend to disappear. This is even more important in arts, culture and sport, where – for most practitioners – livelihoods or sponsorships are very tenuous, and there is not an easily quantifiable way of demonstrating their value.

Before we know it, libraries have closed; grassroots sports programmes have withered away; community arts centres have shuttered.

How do we sustain the things that we value in society? How do we avoid taking them for granted? What can we do to ensure that everyone gets a chance to enjoy sports, arts and culture?

SEPTEMBER

1 SEPTEMBER

A STORY ABOUT A PERSON

'It's a story about self-love. It isn't about a break-up, it isn't about a relationship, it isn't about her going off and meeting somebody. It's a story about a person. We don't often see middle-aged women having adventures like that where it's just about them and their relationship with themselves.'

Bridget Christie, comedian and writer, 2023

• • • • • •

Bridget Christie's comedy effervesces with her intelligent feminism. Her radio series *Bridget Christie Minds the Gap* (2013–15) gives her personal spin on being a feminist; her television comedy-drama series *The Change* (2023) takes on the menopause.

Linda, the central character of *The Change*, wakes up one morning to discover that her life and ambitions have shrunk down to no more than responding to the needs of her teenage children and her hapless husband. Leaving them behind, she rides off on her motorbike to look for adventure.

We're all familiar with the Hero's Journey, where a plucky young boy overcomes obstacles, finds a mentor and defeats his mortal enemy. But what about the Heroine's Journey? What shape would that take?

It would surely be more than romance: meeting the right boy, falling in love and getting married. What if the Heroine isn't young, but is in her fifties, fed up and looking to fall in love with nobody but herself? What shape does her story take? What journeys might she go on?

2 SEPTEMBER

BEAUTY LIKE WHAT I HAVE GOT

'One of the things that I have seen absolutely no movement in at all, either during my period when my only job was hopefully being asked to act, to now, is writers don't find women interesting. I find that utterly bewildering. They are rarely if ever the central driving dramatic engine.'

Glenda Jackson, actress and politician, 2016

• • • • • •

Born in Birkenhead, Glenda Jackson (1936–2023) was a teenager working in Boots when she joined a local amateur dramatic society. A scholarship to RADA followed, and a small part in the kitchen sink film *This Sporting Life* (1963). In 1964, Jackson joined the Royal Shakespeare Company, for Peter Brooks's legendary Theatre of Cruelty season. In *Marat/Sade*, the centrepiece of that season, she played the inmate of a lunatic asylum who is, in turn, playing the part of Charlotte Corday, the assassin of Marat.

Parts – and awards – rapidly followed, including an Academy Award in Ken Russell's 1969 film of D. H. Lawrence's *Women in Love* (1920); Emmy Awards came for her performance (with shaved head) of Queen Elizabeth I in the BBC serial *Elizabeth R* (1971). And, of course, a legendary Cleopatra in *The Morecambe and Wise Show*: 'All men are fools and what makes them so is having beauty like what I have got.'

Entering the House of Commons in 1992 as MP for Hampstead and Highgate, Jackson remained in Parliament until 2015. She served as a junior transport minister in the late 1990s, before becoming more critical of Prime Minister Tony Blair. She returned to the stage in 2016, aged 80, to play Lear.

That an actor as subtle, gifted and brilliant as this should have felt the lack of parts for women is indicative of the deep inequalities that continue to exist in the arts.

3 SEPTEMBER

OTHER PEOPLE'S REACTIONS

'The thing that upset me most was other people's reactions. I'd forget I was bald if I'd gone out sometimes ... People would automatically assume I was very ill, I was going through chemotherapy, and a lot of people thought it was within their rights to come up and say, "So what kind of cancer have you got?" That's when you think, "D'you know what? I'm just bald ..." My mum went through cancer while I was bald at the same time. So you put it all into perspective and you think, "I'm just bald; hair's a luxury." '

Gail Porter, television presenter, 2010

· · · · · ·

Alopecia – which simply means 'hair loss' – is used as a general term to cover a variety of medical conditions. In particular, it's used to refer to 'alopecia areata', thought to be an autoimmune condition, in which hair falls out on the scalp and other parts of the body, such as the eyebrows and eyelashes, either in clumps, or in full. Alopecia affects roughly 1 in 1,000 people in the UK.

Gail Porter (b. 1971) developed alopecia totalis (a form of alopecia areata in which all the hair on the head is lost) in 2005. Porter has spoken movingly about the experience of being so visible while developing alopecia, and the rollercoaster experience of coming to terms with the sudden change in her looks. But it was the reactions of other people that proved most difficult to handle.

Public figures are often treated as public property; women's bodies, too, are subject to unwanted comment and judgement. But we must always remember that our bodies are our own.

4 SEPTEMBER

THE BACKLASH

'This is all terror of women. Terror of women having rights. Terror of women standing up and saying they're human beings.'

Marilyn French, feminist and writer, 2006

• • • • • •

The 'backlash' refers to the pushback against the advances in rights for women achieved from the 1970s onwards during feminism's 'second wave'. The word entered the mainstream with the publication, in 1991, of Susan Faludi's book *Backlash: The Undeclared War Against American Women*. Faludi's particular area of interest and analysis was the increase in sensationalised stories in the press that contributed to a general picture that feminism had 'failed' women, such as 'scares' that single educated women reported significantly lower levels of happiness.

Faludi demonstrated how these stories invariably did not stand up to scrutiny. Looking back from the 2020s to the 1990s, it is clear that the backlash was only just beginning. Narratives about 'cat ladies' abound; feminism, it seems, is to blame for society's ills.

What has caused this pushback against equality? Marilyn French attributes it to the terror of seeing women asserting their humanity.

Where does this terror come from? How is it learned? How can we push back?

5 SEPTEMBER

WOMEN INSPIRE WOMEN

'There is an awful lot the Greenham Women
were addressing at the height of the Cold War
that is really important for us to be inspired
by today. Women inspire women.'

Rebecca Mordan, actor, writer and activist, 2021

. . . . . .

On 27 August 1981, a group of 40 women peace activists set out from
Cardiff to march to the RAF base at Greenham Common, to protest
the stationing there of Cruise missiles. They arrived on 5 September 1981, marking the beginning of the Women's Peace Camp, which
remained there, in various forms, until 2001.

Rebecca Mordan, who was a child at the Greenham, has extensively
documented the encampments and the women who were there. Mordan
draws a direct line between the fears and concerns of the Greenham
Women – of humanity's self-destruction through weapons of its own
creation – and contemporary climate change activism.

The Greenham Women's other aims – to protest against male
violence at the local, national and global level – resonate with contemporary movements such as #MeToo. Working outside of the system
that they sought to dismantle, rather than making the compromises
necessary to reform from within, the women of Greenham provide a
blueprint for activism today.

6 SEPTEMBER

CREDIT WHERE CREDIT IS DUE

'Colossal male egos have always tried to run the show;
they've always tried to have the power. I did experience
writing music and having the music stolen from me and not
being given credit for my music, and having people … just
say, "What are you going to do? You're just a girl."'

Rita Coolidge, musician, singer and songwriter, 2018

• • • • • •

Rita Coolidge's (b. 1945) musical career was at its peak during the
1970s and 1980s, when she enjoyed chart success and became a
double Grammy Award-winning artist (with her then husband, Kris
Kristoffersen). But in her autobiography, *Delta Lady: A Memoir* (2016),
Coolidge writes that one of her most famous compositions is one for
which she has never received credit.

Coolidge recalls a songwriting session in 1970 with her then
boyfriend, Jim Gordon, in which he began playing a striking chord
progression on the piano. Coolidge came up with a countermelody.
They called the song 'Time', and recorded a demo, which they subsequently played for Eric Clapton when they were recording with him
in England.

In 1971, turning on the radio, Coolidge heard what she recognised
as the piano tune she had worked out with Gordon. The song was by
Derek and the Dominos, and is called 'Layla'. 'Layla' moves from the
distinctive opening guitar section into a contrasting piano 'coda', and is
credited to Eric Clapton and Jim Gordon.

In her memoir, Coolidge writes that there were many contributions to 'Layla', but that among its various fathers, it also had a mother.

7 SEPTEMBER

HAPPY ENDINGS

'I think it's very strange to be described as anything in the context of "child". I do not feel child-free any more than I feel dog-free or gap-year-in-India-free . . .
I met the man that I loved; we moved in together; we bought a flat. It doesn't seem to me that we're missing the chapter at the end of a book. So to describe me, or indeed us, as child-free seems to me slightly inaccurate. It just isn't something that we were interested in doing.'

Natalie Haynes, writer, broadcaster, classicist and comedian, 2010

● ● ● ● ● ●

We all know how the story goes – meet the person of your dreams, fall in love, get married, buy a house, have children.

But wait! That hasn't been the story now for a long time. We make different decisions. We focus on qualifications, or a career, or having a good time. We live together without getting married, or we stay single. We get a dog – or a cat. And who can afford to buy a house these days anyway?

Natalie Haynes (b. 1974) draws our attention to the language we use when we talk about having or not having children. Too often, she suggests, we frame it in terms of a lack, something that is missing, when the opposite is true. A lack is not felt at all.

How does the language we use reflect habits of thought? Can we find better ways to describe the experiences of others that give us insight into their lives?

8 SEPTEMBER

WHAT ARE YOU?

'We have many identities in life ... We are a lotus:
different petals keep opening up. We've probably been
a worker, we've been a friend, we've been a parent.
We still are, but these things have lessened their
hold ... You're probably retired, you're probably without
your children at home, many of your friends may have
scattered. So those identities – and we need more
than one – are weakened or lessened, and the caring
side of things may come into the fore. When [caring
for a parent] goes, wow. You're not a child. You're
not a carer. You're not central as a parent.
You're not working. What are you?'

Linda Blair, chartered psychologist, writer and broadcaster, 2023

• • • • • •

As our population ages, we find ourselves approaching – even passing – retirement, and caring for elderly parents. As we move on from being parents ourselves, perhaps, or being at work, we might yet still be someone's child. The death of a parent is like an axe blow to a tree trunk. Losing a parent when you're young brings its own particular difficulties – how to cope with early bereavement; what it means to lose out on one of the most important relationships of your life. But what is the impact of losing a parent late in life?

Linda Blair has worked as a clinical psychologist for over 30 years. Her books have explored subjects such as sibling rivalry, how birth order affects our psychology, and how to cope with stress and anxiety. Blair reflects thoughtfully on what it might mean to lose parents later in life. Other roles and identities may well have moved on – but what if this is your oldest, most enduring relationship? How might we talk about, and grieve, this particular loss?

9 SEPTEMBER

BOYS WON'T BE BOYS

'I think you've got to encourage boys to be open emotionally and . . . that's the absolute crux of it really. And to resist the peer pressure . . . That's the thing. They need the tools to say, "No". [We] talk often about the power of being an individual, but to resist group pressure is very important.'

Grayson Perry, artist, 2016

• • • • • •

Turner Prize-winning artist Sir Grayson Perry (b. 1960) has worked extensively in textiles and ceramics, media that have been traditionally coded as 'feminine' and valued less than forms such as painting and sculpture.

Perry's cross-dressing, and the various alter egos he has created, also form a significant part of his artistic practice, playing with and exaggerating stereotypical 'femininity'. Gender becomes part of a performance, making us aware of the stereotypes that we are taught to perform early, so that they become almost instinctive.

Standing out from the crowd takes self-confidence and self-awareness. As children enter adolescence, the desire to fit in becomes strong, and peer pressure plays an ever more important part in their lives.

How do we nurture young adults who are confident in expressing themselves? How do we help affirm their nascent identities?

10 SEPTEMBER

YOU CAN NEVER JUST TALK ABOUT CLOTHES

'Whenever you talk about plus-size fashion it becomes inherently political, because you can never just talk about clothes. You have to talk about bodies, identity, politics, who's in, who's out, who's allowed, who's not.'

Bethany Rutter, author and blogger, 2017

. . . . . .

Bethany Rutter has blogged extensively on fashion, and edited *Plus+*, a coffee table book that celebrates plus-size fashion from around the world. The author of five novels, Rutter was frustrated at the absence of heroines who looked like her, and now writes chick lit and young adult novels that put plus-size heroines at the centre of their narratives.

Psychotherapist Susie Orbach's book *Fat Is a Feminist Issue* (1979) was a groundbreaking analysis of dieting, food psychology and women's frequently difficult relationship to their weight, and was one of the first books to open up a public debate on the politics of women's bodies.

As we try to sculpt and mould and change our bodies, we are caught in a tangled web not simply of appetite, but of psychological anxiety, and social pressures that have only increased since the book first came out.

Indeed, 40 years after the book was published, Bethany Rutter describes how the situation has barely changed; that talking about plus-size fashion mobilises a whole series of narratives about women's weight, not to mention the invidious moral judgements that often surround such discussions.

Fat remains a feminist issue. The fat acceptance movement offers us a chance to look at our assumptions, and talk about size inclusivity in a more positive way.

11 SEPTEMBER

LOVE YOURSELF

'I've not once received a message from a slender person saying, "Wow, your pictures are so amazing, I want to gain weight." Not a single time. What I have received is thousands upon thousands of messages saying, "Your picture encouraged me to love myself" and, through self-love, generally, loving yourself leads to a healthier lifestyle, both physically and mentally.'

Olivia Campbell, plus-size model, 2017

● ● ● ● ● ●

Olivia Campbell is a plus-size model who has used social media extensively to affirm body-positive messages and reclaim language surrounding weight. As a visible, Black, online, self-described fat woman, she has inevitably been the target of insults and trolling.

The fat acceptance movement aims to counter stereotypes and discrimination experienced by fat and obese people that can affect their day-to-day experiences, and their mental health. Discrimination might include being unable to find anything in clothes shops that will fit, or struggling on public transport. Stereotyping is based on the persistent assumption that a person's weight relates somehow to their character; that 'thinness' in some way represents moral rectitude.

One criticism that Campbell – and others – face is that their body positivity encourages 'unhealthy lifestyles'. Campbell dispenses with this argument and points out instead the benefits of self-acceptance in terms of better mental health, and the positive impact that this can have on physical health.

What assumptions do we make about others based on appearance? What are our own tangled relationships with our bodies? Do we love how we look?

12 SEPTEMBER

FEELING GOOD

'I let somebody loose on me [for a makeover]. I went for it. What would any other girl do? I like wearing nice things, because it makes me feel good.'

Susan Boyle, singer, 2012

• • • • • •

With Susan Boyle's rise to stardom came the inevitable makeover, and she speaks about this as one of the most enjoyable aspects of her suddenly changed life. Her straightforward delight reminds us that we really are allowed to have nice things, to take pleasure in our appearance and to wear what makes us feel good.

'Lipstick feminism' is the nickname given to a movement in third-wave feminism that embraced aspects of traditional femininity – such as taking pleasure in one's appearance – as a means of reclaiming these as sources of empowerment for women.

How does the way that we dress make us feel? Do we dress in a way that makes us feel powerful? Do we dress on our terms?

13 SEPTEMBER

CLOTHES ARE NOT SERIOUS

'I remember seeing [Chanel] a couple of years before she died – she must have been 80 – sitting in the Ritz in Paris, looking absolutely wonderful. Incredible. And yet that suit could equally have been worn by a girl of 14, who in her way would look marvellous . . . I don't believe that clothes are designed for special ages. Fashion is for enjoying, for being alive in. Fashion's for fun. Clothes are not serious. They're for enjoying.'

Mary Quant, fashion designer and businesswoman, 1971

• • • • • •

Clothes can sometimes make us unhappy. Perhaps we keep items that we used to wear, with a promise to ourselves that one day we will fit into them again, only to open our wardrobe and see them hanging there, like a reproach. Perhaps we've lost a sense of style, reaching for clothes that are functional, that will do the job for everyday life.

Quant reminds us that our clothes should be about who we are now, a means to bring pleasure to our lives, and that they are there to be worn and enjoyed.

'Fast fashion' means that fashionable clothes are cheaper to buy than ever before – but the environmental cost is huge. So how do we combine a sense of pleasure in what we wear without simply buying and buying? Can we pass on clothes in our wardrobe that have had their day for us, for someone else to wear and love? Can we find the style that works for us, that brings us pleasure in our day-to-day life, without feeling the need to continually buy something new?

14 SEPTEMBER

POWER DRESSING

'I like to make women feel and look important. I do believe that people need power as much as they need love.'

Vivienne Westwood, fashion designer and businesswoman, 2014

• • • • • •

If Dame Mary Quant captured the zeitgeist of the sixties — youthful optimism, having fun, the freedom enjoyed by young women beyond anything experienced before — then the designs of Vivienne Westwood captured the mood of the late seventies — angrier, grubbier and far more provocative. If the sixties were about fun, the seventies were about politics and power.

Punk was the product of Vivienne Westwood's aesthetic genius and Malcolm McLaren's showman's eye for publicity. With fetish wear retooled to be worn on the streets (think stilettoes, leather and rubber) and images such as the Queen with a safety pin through her nose, or bare breasts imprinted on the front of a T-shirt, or fascist insignia (including swastikas) — the whole purpose was to shock.

A fashion that could be made simply by taking a pair of scissors to your jeans or to your father's favourite jumper, no wonder so many young people were on board. And punk's do-it-yourself ethos stretched beyond dress — never before had so many girls picked up a guitar to play and write the music themselves.

Punk flared up brightly and burned out fast, but Westwood's provocative designs were embraced by subsequent generations of women who wanted to project that brand of confidence and power, from Helena Bonham Carter to Rihanna.

15 SEPTEMBER

PUSH AND PULL

'[Anna Wintour and I] have a really great relationship . . .
I push her and she pushes me. We're both very
professional and we both absolutely love what we are
doing. I'm very passionate about what I do, and she
knows that. The more she pushes me, the better it is for
me. I think people that are edited are stronger than if you
just have complete free rein to do what the hell you like.
Everybody needs editing and I most certainly do, because
otherwise – give me an inch I'll take a mile. She and I are
just the perfect couple. We work really well together.'

Grace Coddington, former model and creative director, 2012

• • • • • •

American *Vogue*, first published in 1892, is the ultimate fashion and lifestyle magazine. Since 1988, its editor-in-chief has been British-born editor and executive Anna Wintour (b. 1949), one of the most powerful women in a billion-dollar industry.

Grace Coddington (b. 1941) was creative director at American *Vogue* from 1988 to 2016. A fly-on-the-wall documentary, *The September Issue* (2009), follows the making of an issue of *Vogue*, and depicts the often fraught relationship between her and Wintour.

Wintour's interpersonal and management style has earned her the soubriquet 'Nuclear Wintour'. Lauren Weisberger's novel *The Devil Wears Prada* (2003) follows a young woman working as the personal assistant for a British fashion magazine editor, 'Miranda Priestly' (Weisberger had worked for Wintour). The book was subsequently made into a film starring Meryl Streep as Priestly, and, in a nod to the character's inspiration, Anna Wintour attended the premiere wearing Prada.

In an industry concerned with appearance and presentation, who can ever know the truth? Perhaps this is why these figures fascinate so much, existing as they do somewhere between reality and fantasy, as glamorous as their own glossy covers.

16 SEPTEMBER

SO MANY VOICES

'[T]here are so many voices that we can read and hear from, and so many experiences that we can share, and reading does transport you to another world. And in order to understand something from another character's point of view, reading is one of the best little keys to open the front door and to let you open the window in somebody else's house.'

Jackie Kay, novelist and poet, 2020

• • • • • •

Jackie Kay was born to a white mother and a Black father, and adopted by white parents. She has spoken movingly about the racism she experienced growing up in the 1960s and 1970s, not just from other children, but from teachers and other adults.

Kay's writing deals extensively in marginalised identities, whether in terms of race, sexuality or gender. In so doing, she invites us to turn the key of the door into the lives of others, and enter into their worlds.

What, and who, do we read? What voices do we listen to, and which do we overlook? Do we stay with what we know, or try to experience new perspectives? What might we learn about the world, about others – and about ourselves – if we listened more carefully, read more widely?

17 SEPTEMBER

PARENTAL DISAPPROVAL

'I had to get a job in a bar, and that's when I changed my name to Nina Simone. My mother and father would've hated me if they'd thought I was playing in a bar. And they would've killed me. So I had to change my name, so they wouldn't know ... They still do not like me playing in nightclubs and bars. They only like me giving concerts.'

Nina Simone, singer-songwriter, composer,
pianist and civil rights activist, 1988

• • • • • •

After being rejected from the Curtis Institute of Music in Philadelphia, Eunice Waymon was forced to give up on her dream of becoming a concert pianist, and turned to playing piano in bars. Aware that her parents, particularly her mother, who was a Methodist preacher, would not approve, she adopted the name 'Nina Simone' so that her parents wouldn't find out.

Parental disapproval is painful, and the fear of it can even prevent us from making decisions that we know in our hearts are in our best interests. Careers, lifestyle, choice of partner – sometimes deeply fundamental issues such as moving away from the faith in which you were brought up. The sense of being at odds with the people from whom we most want unconditional love can be too much to bear. Who wants to feel that they are a disappointment?

What boundaries must we draw between the hopes of those we love, and our own needs and desires? Is it possible to have the difficult conversations, and how might we prepare ourselves for these?

18 SEPTEMBER

WHAT WE LEAVE BEHIND

'The most one can hope for is that when [her two sons] grow up and leave home, they will keep in touch with each other and, if it isn't too much to hope for, love each other.'

Shirley Conran, author, journalist and campaigner, 1979

• • • • • •

Dame Shirley Conran had two sons from her marriage to designer Sir Terence Conran, both of whom have become successful designers in their own right.

We can imagine grand futures for our children, even help them in bringing their own ideas for their grand futures to fruition, but Conran voices what most of us, perhaps, hope – that their future will be one that involves loving, and being loved, even when we are not there any more.

19 SEPTEMBER

THE CHANGE

'We just don't know enough about women's endocrinology. Because women come into the whole medical discourse as a chapter on reproduction, attached to the anatomy of males. They haven't really figured out just how different we are.'

Germaine Greer, writer, academic and public intellectual, 2018

• • • • • •

In 1970, the Boston Women's Health Book Collective published *Our Bodies, Ourselves*, a book written by women about women's health and sexuality. The book covered sexual health, contraceptives, abortion, pregnancy and lesbian sexuality. It arose from the need seen by the collective to inform women about their own bodies, when they were more commonly directed to submit to the diktats of doctors.

This was not a generation of women who, as they reached menopause, were going to be fobbed off with partial information.

Germaine Greer's book *The Change: Women, Ageing and the Menopause* (1991) was at the vanguard of this new front; a social and cultural history that drew widely to continue making the case that when it came to women's health, medical professionals were far from well informed.

But how close are we to understanding our bodies fully? Kate Muir's 2022 book on the menopause, *Everything You Need to Know About the Menopause (but were too afraid to ask)*, grapples with the same questions: the information deficit, misdiagnosis, lack of access to treatment. It seems we are still a long way from what we need.

20 SEPTEMBER

PREGNANT PEOPLE

'From my perspective as a trans man, I don't think anyone in my community is interested in redefining motherhood. We aren't trying to take that word away from anyone. We're simply trying to be seen and trying to make room on the healthcare side of things for people like us as well.'

Freddy McConnell, journalist, 2017

. . . . . .

Journalist Freddy McConnell (b. 1986) is the first British trans man to carry and give birth to his own baby. Freddy's first pregnancy was the subject of a documentary, *Seahorse: The Dad Who Gave Birth* (2019), directed by Jeanie Finlay, which followed Freddy through his attempts to conceive, his pregnancy and the birth of his son.

In 2019, McConnell, who holds a Gender Recognition Certificate confirming that his gender is male, lost a legal battle to be named as 'father' or 'parent' on his child's birth certificate; this ruling was later upheld by the Court of Appeal, with the court referring the issue to Parliament for legislation.

McConnell gave birth to his second child in 2022.

What is the case for using gender-inclusive language when referring to pregnancy and childbirth? Some doctors and health practitioners say it is a matter of medical accuracy, and one that prevents them making mistakes. Others would suggest that using this language erases the specific experiences of women. But, as Freddy McConnell says, does anyone really want to take away the experiences of others? Perhaps the intention of inclusive language is to broaden access, to make visible a very small number of people who might otherwise be overlooked.

Perhaps there are common goals when it comes to the right to receive appropriate healthcare, to bodily autonomy, and to dignity.

21 SEPTEMBER

INTERNATIONAL DAY OF PEACE

'Women have long been involved in international
organisations, going back even before the United
Nations was created. The Women's International League
for Peace and Freedom was founded in 1915, a strongly
pacifist organisation that pushed for women to have a
greater role in working on peace and security. In many
ways, women's role in international relations and beliefs
in international cooperation went hand-in-hand with
their domestic push for suffrage. By the time we got to
the founding of the United Nations, there was already a
40-year history of women's strong involvement in using
international cooperation to push for peace.'

Heidi Tworek, professor of international history, 2017

· · · · · ·

21 September is the International Day of Peace, first established by the
UN in 1981.

In 1999, the United Nations General Assembly adopted the
Declaration and Programme of Action on a Culture of Peace. The declaration gives a broad definition of 'peace', recognising that it 'not only
is the absence of conflict, but also requires a positive, dynamic partici-
patory process where dialogue is encouraged and conflicts are solved
in a spirit of mutual understanding and cooperation'.

The declaration also recalls the UNESCO charter, which states:
'since wars begin in the minds of men, it is in the minds of men that
the defences of peace must be constructed.'

The Women's International League for Peace and Freedom was
founded in 1915 after a meeting in The Hague of more than 1,000 suf-
fragists, from 12 countries, to discuss the causes of conflict and bring
about an end to the First World War.

Now operating in more than 40 countries, its vision is one of 'a world of permanent peace built on feminist foundations of freedom, justice, nonviolence, human rights and equality for all, where people, the planet and all its other inhabitants coexist and flourish in harmony'.

22 SEPTEMBER

WOMAN'S INFLUENCE

'[I]t is in the home that women really teach democracy;
a home can be a miniature of what democratic life in
the nation and between nations should be. [Women
have a responsibility] to take an interest in the civic
and municipal general political situation . . . not only
because our opinions can carry weight, not only
through the influence we have in our own circle,
but through the way we can encourage the way
other people manage their lives both at home and
abroad . . . Woman's influence goes from her home into
the neighbourhood and her state and her nation
and finally out into the world as a whole.'

Eleanor Roosevelt, politician, diplomat,
activist and First Lady, 1947

• • • • • •

Eleanor Roosevelt (1884–1962) was First Lady of the United States
from 1933 to 1945, when her husband, Franklin D. Roosevelt, was
president. During her tenure she redefined the position: partly as a
result of the long period of time she spent in the role (FDR is the only
president to have served more than two terms), and partly because, as a
result of her husband's disability, she took on many public engagements
and speeches.

A skilled communicator, Roosevelt wrote vast numbers of newspaper columns, more than two dozen books, and was a regular radio
broadcaster. (She recorded a special message for *Woman's Hour* in 1947,
the year after the programme began broadcasting.) On entering the
White House, she made her press conferences women-only, supporting
the livelihoods of women journalists during the Depression. After her
husband's death, she was the US representative to the UN Commission

on Human Rights, and played a critical role in drafting the Declaration of Human Rights.

Roosevelt's idea of women having a 'civilising' role on male political discourse, their power grounded primarily in their home life, sounds dated now. For a woman who was expected to play the part of decorative hostess, her life and work represent a phenomenal advancement of women in the political sphere.

23 SEPTEMBER

REPRESENTATIVE REPRESENTATION

'Politics is not seen as something that women naturally
think of becoming involved in. I challenge that because
the reason I became a member of Parliament is that
I think, and I thought then, that Parliament needs
more women who've had children, who've worked in the
workplace, who have experienced the sort of pressures
and the guilt that goes with being a working mum.'

Maria Miller, politician, 2012

. . . . . .

Dame Maria Miller (b. 1964) served as MP for Basingstoke from 2005 to 2024. She was the first chair of the Women and Equalities select committee and also served as Women and Equalities minister.

According to statistics published by the House of Commons Library, the 2024 general election returned the highest number and greatest proportion of women MPs ever: 263 (40 per cent) of 650 MPs. It's a great achievement – although it's still not parity. A record 87 MPs from an ethnic minority background were elected in 2024 (that's 14 per cent of elected MPs; the 2021 census shows that 81.7 per cent of the population of England and Wales are white) – again, a huge achievement in the headline figures.

But how representative are our institutions? If we look at the workings of government, how do these figures play out in positions of power – such as ministerial positions, chairs of select committees, and so on? As Miller points out, Parliament – and all our institutions – benefits by drawing from a wide range of life experience and expertise.

What more can be done to make our representative bodies truly representative?

24 SEPTEMBER

LETTING GO

'I have had to oversee the getting rid of a family home. It had been my grandmother's home, and then my aunt's, and when my aunt died in her eighties we had to dismantle this beloved 80-year-old family home. This was very dismaying. Artefacts – objects – became hugely important . . . All is not lost; something is salvaged.'

Penelope Lively, novelist, 2012

• • • • • •

To dismantle a home must be one of life's saddest and most melancholy tasks. This can happen when an elderly family member passes away, or when they are no longer capable of living independently.

It is easy to say that possessions are unimportant, that what matters is our relationships and memories. But when objects have been cherished, when they have been given in love, and cared for with love, then the line between the material and the emotional is not so easily drawn.

Booker-winning novelist Penelope Lively's (b. 1933) thoughtful reflections on what it means to pack up a family home speak truthfully about this process. When people are gone, what they have left behind can matter even more, providing a tangible link to those we have lost.

25 SEPTEMBER

BETTER LIVING SPACES

'In Denmark it's very common to place an old people's home directly next to a kindergarten. It's routine.'

Sandi Toksvig, broadcaster, comedian, writer and presenter, 2017

• • • • • •

It's a sad fact of contemporary society that care work is pushed to the periphery – underpaid, undervalued and largely unseen. Sometimes, even the way we organise the spaces in which we live shows how care is marginalised.

Sandi Toksvig describes the Danish approach of putting old people's homes and daycare institutions next to each other, where the old people visit the pre-school children and read with them, and the children, in turn, visit those who are unable to come to them. Rather than compartmentalisation, the more vulnerable members of our society are connected – to the benefit of all.

How could we organise our towns and cities so that care is brought to the heart of our communities? How would we all benefit from thinking more carefully about the ways in which we plan where and how to build places such as old people's homes and daycare facilities?

What other places – like libraries, doctor's surgeries or MPs' offices – provide social care? How do we nurture these? How might they be brought together? And would this bring into focus the invisible – and fraying – web of care upon which society is built?

26 SEPTEMBER

LOVING AN AUDIENCE

'I was born a show-off. I think it's a temperamental thing that I enjoy an audience and so from the very beginning, whenever I knew that other people meant there was an audience I would perform in some way or another. I've never been trained.'

Miriam Margolyes, actress, 2017

• • • • • •

Miriam Margolyes claims to be one of the first people to say 'fuck' on television – in 1963, when she was representing Newnham College, Cambridge, on *University Challenge* (a full 13 years before the Sex Pistols dropped that particular bomb on Bill Grundy).

Margolyes has continued to give legendary live interviews (particularly on *The Graham Norton Show*), but her acting credentials should not be overlooked. Known internationally for playing Professor Sprout in the *Harry Potter* series, she won a BAFTA for Best Supporting Actress for her performance in Martin Scorsese's adaptation of Edith Wharton's *The Age of Innocence* (1993).

The project dearest to Margolyes's heart, however, was her one-woman show *Dickens' Women*, which she toured between 1989 and 2012. Co-written by Margolyes with Sonia Fraser, the play traced Dickens's life through performances and extracts focusing on the women from his books, allowing Margolyes to demonstrate her range through portraits of Miss Havisham, Little Nell – and one or two of the men. Margolyes took the show on a world tour in 2012, as part of the Dickens bicentenary celebrations.

27 SEPTEMBER

SELF-DEPRECATION

'One, I am not in an operating theatre holding a scalpel.
Two, I am not giving a really important talk ... to
GCSE kids a week before their exam. I realise what
I do is not important on any level. I have to have
some perspective. So even though I'm terrified and
I think I'm going to mess it all up and I'll never
work again, is that so bad?'

Claudia Winkleman, television and radio presenter,
writer and journalist, 2021

• • • • • •

Claudia Winkleman speaks here about keeping a sense of perspective about her work, and the importance (or otherwise) of her job. But perhaps she does herself an injustice.

We're not all cut out to be surgeons, or even secondary school teachers. But the work that we do can be important in other ways – and bringing pleasure and enjoyment is no small achievement.

What is the balance between self-deprecation and self-perspective? How do we keep a sense of proportion about the significance of what we do, alongside the professionalism and hard work that it takes to do it?

28 SEPTEMBER

MIDWAY ON LIFE'S JOURNEY

'There's a big controversy in my mind as to whether as you grow older you grow more or less ... Certain people can become cynical and jaded and therefore more closed-hearted. I think when you're younger you have that wonderful sort of vulnerable elasticity ... I can only say that I'm sort of in the middle distance.'

Carly Simon, musician, singer-songwriter and author, 2010

• • • • • •

How do we define 'middle age'? Do your forties sound too early? What about your fifties? Are you spreading, ever so slightly? Are you a little more jaded than you used to be?

Or do you feel you're coming into your powers, no longer doubtful about your own competence and expertise? Are you able to command respect, and have people listen when you speak? Is your experience of life granting you wisdom, while you're still sprightly enough to make good use of your insight?

Enjoy middle age. It's uphill from here.

29 SEPTEMBER

THAT'S MY PEOPLE

'One of the Greenham Women said to me, "I saw a lesbian on the telly and I thought, 'Oh my God, I'm not the only one. I'm going to go there. That's my people.'"'

Rebecca Mordan, actor, writer and activist, 2021

· · · · · ·

The press coverage of the Greenham Women's Camp – in particular by the tabloids – was deeply virulent when discussing lesbianism at the camps. As Rebecca Mordan, who has documented the peace camps, points out, this was in a context where there was hardly a public discussion about lesbianism at all. But at least one woman, seeing the camps on television, and despite the negative coverage, was inspired to go to Greenham.

Mass culture tends towards normalisation and homogeneity, and it's hard to be what you cannot see. Still, we are good at seeing what exists beneath the veneer, and the attempts to suppress or demonise diverse ways of being. We are good at finding the spaces in which people like us not only live, but thrive.

30 SEPTEMBER

WHAT MAKES LIFE LIVING

'What kind of life is that without a French fry ever?'

*Oprah Winfrey, talk-show host, television producer, actress,
author and businesswoman, 1999*

. . . . . .

When Oprah Winfrey appeared on the cover of *Vogue* in 1998, she was one of only a handful of African-American women at the time to have had a cover shoot. She was promoting the film *Beloved* (based on the novel by Toni Morrison) and, at the instruction of *Vogue's* editor, Anna Wintour, had gone on a stringent diet and exercise regime, losing 20 lbs (9 kg).

Speaking about the weight loss, and whether she had 'sold out', Winfrey casts her decision in transactional terms: this was how she would need to look to be on the cover of *Vogue*, so that is how she would look. Winfrey's openness about her attempts to lose weight, and its connection to her emotions and past traumas, was a frequent subject on her talk show, and the scrutiny under which her body was put by the tabloids is almost impossible to believe from this distance. For many, she has come to symbolise the unwinnable game played by the dieting industry: if not even Oprah is good enough, who among us can be?

OCTOBER

1 OCTOBER

BLACK HISTORY MONTH

'When I do my programmes, I try to pour unconditional love into that child, so that even if they're going through some sort of trauma, they know that somebody out there loves them unconditionally.'

Floella Benjamin, actor, singer, presenter and writer, 2022

. . . . . .

October is Black History Month, an annual commemoration of the histories, cultures and achievements of African and Caribbean people in the UK. The first Black History Month in the UK took place in 1987; the instrumental figure in establishing the event was Akyaaba Addai-Sebo, at the time a special projects coordinator of the Ethnic Minorities Unit at the Greater London Council.

Trinidadian-born Floella Benjamin, Baroness Benjamin of Beckenham, was part of a commission that established a National Windrush Monument; in addition, not least in her capacity as Vice President of Barnardo's, she has worked tirelessly in support of children's rights and safety.

She is best known to – and loved by – a generation of children as the host of children's television programmes *Play School* (1964–88) and *Play Away* (1971–84), a kind, joyful and loving presence in the heart of the home.

In 2017, a bronze bust of Baroness Benjamin was placed on campus at the University of Exeter to celebrate her tenure as Chancellor there. It is believed to be the first bust of a living, named Black woman in the UK.

2 OCTOBER

NATIONAL CURRICULUM

'What is lacking in this country, is any form of knowledge or education or even discussion about basic feminism.'

Kate Figes, journalist and author, 2013

. . . . . .

Do you remember how you found out about feminism? How and where did you learn about it? Was it the water that you swam in? Were you surrounded by mothers or aunts or sisters — or fathers and uncles and brothers — or other mentors, who talked and lived and breathed these ideas?

Or did you have to go looking for yourself? Did you open books in a library, read them and think, *Now I understand* . . . Did you see someone speak, or read an interview, or watch a TED Talk?

What did you learn in school? Did you hear about the suffragettes? About Wages for Housework? About *Spare Rib*? Or did you watch an episode of *Horrible Histories*?

What knowledge — what wisdom — would be contained within a feminist national curriculum? What might this education look like? What lessons would we provide? What tests would we set (if any)?

What do we think is the most essential knowledge for our society's young people to learn?

3 OCTOBER

A GOOD INNER COMPASS

'Notice what you feel. You've got a good inner compass about people's intentions, and if you're confused, come and talk ... [Strong girls have] some inner resolve, good conversations with adults, and have been switched on to their own judgement.'

Steve Biddulph, psychologist and author, 2013

• • • • • •

Steve Biddulph (b. 1953) has written and spoken extensively on the subject of parenting, particularly on raising boys. Some of Biddulph's ideas are controversial – for example, his argument that daycare is not the best option for children under the age of two. In other ways, his promotion of a more affectionate style of parenting has plenty to offer, particularly his advice to speak to children on their own terms.

Sometimes it's easy to think of children as 'people-in-waiting', not fully developed – a distinct category from adults. But perhaps we are better thinking of children as 'people-in-progress', learning and growing through and towards a series of developmental stages.

It might help with parenting, too, if we thought of ourselves as 'parents-in-progress', learning what's best as we go along, responding to the child in front of us.

How can we encourage children to trust their own judgement, to notice how they feel and to think about their emotions? How do we open up the spaces where they feel they can confide in us safely?

4 OCTOBER

NOBODY'S PERFECT

'Girls are particularly suffering at the moment, not only as a result of sexualisation, but particularly as a result of this total need to be perfect in so many ways: we've got to be thin, we've got to be successful, sexy, good, kind, liked.'

Kate Figes, journalist and author, 2013

• • • • • •

Kate Figes (1957–2019) wrote extensively on relationships and family life, covering topics such as coupledom, childbirth and motherhood. Several of her books examined the relationships between mothers and their teenage daughters, with a view to preventing these relationships from becoming fraught.

Figes writes perceptively about the difficulties faced by girls in contemporary society, where the pressures to be attractive and popular are greater than ever, combined now with an emphasis on exam and career success, perhaps exacerbated by the ubiquity of social media.

How did we learn ourselves that it is, in fact, okay to fail? Is this something we still struggle with ourselves? How do we pass this knowledge on to children? Do we model resilience and show how to fail well, or do we chase perfection?

5 OCTOBER

IT TAKES A VILLAGE

'Get some aunties involved . . . Sometimes they
don't want to talk to Mum but will talk to an aunty
about something embarrassing or they don't
want you to know about.'

Steve Biddulph, psychologist and author, 2013

• • • • • •

Parenting tweens and teens is hard enough, but sometimes the
relationship between mother and daughter can be fraught, full of
miscommunication and misunderstanding, with one person trying to
establish their own fledgling identity while the other tries to protect
someone who is still very young and inexperienced.

We might want to think that our children can come to us with any
problem, that we will always be the port in the storm. But sometimes –
for whatever reason – the last person a child might need to speak to is
their mother. Sometimes – for whatever reason – they might need to
take advice from somebody else.

It's not a rejection; it's about having resources as you grow and
become your own person. Raising children is not a solo act – it's not
really even a double act. Who are the 'aunties' in a daughter's life? Who
are the people that she can trust to ask for advice, that you trust in
turn?

6 OCTOBER

KEEP COMMUNICATING

'You have to have a climate at home of really hard,
open conversation ... Children expect their parents
to protect their health, their safety and their education,
and if you couch any conversation in those terms,
they will listen, they will hear.'

Kate Figes, journalist and author, 2013

· · · · · ·

The teenage years can be hard on a family. Door-slamming, mood swings, anger and frustration (and that's just the parents).

As children metamorphose into adults, and begin the process of moving away, there's a need on both sides to set boundaries, to give the space for freedom and learning to use judgement while still making clear that you are close whenever you are needed.

Talking to each other is key. Where are the spaces for open conversation in the day? Are you able to find time simply to stop and chat?

7 OCTOBER

WHAT KIND OF MEN DO WE WANT TO CREATE?

'Men don't turn out well by chance ... Parents [need] clear ideas of what kind of young man they want to create, and be working on that from the minute he opens his eyes.'

Steve Biddulph, psychologist and author, 2013

• • • • • •

Psychologist Steve Biddulph's book *Raising Boys* (1997) was a global bestseller, written to fill what he saw as a gap in clear books on parenting that addressed the specific needs of raising boys.

The rise of incel culture in the 2010s has led to the emergence of a new misogyny among young men grounded in resentment and self-pity, hostility and extreme misogyny towards women – as well as blaming women for their own unhappiness – and a sense of entitlement towards sex (the neologism 'incel' is a contraction of 'involuntary celibate'). Online influencers have been quick to find that these grievances are monetisable, providing a ready source of income for many, and there are myriad connections between incel culture and alt-right and white supremacist groups.

By teens – even by tweens – it may be too late. Habits of thought are formed that go on to shape a young man's early adulthood – and these can take a long time to unlearn.

How do we raise young boys? What kind of men do we hope to create?

8 OCTOBER

GOOD INFORMATION

'The people who were against us made such
a to-do that I never had to spend a penny on
any kind of publicity. They did it all for us.'

Helen Brook, family planning campaigner and organiser, 1989

· · · · · ·

The first Brook Advisory Clinic opened in November 1964 with the aim of providing free contraception and confidential advice on sexual health to unmarried women under the age of 25.

The founder, Helen Brook, had been involved with the Family Planning Association, which, at that time, did not give contraceptive advice to unmarried women, concerned for the risk to the reputation of the organisation. On the death of Marie Stopes in 1958, Brook took over her clinic and began to run a weekly evening session for unmarried women.

In 1963, she extended this to younger unmarried women. A public outcry followed, but the publicity worked in Brook's favour, leading to the opening of Brook clinics across major cities in Britain.

Brook's motivation was pragmatism, at a time when abortion was illegal and women faced the choice of an expensive private clinic or risking their lives at the hands of a back-street abortionist. Her intention was the provision of good information which would enable young women to make well-informed decisions about their lives.

We have a responsibility as a society to provide verified, accessible information about sex, particularly in a time when opposing information available from sources such as the incel movement. How well do we equip ourselves with the right information to have those conversations?

9 OCTOBER

ADVICE TO YOUR YOUNGER SELF

'Give yourself space to find out who you are ...
outside of society's expectations. Be you,
do you – and do so unapologetically.'

Tanya Compas, youth worker and LGBTQ+ rights activist, 2017

. . . . . .

Tanya Compas's advice is addressed to herself as a young, Black, queer person looking for people who could act as role models and give assurance and advice, particularly on how they could be the person that they wanted to be.

What advice would you give to your younger self? What do you wish that you had known when you were setting out in life?

Is there someone now who would welcome hearing some of what you've learned?

10 OCTOBER

BABY LOSS AWARENESS

'You are at your most vulnerable when you're pregnant
and your baby is vulnerable too and having had that
experience [of stillbirth], it deeply informed my life
and made me pop out of that bubble of ... working
and being an artist ... It sort of expands you into the
universality of being a human being on the planet.'

Annie Lennox, singer-songwriter and activist, 2010

• • • • • •

Annie Lennox's first child, her son Daniel, was stillborn in 1998. She
has frequently spoken openly about the trauma and the immensity of
her loss, and how the impact of the tragedy brought home to her the
fragility of life.

The Miscarriage Association reports that an estimated one in four
pregnancies ends in miscarriage, with a smaller but significant number
of ectopic and molar pregnancies. Some people may experience multiple losses. This may mean the loss of plans and dreams; a sudden and
harrowing change in how their future family life has been envisaged.
Colleagues and managers may not know what their responsibilities are,
or what to say.

Like so many aspects of women's health, we are still finding ways
to have conversations that bring people the support that they need.
Organisations like the Miscarriage Association, with the support of
high-profile women like Annie Lennox, who speak openly and bravely
about their experiences, provide one way in which this conversation
can happen and offer a place for people to find support.

11 OCTOBER

SAYING GOODBYE

'There is a significance that's special to [the parents], but essentially it means that you have some legal recognition of the brief existence of your baby and I think that matters hugely to parents. And actually it can matter very much even before 24 weeks of pregnancy, which is when that kind of certification comes in.'

Ruth Bender Atik, National Director of the Miscarriage Association, 2012

• • • • • •

Babies that die after 24 weeks' gestation are officially recorded as stillbirths, but until recently, no recognition existed for babies lost before that age. In February 2024, baby loss certificates were made available in England for the first time. The certificates are for people who lose a baby before 24 weeks to allow them to record and recognise their loss. The scheme is voluntary, and is an official but not a legal document.

The scheme comes after years of campaigning from many organisations, such as the Miscarriage Association, and the Mariposa Trust, a charity that provides support for anyone who has lost a child in pregnancy, at birth or during infancy. The purpose of the certificates is to recognise that early baby loss is not 'one of those things', that the parents are grieving a loss and that there is official recognition of their child's life.

It seems something small, and yet it can have huge significance.

12 OCTOBER

ALL THE PRIZES, EVERY BLOODY ONE

'It was very nice to win the Nobel. I've just been looking
at my accounts and I'm earning a lot of money
because of the Nobel . . . [B]ut I haven't done any
work since I won . . . I win this bloody thing,
my back collapses, my heart gives in.'

Doris Lessing, novelist and Nobel laureate, 2008

· · · · · ·

The writer Doris Lessing (1919–2013) was born to British parents in
Iran; the family moved to Southern Rhodesia (now Zimbabwe) in 1925.
The racial politics of Rhodesia during the 1940s formed the basis of
her first novel, *The Grass Is Singing* (1950). She left for London in 1949,
where she was active in anti-apartheid and anti-nuclear campaigns.

Lessing wrote over 50 books, ranging from realism to science
fiction to explorations of Sufism. Perhaps her most famous is *The
Golden Notebook* (1962), her experimental novel charting the life of
writer and mother Anna Wulf from the 1930s to the 1950s. Her five-
book semi-autobiographical series *Children of Violence* (1952–69) is a
Bildungsroman that begins in Rhodesia in the 1940s and culminates in
a vision of a post-apocalyptic London.

When Lessing won the Nobel Prize in Literature in 2007, she gave
a memorable interview on her doorstep to the journalists bringing the
news. 'Oh Christ,' she said, and turned away to pay for her taxi, check
on her shopping and usher her son, Peter, towards their home. 'It's been
going on for 30 years. One can't get more excited than one gets.'

She was 87 years old, the oldest person to be awarded the Nobel
in Literature.

'I've won all the prizes in Europe, every bloody one,' she went on as
she walked towards her home, pressed by a journalist to say something
uplifting. 'It's a royal flush.'

13 OCTOBER

BRIDGET JONES'S REVOLUTION

'I saw [*Bridget Jones's Diary*] on the box the other night and it was quite a revelation ... Jane Austen did it better – but here we have girls looking for Mister Right. [Not much has changed, except] a lot of women are not having children. In other words they have choice which they never had before. [T]he Pill is the real revolution of our times.'

Doris Lessing, novelist and Nobel laureate, 2008

● ● ● ● ● ●

When the Swedish Academy awarded Lessing the Nobel Prize, they called her 'that epicist of the female experience, who with scepticism, fire and visionary power has subjected a divided civilisation to scrutiny'. Her intelligence is at work even (especially) when watching *Bridget Jones's Diary* (2001), seeing the continuities between Bridget and Elizabeth Bennett, and foregrounding the revolutionary break in history that was the Pill.

Reports on Lessing's life frequently focus on her decision, in 1949, to move from Rhodesia to London, leaving behind her husband and two young children. Some portray this as cruel abandonment; others as a necessary dash for freedom. Lessing later remarried, and had a second son, Peter, who lived with her until his death in 2007.

Julie Phillips, author of *The Baby on the Fire Escape: Creativity, Motherhood, and the Mind-Body Problem* (2022), takes a more complicated view of Lessing's life, one that cannot be shaped around these two poles. Lessing, like many of us, lived through the ambivalences of combining vocation with motherhood. Her genius, however, allowed her to speak the truth of these feelings and, in voicing them, make them available for discussion and political change.

14 OCTOBER

THE GOLDEN NOTEBOOK

'This was a book about a woman in history or more than one woman in history and that absolutely amazed me ... The part about free women and the concept of the golden notebook as a bringing together of all these fragments of a woman's life was absolutely thrilling and new to me. I had never read any novel that took a woman so seriously as an actor in history, as an intellectual and as a thinker and as someone involved in the great crises of our time.'

Elaine Showalter, literary critic and writer, 2008

• • • • • •

The Golden Notebook (1962) is Doris Lessing's best known novel. Experimental in form, the book presents a relatively straightforward narrative, 'Free Women'. Around this story, however, interleaving and interweaving, are four notebooks kept by a novelist and Communist, Anna Wulf, who is in the throes of writer's block.

The four notebooks attempt to bring some order to Anna's life: the black notebook covers her childhood in Rhodesia; the red notebook her involvement in the Communist Party; the yellow notebook contains the story of her alter ego, Ella; the blue notebook is Anna's diary. The process of the novel is one of integrating these disparate parts into a single thread – the golden notebook.

The impetus for the book was Soviet leader Nikita Khrushchev's denunciation of Stalin and his crimes, and the shattering impact of this upon Western communists and leftists. Lessing describes the book's 'charge' as arising from this disappointment and anger. (Lessing left the British Communist Party in 1956, in protest at the Soviet invasion of Hungary.)

As the world around Anna – and Lessing – falls apart, *The Golden Notebook* attempts to reintegrate. Placing the life and intellect of a woman at its centre, the novel stands at the cusp of the second wave that was about to come crashing down.

15 OCTOBER

#MeToo

'This is not about casting every woman as a helpless victim. This is not about abusing all men and suggesting that this is something inherent to them. This is about specifically rooting out and tackling a very deliberate form of abuse by a small number of men which has affected a large number of women.'

Laura Bates, writer and activist, 2017

• • • • • •

The phrase 'Me Too', as an expression of solidarity with fellow survivors of sexual harassment and sexual abuse, was originated in 2006 by the activist Tarana Burke (b. 1973), on the social media site MySpace.

By 2017, particularly following the numerous allegations of sexual abuse against film producer Harvey Weinstein, the phrase had become a hashtag, #MeToo. This hashtag went viral following a tweet on 15 October 2017 by actress Alyssa Milano (b. 1972) and opened the floodgates for millions of women to say that they, too, had experienced sexual harassment and abuse.

Laura Bates (b. 1986) founded the *Everyday Sexism* website in 2012 to document examples of sexism from around the world. In speaking about the #MeToo movement, Bates is clear that it is not simply a cry of anguish, but the raising of a collective voice demanding accountability from those men who consistently abuse women.

Abuse flourishes when those who are suffering do not believe that they will be listened to. #MeToo provided a means for women to speak to each other about their experiences; what follows must involve accountability.

16 OCTOBER

SHOCKED

'We're so shocked and undermined by these actions that
we can't turn around and take the action that we want.
And that's the thing that sticks with us.'

Emma Thompson, actor and screenwriter, 2018

• • • • • •

Dame Emma Thompson, actress and writer, and the only person to
have won Academy Awards in both writing and acting categories, is
one of the most lauded performers of her generation.

In the wake of #MeToo, many women spoke about their experiences of sexual harassment. Thompson captures the injustice felt by
those who find themselves unable to call out their abusers, who are left
speechless and sidelined by those who wreak such havoc in the lives of
others but who move on, with apparent impunity.

Voicing one's sense of hurt and injury is the first step towards
being able to push back.

17 OCTOBER

A FUGITIVE, FURTIVE KNOWLEDGE

'A fugitive, furtive knowledge – shared amongst women, quietly, with each other – has escaped. And it's escaped into an international conversation ... What now is needed is that cultural experience shared amongst women remain not furtive and fugitive, and is translated into institutional life.'

Bea Campbell, writer and activist, 2017

. . . . . .

Bea Campbell (b. 1947) is one of England's sharpest socialist feminist writers and thinkers. Campbell was a teenager when she joined the Campaign for Nuclear Disarmament's march to London against nuclear weapons, and joined the Communist Party around the same time.

The emergence of the Women's Liberation Movement divided the left, with the feminist movement increasingly defining oppression primarily in terms of sex, and women's liberation becoming the primary, not a secondary, aim of their political activism. Campbell was part of the women's collective that founded and published *Red Rag* (1972–80), the socialist feminist magazine which, in inviting contributors from a wide range of perspectives, was banned by the Communist Party. The magazine's editorial collective replied, 'It's not yours to ban.'

Campbell captures the sense of a radical rupture with the past that was instigated by #MeToo, that certain truths were at last being told, that certain silences were being broken. She tells us the next necessary step, too – that these conversations need to move beyond shared experience and into concrete, institutional change.

18 OCTOBER

A MONOPOLY ON COMPASSION

'I've been a Tory almost all my life and I've certainly been a feminist almost all my life as well. I don't see any problem with the two. Because no one political party has a monopoly on compassion and no political party has a monopoly on equality and doing the right thing.'

Anna Soubry, barrister, journalist and politician, 2012

• • • • • •

In 2012, Harriet Harman (b. 1950), then Deputy Leader of the Labour Party, in an interview about the then Home Secretary, Theresa May, stated that it was impossible to be a conservative and a feminist. Conservatism, Harman argued, is at worst an ideology of self-interest, and at best promotes self-reliance without ensuring there is a level playing field. In other words, Conservatism failed to address the structural inequalities that systematically disadvantage women and minorities.

Harman's remarks earned pushback from various quarters, including from Anna Soubry (b. 1956), at the time MP for Broxtowe. Soubry, pointing to her own history of supporting anti-racist and pro-choice causes, argued that there are certain issues that transcend party-political lines. Soubry's own career as an MP came to an end as a result of her own pro-Remain stance, which eventually resulted in her losing her parliamentary seat.

The British political system is notoriously adversarial, but are there issues that go beyond party-political allegiance? What might our politics look like if coalition-building and consensus-seeking were more the order of the day?

19 OCTOBER

THE SIMPLE LIFE

'I like the simple life, frankly . . . I am myself, except when
I'm performing in a play or a motion picture,
and then I take on the character . . . I don't drink,
and I don't smoke, and I've found that my way of
really living is to live simply.'

Ginger Rogers, actor, danger, singer and film star, 1969

• • • • • •

Ginger Rogers (1911–95) was one of the greatest stars of the Golden Age of Hollywood. Her fame peaked during the 1930s, when she made nine films with Fred Astaire and won an Academy Award in 1940, after which she became one of Hollywood's most highly paid stars.

Image and glamour were central to the Hollywood star system in the Golden Age, but still it's hard to imagine those stars in our contemporary world of non-stop online access that details the minutiae of the lives of the rich and famous.

Our fascination plays its part in this churn of stories about the famous. Rogers's perspective on the distance between her and the parts she plays reminds us that superstars, too, are simply human. And that the fundamentals of life – what really makes life worth living – are within the grasp of all of us.

20 OCTOBER

IF YOU'RE WORRIED, SUNSHINE

'It describes exactly what the problem is. It's very helpful to men. So there is no confusion. If you're worried, sunshine, about what sexual harassment is and what isn't invited and unwanted, and what the implications are for women, that we have to keep on smiling, while our hearts are breaking ... It helps everyone to understand how change needs to happen.'

Bea Campbell, writer and activist, 2017

* * * * * *

#MeToo has rightly centred the voices of those who have been abused, opening up the space where they can tell their stories without fear of reprisal, and in circumstances that are free from blame and shame.

It is an ancillary benefit, as Bea Campbell points out, that this information can assist any man taking the time to listen and to read. The stories that have emerged from #MeToo are a masterclass for anyone wanting to understand what constitutes abuse, what constitutes harassment, what is meant by 'consent' and how consent can be weaponised as a line that is constantly being redrawn, an inch or two further ahead.

The #MeToo conversation – like all open conversations about inequality – are an opportunity for everyone to learn. The question then becomes: what will we do with this knowledge?

21 OCTOBER

WHAT IF WE TOOK GENDER AWAY

'I wrote it [at a time when] everybody was beginning to ask, "What is the real difference between a man and a woman? Is there any real difference?" [A]n absolutely valid question which has become much deepened in asking, "Is all gender constructed by society?" [M]y way of asking all questions is to write a novel about it, and say, "What if you took gender away? What have we got left?"'

Ursula K. Le Guin, writer, poet and critic, 1990

• • • • • •

The science fiction writer Ursula K. Le Guin's novel *The Left Hand of Darkness* (1969) creates a distant world where the inhabitants regularly shift between male and female. Mothers can become fathers, fathers can become mothers, and kings can be pregnant. Into this world comes a human who cannot at first understand how this might work – until he learns more about the world, Gethen, and its inhabitants.

The Left Hand of Darkness won multiple awards, and regularly appears on lists of the best science-fiction novels of all time. Although dated in several ways (not least the use of male pronouns to signify the universal, a creative decision that Le Guin later regretted), the questions it poses remain current.

What if we took gender away? What would be left? Can we imagine a world where parenting and care work is shared equally among us all? Could we imagine what the world might be like if we were all, first and foremost, people?

22 OCTOBER

PAPPED WITH NO BRA

'I don't see myself as [famous] because I live such a normal life . . . Accepting that your anonymity is something that gets slowly stripped can sometimes be tricky. But when you want to walk to the shop without your bra on. And then you get papped with no bra on . . . But I don't want to change the way I want to live!'

Jodie Comer, actress, 2024

* * * * * *

Jodie Comer's (b. 1993) career began in 2008 with a part in the medical drama *The Royal Today*; she followed this up with television roles that steadily increased her recognition in the public eye, in shows such as *Doctor Foster* (2015–17) and the miniseries *Thirteen* (2016).

But without doubt the role that shot her to stardom was as assassin Villanelle, in the BBC America spy series *Killing Eve* (2018–22). *Killing Eve* follows investigator Eve Polastri (Sandra Oh) as she tries to capture the elusive and sociopathic Villanelle. As the show progresses, the duo become mutually obsessed. Based on novels by Luke Jennings, the show was written by a series of high-profile women, including Phoebe Waller-Bridge and Emerald Fennell.

For her portrayal of Villanelle, Comer earned a BAFTA Television Award and a Primetime Emmy Award, cementing her reputation on both sides of the Atlantic. Her performance in the West End in *Prima Facie* (2022) won her a Laurence Olivier Award and, after its transfer to Broadway, a Tony Award.

Comer's versatility (particularly as Villanelle) is such that her natural Scouse accent comes as a surprise. It's a pleasingly down-to-earth aspect to a very natural actor, one who is surely on her way to even greater fame.

23 OCTOBER

THE SACRIFICE OF PRIVILEGE

'It's a matter of proving that you are an African, even though you are white, that you don't expect to live a life of segregated privilege. That you're ready to accept that we are all human and that there are tremendous deficiencies in Blacks' lives that have to be made up, perhaps with the sacrifice of some white privilege.'

Nadine Gordimer, writer, activist and Nobel laureate, 2014

• • • • • •

South African writer Nadine Gordimer was awarded the Nobel Prize in Literature in 1991 for 'her magnificent epic writing [which has] been of very great benefit to humanity'.

Gordimer's novels took as their primary subject the injustices of apartheid-era South Africa. Gordimer became active in the anti-apartheid movement after the 1960 Sharpeville massacre, when the South African police opened fire on a crowd protesting anti-Black pass laws. She joined the African National Congress and, as her literary reputation grew, campaigned internationally against apartheid and South African government repression, and in support of freedom of speech.

Gordimer described how her consciousness of the injustices of apartheid was awoken when, as a child, she observed the differences in treatment that she and her mother received at the local store, when contrasted with the local Black workers.

Some injustices cannot be tolerated; some privileges are not worth the human cost. What place does allyship have in our lives? What scope do we have to be better allies?

24 OCTOBER

NOT A CLUB

'Feminism ... is not a club. It doesn't have rules and
I think one of the most important aspects of feminism is
that it encourages women to define themselves. I
personally would be ... reluctant to start saying
someone can or can't be a feminist if they feel they are
feminists, if they feel aligned to feminist principles.'

Sarah Veale, trade unionist, 2012

· · · · · ·

There isn't a membership card. There aren't subscription fees. We can't police the boundaries of the feminist movement, and there are likely to be feminists with whom we disagree profoundly.

The suffrage movement was divided between those who would not act outside of the law and those who moved to civil disobedience. The priorities of the second wave of feminists might not be entirely congruent with those of the millennial generation. Concepts such as intersectionality have transformed how we think about the ways in which categories such as sex, race, class, gender, disability, age, weight and sexuality work simultaneously both to empower and to disadvantage us.

And who knows where the next generation of feminists – globalised, interconnected, environmentally aware – might take us?

We're not playing golf and this isn't a club. It's not even a single entity. It's many movements, all at once, towards equality.

25 OCTOBER

ABORTION

'I have had two abortions. Lots of friends of mine have had abortions, more than one, some of them before they had children, some of them after . . . I felt it was time to come forward and say this is what has happened to me. I don't feel ashamed about it; I don't feel embarrassed about it. This is something that does occur . . . and we don't talk about it because it does feel so taboo.'

Lucy Cavendish, journalist, 2008

• • • • • •

On 25 October 1967, the Abortion Act (1967) passed its second reading in the House of Commons. The law came into force the following April.

The law legalised abortion for the first time in Great Britain, permitting it under certain circumstances, authorised by two doctors, up to 28 weeks. Later laws reduced the limit to 24 weeks, in the light of medical advancements, while removing other restrictions on late-term abortions. These laws do not apply to Northern Ireland, where abortion was legalised in 2019.

In the wake of the Dobbs ruling in the United States – which has effectively outlawed abortion in many states – it is important to remember that the situation is completely different in Britain. A YouGov survey in 2023 reported overwhelming support for abortion in Britain, with 87 per cent saying it should be allowed. Attitudes are no different across genders, indicating that this is not simply seen as a women's issue, but one of bodily autonomy and choice.

To what extent, however, does the topic remain taboo? Are we able to hold open, supportive and non-judgemental conversations about abortion?

26 OCTOBER

THE BATTLE OF THE SEXES

'He was as old as my father. To beat him athletically was not going to be very exciting. I knew what it represented. I knew it was about social change. I knew it was going to be huge … A woman could not get a credit card in 1973 without it being co-signed by a male.'

Billie Jean King, tennis champion and activist, 2013

• • • • • •

In 1973, at the height of the second wave, retired tennis champion Bobby Riggs challenged any currently playing professional woman tennis player to try to beat him.

In May of that year, Riggs defeated Margaret Court (then the woman's top player) 6–2, 6–1 in a match that came to be known as the 'Mother's Day Massacre'. Billie Jean King accepted his challenge to a follow-up match. This match, which was dubbed 'the Battle of the Sexes', was pure theatre: primetime television, with a prize fund of $100,000. The players were carried in on litters.

Billie Jean King won in straight sets: 6–4, 6–3, 6–3.

The theatricals surrounding the match should not detract from its significance. If anything, they made the stakes higher. Billie Jean King went out to win – and she did what she set out to do.

27 OCTOBER

SIT AND SUFFER

'I think any parent will tell you the same thing: it doesn't matter what your child's doing . . . if they're trying to do their absolute best and it's so important to them, you just want things to be right for them and you know there is nothing you can do about it. So I just sit there and suffer.'

Judy Murray, tennis coach, 2012

• • • • • •

Watching children struggle – and fail – is incredibly painful. We might want to intervene, to help out, to take away what we can see is going to be disappointment and sidestep the demoralisation that will inevitably follow.

Of course, we can't always do this – and it's rarely the right thing to do. Experience is how we learn; failure is how we improve. It stands for many other situations too – it's hard to watch family or friends make mistakes, and be unable to stop them happening.

Part of life is being there to help those that we love pick up the pieces – and to resist saying, 'I told you so.'

28 OCTOBER

NINETEEN YEARS

'It was so bad for us. Any information that came to us, we would pass it on to the police . . . We couldn't understand why they were reluctant around arresting these individuals. People around the area said they knew these people. We didn't understand; we kept pressing. We suspected something, but we could never prove anything. Nearly 19 years to get to the word "guilty".'

Doreen Lawrence, Baroness Lawrence of Clarendon, campaigner and mother of Stephen Lawrence, 2012

* * * * * *

On the evening of 22 April 1993, Stephen Lawrence was murdered while waiting at a bus stop in Eltham, London. Stephen was 18 years old. He intended to become an architect.

The subsequent mishandling of the investigation by the Metropolitan Police Service (MPS) into what was a racially motivated murder was a watershed in British race relations, leading to changes in the law and police practice. A public inquiry, the Macpherson Inquiry (1999), concluded that the investigation conducted by the MPS had been incompetent, and that the force was 'institutionally racist'. This was defined in the report as:

'The collective failure of an organisation to provide an appropriate and professional service to people because of their colour, culture, or ethnic origin. It can be seen or detected in processes, attitudes and behaviour that amount to discrimination through prejudice, ignorance, thoughtlessness, and racist stereotyping which disadvantage minority ethnic people.'

In 2012, two of the original suspects were found guilty of Stephen's murder, 19 years after his death. The Royal British Institute of Architects, acknowledging Stephen Lawrence's early ambitions, have established an award in his name to celebrate new architectural talent.

29 OCTOBER

ON RETIREMENT

'I think retiring is something I shall never do. It's like being in school. If you go from one grade to another, you don't call it the end. You call it the beginning. I wouldn't retire. I think that's like saying you're dying or you're about to die and sit in a corner. No.'

Ginger Rogers, actor, danger, singer and film star, 1969

• • • • • •

Many of us look forward to retirement as the moment when we can stop filling our hours meeting the demands of others, and finally do everything that we have ever wanted to do. Maybe it's painting, or travelling, or learning a new language.

Maybe we've always wanted to learn to dance – perhaps not backwards, and in high heels, but a little soft shoe shuffle.

There's a difference between working and doing a job. What are things that we could not imagine giving up, even – especially – as we age? Could we even find time in the day before retirement to devote to doing the things that we love?

30 OCTOBER

WE THAT ARE YOUNG

'The gender bender thing did not feature at all. Nobody mentioned it. Nobody ever thought about it. [A]t the extremes of age – be it very young or very old – the gender barriers begin to fray … those absolutes of what it is to be male, to be female … We have both in us.'

Glenda Jackson, actress and politician, 2016

· · · · · · ·

In 2016, after 25 years away from acting, most of that time spent as MP for Hampstead and Highgate, Glenda Jackson returned to the stage to play King Lear at the Old Vic Theatre in London. She was 80 years old.

To return to live performance after so long away from the stage was brave enough. To return at the age of 80 to perform such a high-profile and demanding part was nothing short of miraculous. Her performance was met with critical acclaim; Dominic Cavendish, writing in the *Daily Telegraph*, called it 'one of those 11-hour feats of human endeavour that will surely be talked about for years to come'.

Jackson's remarks on the blurred boundaries between genders at the extremes of life calls to mind the idea of 'late style', the forms of art produced as people reach their eighties, characterised by bravery, mastery of one's craft and an urgency born of the pressing sense of one's own mortality.

Perhaps, as we move closer to the frontier between life and death, it is our humanity that becomes most significant.

31 OCTOBER

WITCHES

'It's extremely interesting that when we've got an old woman [like me] there is a resort to the language of haggery, cronery and witchcraft . . . There is something in Western history . . . which somehow doesn't know what to do with women who no longer have a reproductive function. They're past their childbearing years, so what are they for? . . . The menopause is something which changes how women are seen and how they're looked at.'

Mary Beard, classicist, journalist, broadcaster and public intellectual, 2021

• • • • • •

It is extraordinary to believe that for being an older woman with long white hair, Dame Mary Beard (b. 1955) has found herself called a 'witch' on numerous occasions. Robust as ever about online abuse, Beard instead turns to considering the extraordinary extent to which this language endures, clichés which date back to antiquity, in stories about monstrous women such as the Medusa.

Beard suggests that these tales are an attempt to disempower older women, to fortify the male right to destroy female power, to assert that such power is unnatural and should be eliminated. And indeed this language can be seen used regularly in political discourse – both Hillary Clinton and Kamala Harris have had their laughs described as a 'cackle', and vice-presidential candidate J. D. Vance sees no purpose to post-menopausal women beyond their role as grandmothers.

There is no doubt that the witch is a disruptive force. Double, double toil and trouble . . . Enjoy your Hallowe'en.

NOVEMBER

1 NOVEMBER

HAIRS ON HER CHIN

'[My grandma] said that she'd got hairs on her chin and she tried everything over the years to hide it and get rid of it and pluck it. And she looked relieved when she saw that I'd got my beard and I really wasn't bothered.'

Siobhan Fletcher, fundraiser, 2012

· · · · · ·

'Movember' is a global charity campaign that runs throughout the month of November to raise awareness about men's health issues, such as prostate cancer, testicular cancer and men's suicide. Participants grow moustaches throughout the month, a visible sign designed to encourage questions and persuade men to act to take care of their physical and mental health whether by seeking emotional support or going to the doctor for a check-up.

Women, too, can grow facial hair. Siobhan Fletcher has a condition known as polycystic ovary syndrome (PCOS). Symptoms can include irregular periods and enlarged ovaries, and also the production of excess androgen, the so-called 'male' hormones. This, in turn, can lead to excess facial or body hair. Fletcher chose to grow her beard to participate in Movember.

The response from Fletcher's grandmother reminds us that women's appearances are considerably more diverse than stereotypes would suggest, and how liberating it can be not to conform to those stereotypes any longer. Breaking down the self-same attitudes that try to police women's bodies can assist men's physical and emotional wellbeing.

2 NOVEMBER

ONLINE ABUSE

'If you are a woman, if you're Black, if you're gay, you will
be targeted online and if you are a public figure ...
for some reason that breeds massive jealousy
that you have a platform that these people perceive
you're stealing from them somehow.'

Jess Phillips, politician, 2016

• • • • • •

Jess Phillips (b. 1981) has been Member of Parliament for Birmingham Yardley since 2015. A visible figure with a prominent online presence, Phillips regularly faces online abuse, including rape threats. After the murder of Labour MP Jo Cox in June 2016, Phillips increased the security around her constituency office and her home. During her speech following a narrow election victory in 2024, she was repeatedly heckled by political opponents.

In speaking about the misogyny that she has faced, Phillips has noted that it comes not only from men, but from women. When it comes to possible sources of the intense anger her politics arouses, Phillips suggests that there is a perception that in advocating for women's rights she is, somehow, taking away from the rights of others.

Perhaps we think of rights as pieces of a pie, where we are each cut a slice and eye what other people have been given. Is it more useful to think of rights as intrinsic to us all, whereby if we ensure the rights and equality of others, our own rights become enshrined in law?

3 NOVEMBER

TAKE LIFE AS IT COMES

'My secret is to take life as it comes. And try to
deal with everything the way you can for the best
of everybody. I've been in England for quite a time
now – 70 years – and I've been on my own with my four
children for 45 years. And I look at things back, and I
think I had a lot of pain and a lot of chores,
but I try to face it as it comes.'

Jackie Marcus, nonagenarian, 2016

• • • • • •

Nonagenarian Jackie Marcus recalls the difficulties of being widowed young, not least being left alone with her children from an early age.

There is something deeply poignant about being the last one to remember a group of friends, or a set of siblings. Very long life is not, perhaps, something that we can prepare for. But with longer life expectancies, this is an experience many of us may have in time. We may spend longer without our life partner. We might outlive our siblings and friends, and even our children.

How do we remember those we love and have lost? What memories might we leave behind us?

4 NOVEMBER

WHAT DOESN'T GET DEBATED

'There are issues that are not just women's issues ...
that won't get debated unless you have a woman on
the ballot. ... Public sector cuts are a huge issue for
women ... The majority of my constituents work in
the public sector and most of those are women. They're
teachers, local government workers, they're in the
health service and very often they're in female-headed
households. If you make [these cuts] millions of women
risk losing their jobs, and there are not private
sector jobs waiting for them.'

Diane Abbott, politician, 2010

. . . . . .

No female MP has faced more online abuse than Diane Abbott (b. 1953). An analysis conducted by Amnesty International in 2017 showed that Abbott was the target of almost a third of the abusive tweets that they analysed, which rose to over 45 per cent in the six weeks leading up to the general election. The abuse focused on her gender and her race.

The study also showed that Black, Asian and minority ethnic MPs received almost half of the abusive tweets, despite there being eight times as many white MPs at the time the research was conducted.

Diane Abbott has been Member of Parliament for Hackney North and Stoke Newington since 1987. Born into a working-class family, she attended grammar school and then Newnham College, Cambridge, before joining the civil service. She worked briefly as a reporter before her election to Westminster City Council, and became active in the Labour Party Black Sections movement.

She was the first Black woman elected to Parliament, and, after the July 2024 election, became the Mother of the House, the longest continually serving female MP.

5 NOVEMBER

BONKING IN THE POTTING SHEDS

'I often say to older women at signings, "If you don't like sex in a novel don't buy this one, but if you do like sex in a novel there's a bit of bonking in the potting shed." Which book do they buy? They queue up for the one that's got bonking in the potting shed.'

Prue Leith, restaurateur, broadcaster, presenter and writer, 2016

. . . . . .

After selling her catering business, Dame Prue Leith took up writing novels. Since 2000, she has published nine family sagas – often involving cooks and catering – in the style of Barbara Taylor Bradford.

Sex and sexuality in old age has historically been a taboo subject – but with the generation that enjoyed the benefits of the sexual revolution long since having received their free bus passes, it's no real surprise that such prohibitions on frank discussion have disappeared.

And why not? Do we really believe that post-menopausal women retire into a corner to sit quietly by the fireside? The Boomer generation is still enjoying itself – much as it did in its youth.

6 NOVEMBER

JIGGING AROUND

'Don't underestimate the old. We're quite with it.
In spirit I could be jigging around and doing *Strictly
Come Dancing* and anything you like. It's just
that my legs won't let me.'

Marguerite Patten, home economist, 2009

• • • • • •

If Prue Leith is still full of beans in her eighties, then let us pause for a moment to admire Marguerite Patten (1915–2015), the first British 'celebrity chef', and one who – aged 93 – was ready and willing to jig around.

How do you imagine yourself in old age? Do you hope to carry on disgracefully? Or are you looking forward to putting your feet up at last?

7 NOVEMBER

A DEMOCRATIC PROBLEM

'Our state legislatures are the Catch-22 of American democracy. They're extremely conservative ... They have been infiltrated and controlled by business and very right-wing interests ... It's not so much that the Equal Rights Amendment is having a problem, it's that the democratic system is having a problem.'

Gloria Steinem, journalist and activist, 1977

. . . . . .

The Equal Rights Amendment to the United States Constitution was first introduced to Congress in 1923, but made little headway until the rise of feminism's second wave throughout the 1960s. Reintroduced in 1971, by 1977 the ERA had been ratified by 35 of the necessary 38 states, but a conservative backlash against the amendment stalled the process. The amendment remains unratified.

Gloria Steinem (b. 1934) has spent her career at the forefront of the women's rights movement. In 1971 alone, she co-founded both *Ms.* magazine, the first national American feminist publication, and the National Women's Political Caucus, a grassroots organisation aimed at supporting women's entry into all levels of government. She has continued to speak and organise on behalf of women's rights well into her eighties.

Some hearts and minds will not be changed in their opposition to women's rights. But Steinem's tactical combination of journalism with grassroots organisation acknowledges how the 'soft' power of cultural feminism can support the hard graft of political organising to secure these rights.

8 NOVEMBER

WAYWARD SONS

'It's an address to Donald Trump from the rock of the
island of Lewis, and it tries to address a feeling of
brokenness and loss in him. It's a kind of humanising;
it's hard to do – but it's an attempt to address
him as a wayward son.'

Karine Polwart, singer-songwriter, 2019

• • • • • •

On 8 November 2016, Donald Trump was elected President of the
United States.

Trump's mother, Mary Anne MacLeod (1912–2000), was born in
the Hebrides, on the Isle of Lewis, setting sail for the United States in
1930. This was a time when thousands of Scottish crofters, still suffering from the impact of the Clearances, and now reeling from the
economic crash that led to the Great Depression, made the decision
to leave their homes – economic migrants seeking to escape grinding
poverty for a better life for their children.

Scottish folk singer Karine Polwart has written a piece about
Mary Anne MacLeod's journey, 'I Burn But I Am Not Consumed', the
clan motto of the MacLeods. A book with the same title, by Scottish
photographer Alicia Bruce and the residents of the village of Menie,
Aberdeenshire, documents the impact on their home of Trump's
development of a golf course, which has caused lasting environmental
damage.

Polwart's song radically chooses to recognise what is human in
those whose acts we disagree with. It does not mean that we are giving
them a free pass. Rather, it reinforces how they too are no less account-
able to the rest of us.

9 NOVEMBER

YES, PRIME MINISTER

'I was usually asked by a woman journalist, "What's it like to be a woman prime minister?" and I usually replied ... "I have no idea because I have never experienced the alternative." To me, I was prime minister with a job to do, and I was intent on doing the job.'

Margaret Thatcher, politician and prime minister, 2013

* * * * * *

What can be said about Margaret Thatcher, Baroness Thatcher of Kesteven (1925–2013), the first woman prime minister and, still, one of the most divisive figures in British political history?

The contours of Thatcher's biography are well known: born in Grantham, her father ran a grocer's shop; she went to Somerville College, Oxford, and worked, briefly, as a research chemist (one of very few prime ministers in recent years to have a background in science rather than in law). Elected as MP for Finchley in 1959, she held a variety of ministerial positions.

As Secretary of State for Education and Science, she earned the soubriquet 'Milk Snatcher' over the abolition of free school milk to children between the ages of 7 and 11. Unexpectedly put forward to challenge Edward Heath after his electoral defeat in 1974, she was popular with the right of the party and those who had not attended private schools or Oxbridge. This formed part of the political base that was to give her three consecutive election successes between 1979 and 1992.

The sale of council houses, privatisation of utilities, bitter battles with the unions and Euroscepticism . . . we are still living – for better or worse – in the house that Thatcher built.

10 NOVEMBER

PIERCING BLUE EYES

'I can confess it now she's gone, but no one terrified
me more than Margaret Thatcher. The voice, the
preparation you needed to make to avoid being
made to look a fool, and those piercing blue
eyes that bored right through you.'

Jenni Murray, journalist and broadcaster

* * * * * *

Thatcher's transformation from housewife to Iron Lady is well documented. Her dresses lost their large bows and her voice deepened; perhaps the most memorable photograph of her time as prime minister shows her at the helm of a Challenger tank, wearing a headscarf.

What was her legacy for women, either in politics or across the country? She famously rebuffed any idea that women should be promoted or selected on the basis of anything other than merit, and that the lack of women in the ranks of her government was the small pool from which she could select.

But her remark that 'there is no such thing as society: there are individual men and women, and there are families' shows a political philosophy that could not allow for or respond to the structural inequalities that might prevent women from entering institutions like the House of Commons, and moving up within these institutions.

Famously prepared and on top of her brief, apparently able to function on almost no sleep and undoubtedly holding a clear vision of how the country should be — nevertheless, nobody could accuse her of having too much imagination.

11 NOVEMBER

A BLOODY DIFFICULT WOMAN

'I was brought up to believe that whatever you're doing, you should do the best you can . . . Whatever you're doing, aim to do your best.'

Theresa May, politician and prime minister, 2013

• • • • • •

In 2016, during the campaign to replace David Cameron as leader of the Conservative Party, veteran MP Kenneth Clarke was caught on camera making some off-the-cuff remarks about the candidates. As well as describing the idea of Boris Johnson as prime minister as 'ridiculous', he also referred to the then Home Secretary, Theresa May, as a 'bloody difficult woman'.

Clarke's remarks about May, which went viral, provoked a media storm, although May's team were reported to be delighted at the boost that it gave her, and the race eventually became one between May and the Minister of State for Energy, Andrea Leadsom. A sour note entered the contest when Leadsom, mother of three, said that having children gave her a 'very real stake' in the future compared to May, remarks that were universally condemned.

Theresa May (b. 1956) was elected as the party leader on 13 July 2016. After six years at the Home Office (she is the only woman to have held two of the great offices of state), May was now Britain's second woman prime minister. Her period in office was overshadowed by her attempts to handle the fallout from the referendum on leaving the European Union, a referendum called by her predecessor, David Cameron.

We are reminded of Alan Bennett's words from his play *The History Boys* (2004): 'History is women following behind with the bucket.'

12 NOVEMBER

ON BEING 'DIFFICULT'

'I look forward to a generation where people like me aren't called difficult . . . One of the many chores I would pass on to the next generation is I think we should start a column called "Difficult Men" in every single newspaper in the world.'

Carmen Callil, publisher, writer and critic, 2022

• • • • • •

When naming the publishing imprint that she founded in 1973, Dame Carmen Callil (1938–2022) intentionally and provocatively chose a word more commonly used as an insult. 'Virago' – a difficult, domineering and bad-tempered woman; a shrew, harpy, scold, harridan; part of a monstrous regiment . . .

Or, to return to the roots of the word, a woman whose strength and spirit are man-like; a woman warrior.

Skilfully, playfully and with laser precision, Callil chose a name that illustrated not only how women's strengths are twisted into negatives, but the double standards that are so typically at play.

Why is it that women who raise their voices are called 'difficult', when men who do the same are called 'assertive'? What would happen if we turned those words around?

13 NOVEMBER

SOFT POWER

'More MPs came to that meeting because of the pull of *The Archers* than I have ever seen at any of the domestic violence All Party Parliamentary groups of which I'm a chair, or any of the groups that we've had about women in the justice system.'

Jess Philipps, politician, 2016

• • • • • •

In 2015, a high-profile storyline on the long-running radio series *The Archers* (1951–) that charted the abuse of Helen Titchener (Louiza Patikas) at the hands of her husband Rob (Timothy Watson) came to its climax.

The storyline, which had been developing over two-and-a-half years, showed Rob's increasing coercive control over Helen, focusing primarily on his attempts to undermine her personality, rather than on acts of violence. The storyline received praise, in particular from charities such as Refuge and Women's Aid.

Jess Phillips MP, who served as shadow minister for domestic violence and safeguarding from 2020 to 2023, and minister for safeguarding and violence against women and girls since July 2024, organised a meeting between peers and MPs in the light of the story on *The Archers*. The captive audience was addressed by the head of Women's Aid, telling them what legislators needed to be doing to protect victims of domestic abuse.

The storyline certainly brought the topic to prominence – but the presence of women in Parliament to organise and attend the meeting is perhaps the more important part. As female parliamentarians say again and again, we need to be there to affect what's debated.

14 NOVEMBER

A BIT OF PEACE

'I have a really ancient phone. I spend a lot of time on my laptop and when I go out during the day it means I don't have to deal with emails and everyone knows that. So I just get texts and calls on my phone and it means that I have a bit of peace.'

Kate Bush, singer-songwriter, 2022

• • • • • •

In a world of instant communication and hyper-connectivity, Kate Bush strikes out on a typically independent path. No smartphone – no notifications or tweets or likes or mentions, just texts and calls.

Industry figures suggest that smartphone penetration stands at around 97 per cent of the adult population in the UK (the percentage is slightly lower for the over-50s). In less than two decades they have become ubiquitous – more like infrastructure than a luxury. It can be difficult, sometimes, to remember life without them.

How easy would it be to place boundaries upon our online lives? How quickly would we adjust, without the constant churn of social media? Would it really matter, if that email went unanswered for a few more hours?

Would we find the disconnection too difficult? Or would it make a measurable difference to our lives, if we had a bit more peace?

15 NOVEMBER

GENDER WARS

'I need to state here that I do not believe those theories that would set out to say that trans women are actually men and are not real women. I do not subscribe to that view and neither do many radical feminists. [Trans-exclusionary radical feminists] have an analysis of power and think that if you have enjoyed a certain amount of power for some time of your life that has a bearing ... As a radical feminist I think that a world that isn't scarred by compulsory heterosexuality and the narrow and limiting binary gender system would be better for all of us ... We share common ground and shared enemies, which is the limiting and repressive binary Western gender system.'

Finn Mackay, sociologist and radical feminist, 2014

• • • • • •

Over the past decade, British feminism has become increasingly divided over the topic of gender identity, with gender self-identification and the presence of trans women in women's sports becoming particular flashpoints.

Finn Mackay (b. 1976/7) is a sociologist and radical feminist with over 20 years' experience of feminist activism. As a teenager, Mackay lived in a women's peace camp; in 2004, they founded the London Feminist Network and revived the London 'Reclaim the Night' march. Mackay's professional background is in youth work; they have implemented award-winning anti-bullying and domestic violence prevention education schemes for a London LEA.

Trans-exclusionary radical feminism emerged from discussion in women's groups and consciousness-raising groups during the 1970s as to what constituted a woman. The classic expression of this strand of feminism is Janice Raymond's book *The Transsexual Empire* (1979). Central to this is the argument that growing up and being socialised as a male confers upon trans women a degree of power and privilege that is not available to girls and women. Raymond advocated 'morally mandating [transsexualism] out of existence'.

Not all radical feminists share this position – Mackay included. Women have different levels of power, and may benefit from racial privilege, heterosexual privilege or age privilege. All of these have a bearing upon different women's lives.

16 NOVEMBER

TRANS AWARENESS WEEK

'It is all very well and good having these discussions, and it's right that we do so, but the reality is that there are kids today that would be too scared this morning to get on the bus to school. There will be kids today who are going to be too scared to go home because their families are their biggest source of hostility.'

Paris Lees, author, journalist, presenter and campaigner, 2014

• • • • • •

Transgender Awareness Week aims to raise awareness about the issues that transgender people face associated with transition and their identity. It is held in the week leading up to the Transgender Day of Remembrance (20 November), a memorial day for those murdered or harmed as a result of transphobic violence.

Statistics from the 2021 census in England and Wales showed that 0.54 per cent of the population identified as trans, with the proportion decreasing by age group. This is roughly 264,000 people. Statistics published by the Home Office on hate crimes reported to the police in the year ending March 2023 indicated that transgender hate crimes increased by 11 per cent. This may be attributable to an increase in such offences, or to police awareness in identifying and recording these crimes.

On 11 February 2023, Brianna Ghey, a 16-year-old transgender girl, was tragically murdered by two 15-year-olds who had attended the same school as her. The judge, handing down the sentences, noted that while sadism was the primary motivation, transgender hate was a secondary motivation on the part of one of the killers.

Here, and in her memoir *What It Feels Like For a Girl* (2021), Paris Lees reminds us that beyond the debates are the lives of real people.

17 NOVEMBER

SORRY, MATE, NOT ON

'Women are always being told to shut up and take the abuse because otherwise you'd make it worse. We've been told that for millennia. It's about time to say, "Sorry, mate, not on."'

Mary Beard, classicist, journalist, broadcaster and public intellectual, 2013

· · · · · ·

In January 2013, after appearing on *Question Time*, academic Mary Beard found herself subjected to a veritable torrent of online abuse, an experience which she likened to a punch in the gut.

Beard is of the opinion that we need the same rules for online interactions as we have for face-to-face conversations, and that we should strive for normal manners and courtesy. After being abused by a 21-year-old student, Beard called him out (he immediately apologised) and subsequently met him for a drink in Cambridge (he apologised again).

We all have moments of intemperance – but online these moments remain for anyone to see. The student who abused Beard found a job with the support of a letter of encouragement from her. And while it is tempting to blame this on social media, Beard has been regularly written about by journalists in print media in language similar to the online insults she has received, denigrating her appearance rather than engaging in her arguments.

The new misogyny looks remarkably like the old misogyny.

18 NOVEMBER

HOW LONG HAVE WE GOT?

'I thought [it] was too bizarre, eccentric and risky for me to write . . . By the time it was published, reality had caught up with it enough so that nobody thought it was too bizarre, too eccentric and too risky. Instead they said things like, "How long have we got before this happens?"'

Margaret Atwood, novelist, poet and critic, 1986

• • • • • •

Margeret Atwood's dystopian novel *The Handmaid's Tale* (1985) depicts a future United States – now renamed 'The Republic of Gilead' – in which an evangelical Christian coup has taken place. Women's rights to self-determination have been removed, and unmarried fertile women are given the role of 'Handmaids', commodities to produce children for the households to which they are assigned.

The book won multiple awards, both mainstream and genre. A sequel, *The Testaments*, was published in 2019, and was the co-winner of that year's Booker Prize (with *Girl, Woman, Other* by Bernardine Evaristo). A hugely popular television series based on the book began streaming in 2016, bringing *The Handmaid's Tale* to a new audience – and inspiring demonstrations against the Trump administration in which protestors dressed in the distinctive red gown and white bonnet of the Handmaids.

With the launch of the television series, many insightful criticisms pointed out that the world of the book was not the future for many American women, and that it depicts what might happen to white women if they experienced the conditions under which Black women historically lived in the 'land of the free'.

In 2016, a majority of white American women voted for Donald Trump. As the world of the book catches up with them, what solidarity will they choose to show? Will they make alliances with other women, or with the men of Gilead?

19 NOVEMBER

INTERNATIONAL MEN'S DAY

'About two-thirds of men tell us they want to spend more time with their children ... What keeps men away from the "fun stuff" ... is the number of hours they have to work to stay middle class, to bring in enough for the household. Caregiving is something men and boys need to do. We've got data from Norway ... that showed that when men's caregiving approximated women's, household violence went down.'

Gary Barker, author, researcher and campaigner, 2015

· · · · · ·

Gary Barker is CEO and president of Equimundo, a research body which works on projects aiming to bring about a gender-equitable world by focusing on work that promotes care, empathy and accountability among men and boys. Barker was also the author of UNICEF's first 'State of the World's Fathers' report, published in 2015, and followed by a second report in 2023.

Why has 'care' become so devalued in society? Why are tasks such as teaching, nursing, childcare and care for the elderly so comparatively unrewarded? Barker asks us to reflect upon what it would mean to put 'care' at the heart of policymaking, and how this might transform the lives of both men and women.

What social and economic structures would need to be created so that we could centre our lives around caring responsibilities? How might our living or urban spaces be rebuilt in order to facilitate access to childcare, or to support those who care for elderly or vulnerable family members? How would our jobs and working lives need to change?

What must be done to make care central to our lives, our economies, our world?

20 NOVEMBER

A VERY NARROW CONCEPT

'Men didn't take women seriously and they never thought women would mean [they had to change their behaviour]. And if you trace it through you get now: the hatred, the incels, all those things, because while being woman has become extraordinarily difficult . . . being a man is still a very narrow concept and we're paying the price of that.'

Rosie Boycott, journalist and editor, 2022

• • • • • •

Rosie Boycott's career in journalism – from working in countercultural publications in the late 1960s, to co-founding *Spare Rib*, to editing national newspapers – covers precisely the period in which second-wave feminism rises and peaks.

Reflecting, in 2022, on 50 years of the women's movement, Boycott identifies the backlash against feminism that has led to a new wave of misogyny in the twenty-first century, and correctly attributes its emergence to those men who are not prepared to make the changes necessary so that women's equality can flourish.

Boycott also identifies that – as the backlash against women took hold, what it meant to be a man continued to be subject to policing and regulation.

Those who enjoy the benefits of power will never willingly surrender that power, and part of that power lies in narrowly constraining what it means to be a man – and persuading men to blame those constrictions on the women around them.

21 NOVEMBER

ON TURNING NINETY

'Keeping having a go at everything. Keeping interested. It keeps you alert really . . . I was fit and well. I had my three daughters, grandchildren . . . Then I've lots of interests. I belong to the local amateur dramatic society. Had lots of nice parts acting. We've got a production next May. I play bridge – it's quite a good thing to do when you're on your own, you get around a lot. I want to keep fit, cookery classes. You've got to keep interested in everything.'

Honor Harlow, nonagenarian, 2016

* * * * * *

Nonagenarian Honor Harlow reveals the secret to living into her nineties. Good health is key; family connections are important to her, as are a wide circle of friends.

Most of all, she talks about keeping interested. Doing things. Going out and being with people. Learning new things. Neuroscience backs this up too – we know now that our brains retain their plasticity for much longer than was believed in the past.

Do we expect to live so long? The Office for National Statistics calculates that a woman aged 50 in 2024 can expect to live to 87, with a one in four chance of reaching 95, and a one in ten chance of reaching 99. Those aren't bad odds.

What kind of life do you lead now? What kind of life do you want to keep on living? How can you keep interested in everything?

22 NOVEMBER

OUTRIGHT HOSTILITY

'There was outright hostility, including from the Labour
benches, but there was my maternal anguish about
whether it was right to be in the House of Commons as
well as having young children . . . Sacksful of
mail telling me, "You're ruining your children, they're
all going to be truanting at school."'

Harriet Harman, politician, 2017

. . . . . .

Harriet Harman, Baroness Harman of Peckham entered Parliament in 1982, winning a by-election in Peckham, whereupon she quickly took on a number of shadow ministerial roles. After the election of Tony Blair in 1997, Harman was a key member of his Cabinet – Secretary of State for Social Security and the first ever Minister for Women. She initiated all-women shortlists in the Labour Party, which contributed to bringing the percentage of female Labour MPs up to 45 per cent, and oversaw the passing of the Equality Act in 2010.

In 2017, Harman became 'Mother of the House' (that is, the longest-serving female MP), a nickname given to her by Theresa May, which has now passed on to her successor, Diane Abbott. On her retirement from the Commons in 2024, Harman had been one of the longest-serving MPs in British history.

Harman was 32 years old – and pregnant – when she entered Parliament. At that time, 97 per cent of MPs were men, and the House of Commons was very much a boys' club. Harman endured casual abuse from across the chamber, and even her colleagues were not always supportive.

While the online abuse endured by contemporary female MPs is certainly different in scale, and perhaps in ferocity, the underlying cause is similar – hostility to women in power, and deep-seated misogyny that has still not yet been fully addressed within our culture.

23 NOVEMBER

WONDERFUL TO WATCH

'Seeing [her daughter, Sophie Ellis-Bextor] as a mother is an extraordinary and lovely thing. Watching her become a parent has been exceptional because I think she just gets it right. She has such energy for her children and such love for them and I can see that . . . they are all allowed to be themselves, so it's wonderful to watch.'

Janet Ellis, television presenter, actress and writer, 2016

• • • • • •

Janet Ellis is best known as a former presenter of *Blue Peter*. She is also the mother of three adult children, one of whom is singer-songwriter Sophie Ellis-Bextor.

At all stages of their children's lives, parents delight in seeing them develop, mature and become increasingly capable and confident. Watching them grow into the role of parent themselves is no different in this respect. Ellis speaks about the deep pleasure to be had in watching her own child parent, and her daughter's emphasis on giving her children what they each need.

We might parent differently from the ways that our children parent in turn, but this doesn't imply a rejection of us, or of the choices that we made when our children were small. Children have their own needs; parents must respond to the child that they have.

Grandparenting is the new pleasure of watching these new relationships emerge and thrive, of seeing your children grow even further as their own children grow.

24 NOVEMBER

I WASN'T ALLOWED THAT AS A KID

'It started at the get-go with chocolate advent calendars. I was never allowed a chocolate advent calendar when I was a kid.'

Sophie Ellis-Bextor, singer-songwriter, 2016

• • • • • •

Sophie Ellis-Bextor is the mother of five sons and the daughter of TV presenter Janet Ellis.

Ellis-Bextor observes what seems to be a chief pleasure of grand-parenting: getting to be the fun one, the source of limitless treats, while the parents have to remain authority figures. In her case, she observed that her own mother was happy to give the grandchildren treats that Ellis-Bextor was given as a child herself.

As well as the fun, a grandparent – or an older relative or friend – is someone who can provide an informed perspective when advice is needed; someone who knows where both the parents and the grand-children are coming from, who has experience that expands beyond them.

The other joy of grandparenting comes from being the ones who can provide a sense of continuity: someone in a position to pass on the family narratives; the one whose memories stretch back further – to grandparents of one's own, perhaps – connecting the family back in time.

25 NOVEMBER

SO MUCH RESPECT FOR WOMEN

'It's made me think about [motherhood] differently . . .
[I have] a newfound appreciation of how selfless it is,
and what it demands of you. Also, what really struck
me was the complex relationship they have with their
own bodies: they feel unrecognisable to themselves,
or unrecognisable to their partner. I have so
much respect for women.'

Jodie Comer, actress, 2024

• • • • • •

The End We Start From is a 2024 film based on the book of the same
title by Megan Hunter. The creative team behind the film was largely
female: the screenplay was written by Alice Birch, the director was
Mahalia Belo, and BAFTA-, Emmy- and Tony Award-winning actress
Jodie Comer was cast as the lead.

Film and novel follow the experiences of a woman who goes into
labour as London floods in the wake of severe and persistent storms. With
her newborn baby in her arms, the woman and her husband attempt to
survive in an apocalyptic Britain ravaged by climate change.

Comer, speaking about the role, has described how she came into
the film with no particular maternal instinct, and that playing the part
altered her understanding of motherhood. Her description of how
women's relationships with their bodies are profoundly changed by
pregnancy and early motherhood is deeply empathetic.

Good artists are able to access aspects of the human condition which
they themselves have not experienced, and to express that to their audience or readership. Comer's performance – and Hunter's book – asks
us to consider the experiences of those in the world who are right now
struggling to keep themselves and their children alive in impossible situations; to empathise, to sympathise and to be moved to action.

26 NOVEMBER

RESILIENCE

'There's no recipe for resilience. Life is a place where terrible things can happen to people that destroy them.'

Liz Lochhead, poet and playwright, 2016

• • • • • •

Resilience refers to our capacity to cope emotionally and mentally with crises, and our capacity to return to our pre-crisis mode rapidly.

In psychology, resilience theory is associated with the work of Emmy E. Werner (1929–2017), an American psychologist who conducted a ground-breaking longitudinal study of resilience. Werner followed the lives of nearly 700 children born on the Hawaiian island of Kauai across 40 years. The study examined some of the factors that prevented children from high-risk backgrounds from later experiencing difficulties with physical and mental health. Autonomy, self-determination and exposure to new experiences were key – but so were structures beyond the family, such as mentors or community support.

But these are not prescriptions and, as Liz Lochhead notes, there are experiences that can destroy even the most resilient among us. Sometimes reality is too much to bear.

What have we survived that, on reflection, amazes us?

27 NOVEMBER

POLITICAL AWAKENING

'I was my father's daughter . . . I followed in his footsteps,
listened to his songs, to what he had to say
. . . I was made in 1926, when I saw the suffering
imposed on people who had been my chums at school
. . . What was done to the miners in 1926 shaped
the whole of my future life.'

Jennie Lee, politician, 1980

. . . . . .

Jennie Lee, Baroness Lee of Asheridge first entered the House of Commons in 1929, when the number of women MPs was in single figures. Returned to Parliament in 1945, she played a significant part in Harold Wilson's first administration (1964–70), where, as Minister for the Arts, she was instrumental in the foundation of the Open University.

Her husband was Aneurin Bevan, who led the creation of the National Health Service in Attlee's post-war administration.

Lee's political memories stretched back to the 1920s, and, in particular, the Miners' Strike of 1926, a critical moment in her political awakening.

By the end of her life, Lee had lived through the arrival of a woman prime minister and another bitter Miners' Strike (1984–5), which, in turn, shaped the social contours of Britain for decades to come.

What are the political events that have shaped our own consciousness of the world? How do they impact the choices that we make, when we come to vote? What might we learn of the motivations of others, if we knew more about the events that had an impact on them?

28 NOVEMBER

MORAL STRENGTH AND RATTLESNAKES

'I didn't mind the election at all ... But to walk up the House of Commons between Arthur Balfour and Lloyd George ... both of them ... would rather have had a rattlesnake in the House than me ... Sometimes I would sit five hours in my seat in that House rather than walk down. What really kept me going was I was an ardent feminist. I always knew women had ... more moral strength.'

Nancy Astor, politician, 1956

• • • • • •

On 28 November 1919, a by-election was held in Plymouth Sutton after the previous MP, Waldorf Astor, entered the House of Lords following the death of his father. The Conservative candidate selected was his wife, Nancy, Lady Astor (1879–1964). Nancy Astor won the election, making her the first woman to take her seat in the House of Commons. She represented Plymouth Sutton until 1945.

In an interview conducted in 1956, Nancy Astor recalled that while she had thrived upon the cut and thrust of election campaigning, entering the House of Commons as the only woman was another matter. Walking between two former prime ministers, Arthur Balfour and David Lloyd George (both equivocal supporters of women's suffrage at best), Astor vividly described her sense of isolation. It was almost two more years before another woman was elected to the House of Commons.

Astor's experiences speak to all women who have been first through the door – the hostility they face, and the endurance it takes to remain in the place that they have earned.

29 NOVEMBER

CLOSE TO PERFECT

'Obviously nobody's perfect. I do think [Michelle Obama] is very close to perfect! [And] for many Black women it means something, because we know many Michelle Obamas but we think that we have not had many opportunities to show the world those Michelle Obamas.'

Chimamanda Ngozi Adichie, writer, 2016

• • • • • •

Chimamanda Ngozi Adichie's (b. 1977) body of work draws on her experiences of growing up in the aftermath of the Biafran War in postcolonial Nigeria. Here she speaks of the significance of Michelle Obama for Black women.

Michelle LaVaughn Robinson Obama (b. 1964) — attorney, author and First Lady of the United States from 2009 to 2017, the first African-American woman to serve in that role.

In an article published in the *Washington Post* in 2016, journalist Peter Slevin described her consistent agenda during her time in the White House as being against the 'stacked deck'; deeply concerned with the enduring inequalities of race, class and gender in American society.

To call her iconic would be an understatement.

30 NOVEMBER

MIGHT-HAVE-BEENS

'Somehow [I] got it in my head I was going to preside
over the next leader being elected and I was bringing
forward the next lot of people. I think I should have done.'

Harriet Harman, politician, 2017

• • • • • •

After Labour's defeat in the general election of 2010, Gordon Brown
stood down as party leader. The deputy leader, Harriet Harman, automatically became 'acting leader' of the Labour Party and Leader of
the Opposition. In 2015, after another election defeat, Ed Miliband
resigned as Labour leader, and Harman held the post of acting leader
for a second time.

Harman was not the first woman to hold the post of acting leader
of the Labour Party. Margaret Beckett (b. 1943) held the position after
the sudden and tragic death of John Smith in 1994. Beckett went on
to run for leader, but came last. Harman, however, ruled herself out
of the leadership contest, a decision that she later came to regret, and
one that was surprising from a voice consistently raised in favour of
affirmative action within both party and country.

There are many missed turns in British political life: Harriet Harman's leadership; 'chaos with Ed Miliband'; and, most tragically, the
premiership of John Smith. As yet, no woman has been elected leader
of the Labour Party, and there has not been a female Labour prime
minister.

DECEMBER

1 DECEMBER

THE PROOF OF THE PUDDING

'My mother was a good home cook ... she was a
very academic person. But always we had a good lunch,
meals. In winter she'd do casseroles. Now if people say
today, "I can't do a casserole, I'm a working woman!",
remember that today most of us have refrigerators,
most have freezers. Why can't they? Why can't they do
like Mother did? Do most of it tonight ... If you work out
things properly, you can deal with them.'

Marguerite Patten, home economist, 2013

. . . . . .

As the festive season approaches, and with it the likelihood of social
and family gatherings that require planning, the stress of food preparation and catering can become a burden.

Marguerite Patten was among the first of what we might now call
'celebrity chefs'. An author and broadcaster, she was a familiar voice on
the radio (including *Woman's Hour*) and on television from as early as the
1950s. During the Second World War, she worked for the Ministry of
Food, producing recipes from rationed food and, after the war, became
something of an evangelist for the pressure cooker.

While the world in which Patten lived is gone, and most women are
no longer stay-at-home housewives, her advice is brisk and practical,
and even, in its own way, encouraging. Whatever the challenge – you
can meet it.

2 DECEMBER

EVERYTHING BUT THE KITCHEN SINK

'I don't think [men] give 50 per cent. But the fact that they give anything is remarkable compared to the way they used to be.'

Marilyn French, feminist and writer, 2006

• • • • • •

In comedian Bridget Christie's sitcom *The Change* (2023), the lead character, Linda (a middle-aged mother of two teenaged children), reveals that for the past 20 years she has kept a ledger in which she has documented the time she has spent on household tasks. She decides to claim back some of that time.

The Wages for Housework campaign began in the early 1970s and was led by a group of Italian feminists. It was grounded on an analysis of women's 'reproductive labour', the unpaid labour that happens in the home that underpins the economic structure of capitalist society. Work outside of the home, the campaigners argued, is entirely dependent on labour within the home: the people who go out to work need their food to be cooked, their home to be kept in order. But this work – housework, which is historically women's work – goes entirely unremunerated.

Contemporary capitalism depends on the hidden and unpaid work of many women. How might this work be rewarded? In the past, schemes such as family allowance or child benefit were paid directly to mothers; a universal basic income might be another solution.

Men have come a long way in terms of participating in childcare and household work. But even if, as Marilyn French says, the change is in itself remarkable, are we yet at the stage where the majority of men take on household responsibilities as a given?

What would the ledgers show? What would happen if the unpaid labour that goes on around us was withdrawn?

3 DECEMBER

AN UNSUITABLE JOB FOR A WOMAN

'If you advertised the role of parent to a newborn it would say twenty-hour-day shifts, seven days a week ... That job would be illegal. And yet we expect people to do it largely unpaid.'

Nell Frizzell, writer and journalist, 2023

• • • • • •

More than 50 years on from the start of the Wages for Housework campaign, Nell Frizzell points out the huge amount of intensive and varied labour involved in one aspect of domestic life – the care of newborns.

Frizzell's description of the kinds of tasks that the parent of a newborn might expect to carry out is mind-blowing, when framed in terms that might be used in the workplace. There's extensive administration (filling in forms, registering births). There's regular meetings with outside bodies (doctors, midwives, wellness checks, vaccinations). There's teaching the child to move and speak – the domain of occupational and speech therapists. There's research assistant – keeping up with the latest in child development or sleep studies. And that's not to mention the physical labour of caring for a newborn, all of which is done while physically vulnerable, potentially recovering from major surgery, sleep-deprived and under stress.

Reframing care work in these terms shows how much labour underpins the domestic sphere – how little it is remunerated, and how little it is valued. It's a principle that applies not only for caring for newborn children, but for all the care work carried out with limited recognition or remuneration.

4 DECEMBER

WOMEN'S WORK?

'Children are aware of gender by the time they're about eighteen months to two [and] can label things in the house as being for men or for women. [T]hey won't do it according to society's generalisations, they'll do it according to what goes on in their household. So if they've got a dad who does all the ironing . . . then the ironing board and the iron will be men's stuff.'

Carrie Paechter, sociologist and professor, 2012

• • • • • •

Gone are the days when children's picture books would show preschoolers at home with mother, cooking and baking and washing, while father was out all day at work. Yet the stereotypes prove enduring.

Carrie Paechter's work focuses on children and gender, particularly how children and young people themselves understand gender. Research shows that children become aware of gender at a very young age – and quickly learn to generalise about categories and become set in their ideas of what counts as masculine and what counts as feminine.

But the picture is more complex, Paechter suggests: if a child repeatedly sees a parent doing work not commonly associated with their gender, the child will associate that work with that gender. A dad ironing regularly means ironing is seen as men's work. A woman mending the taps means plumbing becomes women's work.

Our tendency to categorise begins – and solidifies – at a very young age. But there is far less inherent in those categories than those old picture books would have it.

5 DECEMBER

GODDESS GOODENOUGH

'People have assumed that I'm writing about the joys of housework and how domestic life is the only true and proper way for a woman to achieve anything worthwhile ... What I'm saying is women are interested in the world at large, we operate in the world at large, but we also have domestic sides and we enjoy that too. And the idea is not that you do everything brilliantly but you are allowed to do a bit of everything.'

Nigella Lawson, food writer and television cook, 2000

• • • • • •

What Delia Smith's cookery books and television shows were to the 1970s and 1980s, Nigella Lawson's (b. 1960) were to the late 1990s and 2000s.

Lawson's first cookery book, *How to Eat* (1998), gave practical tips; the second, *How to Be a Domestic Goddess* (2000), focused on baking. Her television show *Nigella Bites*, which ran from 1999 to 2001, filmed inside Lawson's west London home, was simultaneously aspirational and intimate, with tongue-in-cheek shots of Lawson padding downstairs at night in her pyjamas, to open the fridge and feast on leftovers.

The title 'domestic goddess' earned criticism from some quarters as imposing, yet again, impossible standards on working women. Lawson, however, insisted that the title was playful and ironic, and by no means intended to be prescriptive. We don't have to be perfect. We just have to give things a try.

Ideally the cakes we bake will be edible, at least. Still, sometimes the cake's worth baking for its own sake.

6 DECEMBER

WHAT AM I FOR?

'More and more we are seeing younger men doing the
cooking, looking after the kids, changing their nappies,
accepting all the responsibilities, the unattractive
responsibilities, of raising children as well as the
lovely ones ... I think it's the only way to save
the desperate incoherence of young men who
don't know what they're for.'

Shirley Williams, politician and academic, 2004

· · · · · ·

Shirley Williams, Baroness Williams of Crosby was a Labour and later
SDP and Liberal politician. At the centre of the Labour Party, Williams
held ministerial posts at the Department for Education and the Home
Office during Harold Wilson's first administration; in 1976, she became
Secretary of State for Education and Science.

Williams lost her seat in the 1979 election which put Margaret
Thatcher into power; becoming concerned with the leftward move in
the Labour Party, she became part of the 'Gang of Four', the breakaway
group which formed the centre-left Social Democratic Party in 1981.
She became the first SDP MP, winning a by-election in Crosby in 1981.

When the SDP merged with the Liberal Party in 1987 to form
the Liberal Democrats, Williams supported the merger, eventually
entering the House of Lords as a Liberal Democrat peer. Energetic,
articulate and hard-working, Williams was a regular panellist on political programmes such as *Question Time*.

Williams's words on how a busy household manages reminds us
not only that there's always plenty of work to go round, but that isolation and desperation arise from a sense of disconnection.

7 DECEMBER

PERSEVERANCE

'I had boxes of rejections in the basement; boxes.
I understood inside myself that I could do this if
I just kept trying. Stubborn. Obsessive!'

Elizabeth Strout, writer, 2019

• • • • • •

From a very early age, writer Elizabeth Strout (b. 1956) was scribbling in notebooks, and, at the age of 16, began sending out short stories to magazines. Her first short story was published when she was 26. She acquired degrees in English, law and gerontology (the science of ageing).

Strout's first novel, *Amy and Isabelle* (1998), was published when she was in her early forties. It became a bestseller, and was adapted into a film. Major success came with her third novel, *Olive Kitteridge* (2008), which won the Pulitzer Prize for Fiction in 2009. *My Name is Lucy Barton* (2016) concerned the dysfunctional childhood and family of the titular character, and the making of her as a writer. The book was a *New York Times* bestseller, and has been followed by three sequels.

Henry Oliver, in his book *Second Act: What Late Bloomers Can Tell You About Success and Reinventing Your Life* (2024), examines several examples of long and meandering apprenticeships undertaken before huge success. Strout, in many ways, fits the bill: her various degrees, but always, beneath, the persistent chipping away at what she knew was her life's work.

Success is not solely the property of the young, and stubborn persistence may, in the end, pay off.

8 DECEMBER

CONTINUE TO GROW

'There is a myth that people reach a certain age and
they just stop. It's just not true . . . I think that
even if you have been growing even slowly then
you continue to grow until your last breath.'

Elizabeth Strout, writer, 2019

• • • • • •

Perhaps you can still remember a time in life when you were able
to absorb huge amounts of information, concentrate for extended
periods, and work steadily and productively into the early hours of the
morning. Perhaps you're now wondering where that capacity has gone.

Or perhaps you've noticed that you work more efficiently now –
that experience counts for a great deal when you're presented with a
new problem. That you've seen something similar before, and you can
apply this knowledge with immediate effect.

Neuroplasticity – or brain plasticity – is the ability of the neural
networks in the brain to change, grow and reorganise. We can see this
in small children – learning to speak and talk and walk, soaking up
information like sponges – and it was long thought that the adult brain
lost this capacity.

But research in the latter half of the twentieth century increasingly
showed that the adult brain retains more plasticity than previously
realised. Marian Diamond (1926–2017), a neuroscientist and professor at Berkeley, was a pioneer in this field, producing the first scientific
evidence of neuroplasticity.

Our brains thrive on enrichment and experience. Maybe it's time
to learn that new language after all.

9 DECEMBER

ANOTHER SPRING

'All we wanted was another spring. I really did think we'd have one. But time just ran out.'

Olivia Harrison, author and film producer, 2022

• • • • • •

Olivia Harrison (b. 1948) was working in the record industry when, in 1974, she met Beatle George Harrison. Harrison, impressed by her work, hired her to work for his company, and the pair were soon romantically involved.

Following Harrison's divorce from his first wife, Pattie Boyd, he and Olivia married, in 1978, shortly after the birth of their only child, a son, Dhani. In 1997, Harrison was diagnosed with, and successfully treated for, cancer. However, in 1999, the Harrisons were subjected to a terrifying break-in and knife attack at home, in which Harrison was stabbed multiple times, puncturing a lung. Olivia incapacitated the intruder.

Harrison's cancer returned, this time in his lungs, and, subsequently, in the form of a brain tumour. He died in 2001, aged 58. Olivia was 53 when she was widowed.

The loss of one's life partner is a terrible blow, a 'wound that will never heal', in Edna St. Vincent Millay's words. Life after death is possible. It can't be the same – but it is possible.

10 DECEMBER

I'VE GOT A LITTLE LIST

'I love a list ... They're reassuring, they're soothing, they can have this very therapeutic sense – catharsis, almost – and it's a wonderful record for our days ... But there can also be this other side to a list where when we don't get through it, when we don't tick off every item, there can be this deflating sense that can come at the end of the day, almost as if the day's a failure, because we didn't finish our to-do list ... It's about having the list, but holding it lightly.'

Madeleine Dore, writer and journalist, 2024

. . . . . .

Are you anxious about the holidays approaching? Are you trying to wrap up work while thinking about presents, decorations, possibly travel? Have you made a list yet – or perhaps several? Do you tick anything off, or do you transfer tasks from list to list?

Madeleine Dore spent several years exploring how people cope with everyday life, and experimenting with various techniques and routines to examine their effects on her mindset and her productivity. Her book *I Didn't Do the Thing Today: On Letting Go of Productivity Guilt* (2022) aims to reframe conversations about productivity and consider ways to cultivate genuine creativity.

List-making can be calming, helping us to prioritise, making huge tasks seem more concrete and manageable. But do we become too despondent when we fall behind. How – in Dore's terms – can we learn to hold the to-do list lightly, or even let it go?

11 DECEMBER

BLESSED ARE THE CHEESEMAKERS

'Either get one fabulous cheese (preferably that's local) or if you're going to do a really spectacular cheese board then why don't you choose one for each of the main categories: fresh cheeses; soft white like Camembert; semi-soft, which ranges from Edams to the washed rind stinkies ... Then we have hard cheeses, and blue. In the best cheese board, you'd have one from each of those categories, but otherwise maybe three cheeses from three different categories.'

Juliet Harbutt, cheese connoisseur, 2012

• • • • • •

Juliet Harbutt (b. 1951) is one of the world's foremost authorities on all things cheese. Born in New Zealand, she abandoned a promising career as a geologist to open a deli in Wellington. But Europe – and cheese – beckoned, and she relocated to London in the mid-1980s, where she opened Jeroboams, a cheese and wine shop which quickly established itself as a supplier for the Ritz, Claridge's and Harrods.

Her curiosity and enthusiasm for cheese took her around Europe and, in 1992, she was made a member of the Confrérie des Chevaliers du Taste-Fromage de France. Her book *World Cheese Book* won Best Food Book at the Guild of Food Writers awards in 2010.

Harbutt's advice on how to create a small but perfectly formed cheese board should therefore not be ignored. And don't forget the accompaniments: crackers, dried fruit such as apples and pears; crunchable crackers (but not too flavoured); and rustic bread with a crunchy crust. Enjoy!

12 DECEMBER

DEATH IS GOOD FOR THE GARDEN

'Looking back on these 20 years, I thought of
what I've done in the garden ... If everyone could
get out in nature every single day and have a moment
on their own being overwhelmed by nature,
we'd all be much healthier.'

Olivia Harrison, author and film producer, 2022

• • • • • •

Twenty years after the death of her husband, George Harrison, his widow Olivia released a book of poetry, *Came the Lightening: Twenty Poems for George*. One of the poems, titled 'Death is Good for the Garden', was written after Harrison saw all the work she had done in the garden since her husband's death.

Being in and around nature is profoundly beneficial and, for the grieving, can have some powerful effects. Grounding us in the present moment, we might sidestep, however briefly, our turbulent thoughts and emotions, and forget for a while our sense of loss. We can find ourselves reflecting differently upon life-cycles, and death, decay and regeneration. Through gardening, we might find ourselves nurturing new life and growth.

We might find some peace.

13 DECEMBER

NO WRONG FEELINGS

'Whatever feelings you have when somebody dies are not good or bad, they just are. You can't have the correct or the incorrect feeling. Our feelings are a little like the dashboard on a car; they are there to inform you where you're at, so you know to take great care of yourself or something else.'

Philippa Perry, psychotherapist and author, 2017

• • • • • •

Since 2021, Philippa Perry (b. 1957) has been the agony aunt for *The Observer*. Perry's warm persona, grounded advice and accessible style have made her books on psychotherapy and interpersonal relationships bestsellers. She is the author of *The Book You Wish Your Parents Had Read (and Your Children Will Be Glad That You Did)* (2019).

Grief can throw up many overwhelming emotions, and when your relationship with the deceased has been problematic, then these difficulties are compounded. We may feel guilty about having parted on bad terms; we may feel relieved, if a loved one has been ill and their quality of life had diminished; we may feel cheated of a resolution to our relationship with them.

Perry astutely advises that we think about these emotions in neutral terms. There are no rights and wrongs. It's advice that works beyond bereavement too: emotions as warning signs, signals from yourself to yourself, that it's time to pay attention, step back and work out what's going on.

14 DECEMBER

FIRST AMONG EQUALS

'[Constance Markievicz] was sentenced to death, but her sentence was commuted on the basis of her sex which she found quite insulting because she'd fought as a comrade with these men in the [Easter] Rising. She's imprisoned near them in Kilmainham Jail and she can hear her friends being executed each morning . . . She was very proud to be selected as a candidate but she felt that it was all an *Alice in Wonderland* experience.'

Lauren Arrington, historian and biographer of Constance Markievicz, 2013

· · · · · ·

The UK general election of 14 December 1918 was the first in which women over the age of 30 were able to vote. It was also the first election in which women were able to stand for Parliament.

Two weeks after the election, the results of the Dublin St Patrick constituency were called. The Sinn Féin candidate, Countess Constance Markievicz (1868–1927), became the first woman elected to Parliament although, since Sinn Féin abstained from Westminster, she did not take her seat. Markievicz was in Holloway Prison at the time, jailed for her part in the 1916 Easter Rising.

Born Constance Gore-Booth into an aristocratic Anglo-Irish family, Markievicz started out wanting to be an artist – and became a politician, suffragist, socialist, revolutionary, the first woman elected to Westminster and the second woman Cabinet minister in Europe.

If pressed, most would name Nancy Astor as the first woman MP. Mainstream histories have a way of eliding the radical figures. But if we step beyond the familiar, however, we can discover the lives of singularly vivid and courageous women.

15 DECEMBER

SHOULDERS OF GIANTS

'Nobody was more distressed than I was that I should have been the first ... I'm a proud Virginian, and I realised no matter how long an Englishwoman lived in Virginia, I wouldn't want her the first in the legislature. I remember telling Mrs Fawcett, that I apologised to [the suffragists] for being there.'

Nancy Astor, politician, 1956

• • • • • •

When Nancy Astor entered the House of Commons in 1919, she was the first women to take her seat in Parliament (and the second to be elected). An American, married to a British peer, Astor had no real connection with the women's suffrage movement in her adopted home and, as a Conservative, her politics were distant from those of the leaders of that movement, such as Millicent Fawcett and the Pankhursts.

Yet after her election, Astor was met at Paddington station by a crowd of suffragettes, and she spoke of her own sense of the injustice that she should be the first woman to take her seat rather than someone from the suffrage movement.

Astor was not self-effacing or unduly modest. But her acknowledgement of the years of hard work by the many women of the suffrage movement to bring about the conditions that allowed her to enter Parliament speaks to the fact that social change is the work of many, and solidarity can exist across political differences.

As the assassinated MP Jo Cox said in her maiden speech almost a century later: 'we are far more united and have far more in common with each other than things that divide us.'

16 DECEMBER

LIVING ROOMS

'I think a room should reflect the owner's way of living and look practical and *used*. Heaven knows, mine does.'

Joyce Grenfell, actress and entertainer, 1946

● ● ● ● ● ●

Joyce Grenfell (1910–79) was a fixture of post-war British light comedy films, with memorable appearance in *The Happiest Days of Your Life* (1950) and the *St Trinian's* films (from 1954 onwards).

But it was as a comic monologuist that she became best known, particularly her 'Nursery School' routines, in which Grenfell portrayed a benign if somewhat beleaguered teacher corralling her crew of small children (with the catchphrase: 'George? Don't do that'). Her West End show lasted a year, and sold out on its run on Broadway.

Grenfell wrote over a hundred comic parts for herself, mostly women of all classes in domestic situations; sharply observed slices of daily life, they were mischievous but never malicious. Her material received a revival in the 2000s when comedian and actress Maureen Lipman toured her show based on Grenfell's monologues, *Re:Joyce*.

We might think we want to live in a house lifted straight from a store, stylish and clutter-free, but would it reflect who we are? Look around the rooms you inhabit. What makes you smile? What do you love? How do you make it your own? What goes with you, wherever you go?

17 DECEMBER

WHERE THE HEART IS

'There are days when I want to be a housewife doing purely domestic jobs. I can't tell you how much I long sometimes just to have a morning at home to practise my cooking. At the moment I am simply dying to make a cake.'

Edith Evans, actress, 1949

• • • • • •

Dame Edith Evans (1888–1976) was one of the pre-eminent actresses of her generation. Primarily performing on stage, she rose to prominence in the 1920s; joining the Old Vic Theatre in 1925–6, she took on many of the best female parts in Shakespeare, including Cleopatra, Beatrice and Portia.

She is perhaps now most immediately remembered for her performance as Lady Bracknell in the 1952 film adaptation of Oscar Wilde's *The Importance of Being Earnest.* Her delivery of the line '*A handbag?*' is the definite word on the subject. Married to a man who had no connection to the theatre, home seems to have been a refuge for her, away from the gossip and intrigue that her colleagues enjoyed.

Lockdown and working from home have blurred the boundaries between our professional lives and our home lives more than ever before. Sometimes this can work in our favour – who wants a long commute? – but it can bring its own problems, preventing us from switching off, making us feel that we're always on call.

Remember to close the laptop, put the phone on silent – and take some time back in your domestic, private space.

18 DECEMBER

CLUBBING

'It's a very informal network of gals who like to get
together over a well-crafted drink . . . The idea is
that women can get together in a very casual way, not
having to go down the *Sex and the City* route of sitting
in cocktail bars in our high heels and our finery – you
could literally show up in your pyjamas and sit and have
a drink together, and talk about whatever we feel like.'

Signe Johansen, author, 2019

• • • • • •

The gentlemen's club: it conjures up images of wood-panelled walls, deep comfortable armchairs, and affairs of state being sensibly settled over cigars and brandy.

They've played an unobtrusive but not-negligible part in British life. When the all-male membership of the Garrick Club was revealed in 2024, it turned out to include the head of the civil service and MI6 (both of whom quit), as well as judges, MPs, peers, actors, journalists, rock stars . . . but no women. (The club voted to allow female members in 2024, with Judi Dench and Siân Phillips becoming the first women to join.)

Signe Johansen (b. 1980) is best known as the author of *How to Hygge* (2016), which introduced the Scandinavian concept of 'hygge' – cosiness, comfort and conviviality. She is the founder of 'Spirited Women', a social group for women to enjoy whisky and other spirits. And, we hope, sensibly settle affairs of state.

19 DECEMBER

CHAMPAGNE WIDOWS

'At the time, especially in the nineteenth century,
you didn't find many women, widows or not, running
businesses, so they were formidable businesswomen.
They were also very much instrumental in exporting
champagne. When we go to Champagne and visit the
cellars, we see the names of the export markets that go
back to the beginning of the nineteenth century . . .
[The champagne widows gave the impetus]
to go towards international markets.'

Françoise Peretti, champagne expert, 2019

• • • • • •

Françoise Peretti (b. 1958) spent 30 years at the Champagne Bureau, the UK office of the Comité Champagne, a trade association which represents the grape growers and houses of Champagne, France. She retired from the post of the director of the bureau in 2022, upon which the role was taken up by another woman, Victoria Henson.

That the champagne industry is amenable to women at the top is no surprise when we look at the history of the trade. One of the best-selling brands, Veuve Clicquot (that's 'Widow Clicquot'), is named for Barbe-Nicole Ponsardin, the daughter of a wealthy textile merchant in Reims, who, in 1798, married François Clicquot, the son of another local textile merchant, Philippe Clicquot.

Philippe also sold wine, though it was not his main interest, and dismissed his son when François announced his intentions to expand that area of the business. But François had a secret weapon – Barbe-Nicole's grandmothers had been part of the wine industry. They set out to make the business a success – but in 1805, François died suddenly. Philippe was set to wind up their joint enterprise – but François's widow made him an offer he couldn't refuse. She offered her inheritance to keep the business going – if Philippe would continue to invest.

Widow Clicquot's innovations in the champagne industry ranged from techniques to remove yeast, to export deals that turned champagne into a global business. If you pop a cork during the festive season, remember the Champagne Widow.

20 DECEMBER

YOU'RE BACK

'I thought [Olive] had left . . . I was sitting in a cafe in Norway checking my email and she showed up. I saw her, absolutely vividly nosing her car into that marina. I saw her get out of the car and she now had a cane and I realised, "Oh my word, you're back."'

Elizabeth Strout, writer, 2019

• • • • • •

Already a critically acclaimed writer, Elizabeth Strout won the Pulitzer Prize for Fiction with her third novel, *Olive Kitteridge* (2008). A television adaptation, starring Frances McDormand as Olive, was made by HBO in 2014, and won multiple Emmy awards.

Olive Kitteridge is an unlikely heroine. A retired maths teacher, living in a small coastal town in Maine, she is cantankerous, often downright rude, but deeply perceptive and knowledgeable about her friends, family and neighbours. One is reminded of Miss Marple, with her infinite awareness of human nature, based on her careful observations of village life.

We do not often see elderly women as the protagonists of novels. Yet Olive was to return, in *Olive, Again* (2019). She ages, remarries, fails to make a connection with her estranged son, is widowed for a second time and suffers a heart attack.

Many of Strout's novels overlap, with characters shifting between them, appearing unexpectedly in the lives of others. The whole effect is to build up to a quiet but emphatic symphony, variations on the theme of how we are all interconnected.

Our lives are linked in ways that perhaps we don't fully understand until they near their end.

21 DECEMBER

A WOMAN OF A CERTAIN AGE

'If you're on a train and an inquisitive middle-aged woman starts talking to you, you don't immediately think, "She's trying to spy into my life! She's the enemy!" You just humour them. Nobody sees the threat of a woman once she gets to a certain age.'

Val McDermid, crime writer, 2021

. . . . . .

Jane Marple, Agatha Christie's elderly spinster detective, is the protagonist of 12 novels, and many short stories, spanning the whole of Christie's writing career. She first appeared in *The Murder at the Vicarage* (1930), and her last appearance was in the anthology *Miss Marple's Final Cases and Two Other Stories* (1979).

In 2021, an anthology of new stories about her was published, reflecting the enduring appeal of this unique character. Val McDermid contributed one of the stories.

On-screen interpretations of Miss Marple have ranged from Margaret Rutherford's energetic performance to Joan Hickson's demure, rather faded interpretation, to Julia McKenzie's brisk, retired headmistress. But the essence and appeal of Jane Marple lies in the discrepancy between her outward appearance – maiden aunt-ish; perhaps rather too nosy – and the reality of her intelligence, observational skills and shrewd insight into human nature.

Do we write off people past a certain age? Do we forget that life experience counts for something?

And, once we reach that certain age ourselves, are we frustrated at being passed over? Or can we take advantage of the anonymity – the cover that the stereotype lends to us?

22 DECEMBER

OH YES IT IS

'Pantomimes are so important for kids, because
it's often their first experience of theatre and live
performance . . . I got chosen [from the audience as a
child]. I walk down the dark stairs into the circle of light,
and I feel the light on my face, and the actors are this
close, and I can see their make-up running and their
laboured breath, and I go, what is this place? I don't
know what this is, but this is *home*.'

Meera Syal, actor, comedian and writer, 2023

· · · · · ·

Bad jokes, corny storylines, slapstick comedy – the Scrooges among us find it far too easy to sneer at pantomime. (Oh yes we do!)

But did you know about its roots in *commedia dell'arte* (oh no we didn't!)? Or its connection to Harlequin and Columbine (oh yes we did!)? Do you know how popular music hall used to be, before the advent of cinema, and how modern pantomime draws from that tradition too (oh no we didn't!)?

Panto's contribution to the local cultural ecosystem shouldn't be underestimated either (oh no it shouldn't!). They're so popular that the pantomime season can help keep many regional theatres afloat for the rest of the year (oh yes they do!).

And sometimes, a little girl in a provincial theatre, called up onto stage during a production of *Dick Whittington*, will step into the light and realise that this is the place she wants to be for the rest of her life.

(Oh yes she did!)

23 DECEMBER

COMFORT AND JOY

'A comfort food has to serve the function of making you feel better about yourself and also being an indulgence ... something you're not allowed a lot of the time, something that's a treat, and something that probably was used in childhood as a way of making you feel better ... And then, as you go into adulthood, lo and behold, it serves the same function.'

Jane Ogden, professor of health psychology, 2013

• • • • • •

It's a time of year when our relationship to food can become complicated, when we might overeat – and then feel various pangs of remorse. Food also brings back memories – of childhood meals, of the people who cooked for us who are no longer with us, whether friends, relatives or those who cared for us, or for whom we have cared.

Health psychology, as a field of research, studies exactly these complex psychological, social and cultural influences on our mental and physical health. Jane Ogden, an expert in the field, has specialised for many years in eating behaviour, and how our eating habits are formed.

Reflecting on comfort foods, Ogden draws our attention to its double function – how our chosen food makes us feel better, but how it's something that carries with it a sense of transgression. Her non-judgemental take reminds us that there is no harm in seeking comfort; as in many things, self-awareness of why we choose to behave the way we do is the key to wellbeing. And it may well be that if your body is telling you something, it's worth listening.

24 DECEMBER

POTTERING ABOUT

'We know about comfort eating, which is actually
a misnomer because it simply makes one feel more
miserable and desperate. But comfort cooking is a way
of pottering around in the kitchen making yourself feel
better; maybe a bit more grounded.'

Nigella Lawson, food writer and television chef, 2000

• • • • • •

Nigella Lawson makes a useful distinction between comfort eating (which may not always bring the comfort that we're looking for) and comfort cooking, which is a form of creative activity, aimed at making you feel more at ease in your surroundings, at creating a space which feels safe and warm.

There's a great deal to be said for pottering around the house. Whether it's taking the chance to do some baking, spending time in the garden, sorting through drawers and shelves, or tidying a cupboard – there's pleasure to be had in simply being at home.

Some people, it's said, even enjoy doing the ironing.

25 DECEMBER

MAKING MEMORIES

'I was a bit showy-offy ... We all went into the sea, it was freezing, got home, and I had a glass of champagne. I fell into a drunken stupor, and I woke up having not got the lobster out of the freezer. I'd bought lobsters! ... But I fixed it. I made Dairylea sandwiches, because that's all we had, but I cut them into Christmas shapes with the cookie cutters ... You'll do the perfect Christmas this year, and your kids and family will have forgotten it by January 3rd. Whereas if you mess it up and have to do my Dairylea sandwiches, they'll remember it forever.'

Nina Stibbe, writer, 2017

• • • • • •

The festive season can bring with it huge pressures that often fall on the shoulders of women: making arrangements to see family; preparing to have visitors; organising cards and presents and food; being responsible for the happiness of others. And sometimes – often – reality ends up falling short.

The writer Nina Stibbe (b. 1962) focuses in her books on the humour that lies in the imperfections of domestic life. Her skilful and witty observational style has earned her the Comedy Women in Print Prize (2020) and the enviable epithet 'the heir to Sue Townsend'. *An Almost Perfect Christmas* (2017) is collection of stories, essays and observations about the festive season.

Stibbe recalls a Christmas after her family had relocated to Cornwall, where the fatal combination of early exercise and morning champagne leads to a Christmas dinner more reminiscent of wartime rationing that the planned feast. That the family will remember this where they will have quickly forgotten the perfect day is of course self-deprecating, but remains true. The lobsters won't cook themselves, but perhaps they didn't need cooking after all.

26 DECEMBER

MAGIC MOMENTS

'The idea that there's something in the food that is magical or that will make you feel comforted ... is bizarre, because if you change the shape of that food – if you mashed it up or put it in a drink – urgh! So it can't be what's in it; it has to be the meaning of that food.'

Jane Ogden, professor of health psychology, 2013

• • • • • •

This time of year more than any other can bring home to us the ritual and symbolic nature of sharing food and drinks. We might be inviting others into our homes, or preparing food and drink for large numbers of people, or simply going out for drinks.

Jane Ogden, a professor of health psychology and expert in the psychology of eating, reflects how these meanings and symbols cannot be inherent in the food itself, but must result from the social and cultural meanings surrounding the activity of eating and drinking together.

What rituals surround the way we share food and drink? Are they grounded in joyfulness and celebration, or do they feel more like the dead weight of tradition? Are there rituals that we can keep, and others that are better discarded?

27 DECEMBER

A FINGER IN THE CHEESECAKE

'Putting a finger in a leftover cheesecake is a delight.
I'm just putting that one onto the table there.'

Helen Lederer, comedian, writer and actor, 2013

• • • • • •

At a time of year when overindulgence can lead to feelings of guilt, not to mention promises and plans for New Year austerity diets, it is refreshing to hear comedian, writer and actress Helen Lederer (b. 1954) cut to the chase.

Food can be for pleasure too; no strings attached. Get stuck in.

28 DECEMBER

AS FUNNY AS A ROOT CANAL

'I think [*Mrs. Brown's Boys*] is about as funny as a root canal job ... And yet it was shown twice on Christmas Day. Misogyny is pretty common, and old ladies do come in for casual abuse ... Sadism and British humour have always been intertwined.'

Germaine Greer, writer, academic and public intellectual, 2018

. . . . . .

Leaving aside the fact that *Mrs. Brown's Boys* (2011–) is an Irish (rather than British) comedy, there's no doubting its popularity in the UK – and Greer's point still stands. A strain of cruelty does run through the British sense of humour – and it's not always punching upwards. And when you're punching down, old women are an easy target.

In the hands of the right comedian, old ladies can be comedy gold. Caroline Aherne's character Mrs Merton, an elderly housewife who was the epitome of primness, nevertheless dealt blows to the celebrity guests on her chat show from which they often looked unlikely to recover.

And as anyone who has read Miss Marple knows: old ladies are not to be underestimated. They've seen it all before.

29 DECEMBER

THE COMMON HUMAN EXPERIENCE

'Everybody gets knocked down. You are not the only person with a loss or a disappointment. It is the common human experience. What matters is whether you get back up ... with energy and confidence, that you're going back to doing what it is you want to do in your life. Or do you feel so disappointed and so anxious and so bitter that it turns you in on yourself.'

Hillary Clinton, United States Senator, Secretary of State and First Lady, 2017

• • • • • •

The holiday period, and the run-up to New Year, can leave people exhausted, and – even in the midst of festivities – lonely and depressed. The short dark days (in the northern hemisphere, at least) can add further to this mood. Even more, the end of the year can bring about a sense of melancholy as we reflect upon what has gone or is missed, or upon the course that one's life has taken.

Hillary Clinton's loss of the US presidential election in 2016 was a knockback on an unimaginably public stage. The first woman to win the presidential nomination by a major US party, surely if anyone was going to make history, it was going to be her. And yet, despite winning the popular vote, the unthinkable happened.

How do we rebuild our lives after a devastating setback? How do we turn towards the future in the face of failure? Clinton reminds us that loss is the common human experience, and that it is possible to move ahead and discover, yet again, what to do with your life.

30 DECEMBER

GRASPING LIFE

'I really believe in continuing to take risks. I'm grasping life. I'm just saying this is fantastic. Have as many different experiences and adventures as I can, but I'm also quite conscious that I need to leave space in my mind to be creative and there are things that I want to do that need me to actually take a few days off.'

Clare Balding, broadcaster and author, 2014

• • • • • •

Clare Balding (b. 1971) is one of the most recognisable faces in British broadcasting. Born into a racing family, Balding studied English at Newnham College, Cambridge, before joining the BBC in the early 1990s. From presenting sports on radio, Balding progressed to television and has, to date, reported from eight consecutive Olympic Games.

Add to that journalism, writing and presenting documentaries on rambling, as well as writing children's books, and this builds up to an extremely busy life.

We are right to seize the opportunities that come our way, chances to enrich our lives and expand our horizons. Without taking these risks, we can contract and become limited. At the same time, moving constantly can act as its own defence mechanism, preventing us from stopping for a moment to take stock, to think about what it is we really want to do.

At the end of the year, we might find ourselves asking: What risks would I like to take with my life? What spaces do I need to open up to be able to regenerate?

31 DECEMBER

IN IT FOR LIFE

'We move forward in uneven waves. Women now, feminists now, understand that we're in it for life. This is not something we're doing for a year or two.'

Gloria Steinem, journalist and activist, 1977

• • • • • •

Gloria Steinem, across her long career, has seen the highs and lows of the women's movement in the United States, as exemplified by the shift from the landmark ruling of Roe vs. Wade in 1971, which protected women's constitutional right to abortion, to its repeal in 2022.

Beyond these high-profile rulings, feminists also react to other pushback against women's rights throughout the fabric of society. Struggles to pay for childcare. Enduring pay gaps. Lack of support for those caring for elderly and sick relatives. Growing misogyny in institutions and on social media.

The backlash in many spheres since the heyday of the second wave reminds us that the hard-won gains of the past can be easily lost, and that concerted effort on the part of those who stand for patriarchal structures can and will erode rights that have been taken for granted.

Feminism is the long revolution. It succeeds when feminists across all sections of society make alliances and coalitions, when they do not become complacent about the gains of the past, when they keep standing shoulder to shoulder – for as long as it takes.

ABOUT THE AUTHOR

Dr Una McCormack is a *New York Times* and *USA Today* bestselling writer who has written more than 20 novels based on TV shows such as *Star Trek*, *Doctor Who* and *Firefly*. She is on the editorial board of Gold SF, an imprint of Goldsmiths Press aimed at publishing new voices in intersectional feminist science fiction. An associate fellow of Homerton College, Cambridge, her academic interests include feminist science fiction, transformative works and creative writing practice and methodology; she writes and broadcasts regularly on these and other topics.